THE TROUBLE IN ROOM 519

Gordon Malherbe Hillman, May 1950

THE TROUBLE IN ROOM 519

MONEY, MATRICIDE, & MARGINAL FICTION IN THE EARLY TWENTIETH CENTURY

THOMAS AIELLO

Louisiana State University Press Baton Rouge

Published by Louisiana State University Press
lsupress.org

Copyright © 2021 by Louisiana State University Press
All rights reserved. Except in the case of brief quotations used in articles or reviews, no part of this publication may be reproduced or transmitted in any format or by any means without written permission of Louisiana State University Press.

LSU Press Paperback Original

Designer: Barbara Neely Bourgoyne
Typeface: MillerText

Cover photographs: Gordon Hillman and the Copley Plaza Hotel, Boston, MA. Photographs from contemporary newspaper clippings.

Library of Congress Cataloging-in-Publication Data
Names: Aiello, Thomas, 1977– author. | Hillman, Gordon Malherbe, 1900–1968. Short stories. Selections.
Title: The trouble in room 519 : money, matricide, and marginal fiction in the early twentieth century / Thomas Aiello.
Description: Baton Rouge : Louisiana State University Press, [2021] | Includes bibliographical references and index.
Identifiers: LCCN 2020057141 | ISBN 978-0-8071-7710-5 (cloth) | ISBN 978-0-8071-7598-9 (pdf) | ISBN 978-0-8071-7603-0 (epub)
Subjects: LCSH: Hillman, Gordon Malherbe, 1900–1968. | Authors, American—20th century—Biography.
Classification: LCC PS3515.I643 Z55 2021 | DDC 813/.52 [B]—dcundefined
LC record available at https://lccn.loc.gov/2020057141

CONTENTS

Acknowledgments / vii

INTRODUCTION:
The Life and Times of
Gordon Malherbe Hillman / 1

1. CHICAGO / 10
"Broadway Doll" / 18

2. NOBLES / 29
"Day to Remember" / 40

3. THE *TRANSCRIPT* / 54
"Lead All—Baby" / 65

4. THE CAPE / 76
"A Ship Comes In" / 84

5. THE MAGAZINES / 96
"Tough Guy" / 108

6. HOLLYWOOD / 120
"The Great Man Votes" / 128

7. THE COPLEY / 142
"Panic in Wild Harbor" / 151

8. BEACON HILL / 159
"The Wild Bunch" / 166

Notes / 177

Bibliography / 197

Index / 211

ACKNOWLEDGMENTS

This book has been more than a decade in the making. I first encountered Gordon Hillman in a brief newspaper mention of a novelist murderer while working on a separate project. That mention ultimately led to a years-long obsession with the author, as I began collecting all of his work, then trying to piece together his life in the historical record. What follows is the product of that obsession, and it was abetted by many over those years.

Gregory Richard hosted me in Oxford, Mississippi, as I trolled the library there for hard-to-find stories. Pete Aiello and his wife, Saya Hillman, hosted me in Chicago as I tried to piece together the Hillman family's life in the city. A fortuitous invitation to speak at the Law and Society Association's annual meeting in Boston allowed me to sit in the lobby of the Copley Plaza Hotel, staring in wonder at the gilded baroque appointments. Several graduate students helped me transcribe some of the stories, often from problematic, blurry copies. Of special note in this regard was Erin Blanton. Jenny Smith also did tireless work tracking down leads.

Denise Montgomery, formerly of Valdosta State University's Odum Library, was inordinately helpful, as were the archivists and librarians at Wellesley College, the University of California at Berkeley, Northwestern University, the Massachusetts Supreme Judicial Court, the Boston Public Library, the Boston Police Department, Emory University, the Academy of Motion Picture Arts and Sciences, and Noble and Greenough School. I took all of that information and used it to write

ACKNOWLEDGMENTS

this book, but the version you are reading is far superior to that original draft thanks to the helpful commentary of peer reviewers and the amazing staff of LSU Press.

My long-suffering wife, Kelley "Pickle" Clark Aiello, had to listen to my stories about Hillman. She deserves special thanks for putting up with me.

Finally, Diane Kessler was so gracious with her time in describing the later lives of Hillman and his wife, and Dixie Ellen Milner was just as gracious in conducting those interviews. She is one of the best friends anyone could have and suffered through much of this work alongside me.

This book is for Dixie.

THE TROUBLE IN ROOM 519

INTRODUCTION
THE LIFE AND TIMES OF GORDON MALHERBE HILLMAN

Around seven o'clock in the evening, May 7, 1950, author Gordon Malherbe Hillman filled an empty bottle with water, capped it, then walked into his mother's room in the pair's fifth-floor suite at Boston's Copley Plaza Hotel. He walked up behind her. Then he bludgeoned her to death. The pair was scheduled to be evicted the following day. Mounting debts had finally broken the forty-five-year-old. But it hadn't always been that way. He had, as a youth, attended the prestigious Noble and Greenough School. He had published a novel, written for Hollywood, and had two of his dozens of stories made into films. But Hillman was, for the most part, a middling magazine fiction writer, as were the majority of working fiction writers in the 1920s, 1930s, and 1940s.

Gordon Malherbe Hillman's work has never been studied in any formal way. His life has never been examined. Perhaps more importantly, however, his career trajectory is far more emblematic of the situation of most twentieth-century writers than are those of writers who have made the canon. Most didn't kill their mothers, of course, but most found sustenance in publication without ever reaching a level of fame that allowed them to write creatively full-time. This study of his life is a good story, but it also serves as a prism through which to evaluate the fiction of popular magazines in the first half of the twentieth century and the life lived by the writers of that fiction. It is a subject that has received very little attention. While scholars have studied science fiction of the era, horror, children's stories, and pulp novels, general popular-magazine fiction, by far the tamest of the listed genres and the most widely read in this golden age of reading, has been given short shrift. This work begins to remedy that deficit. *The Trouble in Room 519* tells Hillman's story, examining his writing as exemplary of Depression-era popular fiction and of his declining mental state, and uses Hillman as a foil to discuss magazine fiction and its authors prior to World War II.

In 1920, Arthur B. Maurice announced—in a magazine, fittingly—that the nation had "passed the threshold of a new 'golden age' of American reading." He produced as evidence the sales figures for bookstores and book publishers, which demonstrated the success of both. It was also, he argued, a golden age for male writers in a field that was often seen to be dominated by what Nathaniel Hawethorne called "a damned mob of scribbling women." There were "probably many causes" for this particular renaissance, Maurice argued, "but the chief cause is obvious"—the Great War: "Three or four million boys in camps found, many of them for the first time in their lives, time and opportunity for reading." Then those same boys went overseas and in the process gained a measure of European sophistication about their reading.[1]

Maurice's pronouncement dealt almost entirely with novels as a manifestation of the popularity of popular literature, but his conclusions could just as well have applied to magazine fiction, from whence many of those novels came. He celebrated the success of Kipling and Conrad, the revival of interest in poets like Walt Whitman. But he was most interested in newer authors like John Masefield, who would by 1930 become the United Kingdom's poet laureate. He emphasized Rex Beach, George Barr McCutcheon, H. G. Wells, Edward Streeter, John Galsworthy, Booth Tarkington, Zane Grey, Hugh Walpole, Harold MacGrath, Ernest Poole, and the Spanish author Vicente Blasco Ibañez, along with women writers like Daisy Ashford, Mary Roberts Rinehart, and Ellen Glasgow.[2]

It was a list that provided an aspirational nexus for a young Hillman, who would become one of a series of popular fiction writers who followed a decidedly well-trod path. Rex Beach, for example, was an American who wandered to Alaska during the Klondike Gold Rush of the early century, which became the subject of his 1906 novel, *The Spoilers*. The adventure novels and short stories that he regularly pro-

INTRODUCTION: THE LIFE AND TIMES OF GORDON MALHERBE HILLMAN

duced following the success of *The Spoilers* led to film adaptations and to a stint as a movie producer. In 1949, the year before Hillman murdered his mother, Beach killed himself in Sebring, Florida.[3]

George Barr McCutcheon had a similar profile. The Indiana novelist worked in journalism during his collegiate days at Purdue before making his name as a novelist and playwright, which, like Beach, also led to film adaptations.[4]

Harold MacGrath was another early model for Hillman, beginning work as a young reporter for the *Syracuse Herald* before publishing his first novel in the late 1890s. The popular novels that he would continuously produce during the first decades of the twentieth century were supplemented by short fiction work published in popular magazines. Some of his novels were even serialized in the publications. His success led him to write for the movies, and several of his novels and short stories were adapted for the big screen. His writing made him wealthy and famous, affording him a lavish public life before his passing in 1932. It was a model Hillman hoped to follow, a success he hoped to reach.[5]

Edward Streeter also began his career as a journalist, starting as a reporter for the *Buffalo Express* before becoming a syndicated columnist. After World War I, Streeter worked as banker, publishing a variety of short stories in his spare time. The success of his short fiction led in 1938 to his first novel, *Daily Except Sundays,* which was followed by a series of books that would continue through 1969.[6]

Ernest Cook Poole was schooled at home for the first years of life before attending the exclusive University School for Boys in Chicago, where he worked on the school newspaper. He and his family spent summers on Lake Michigan. It was after he began attending Princeton that Poole combined his journalistic work with efforts at creative writing. After college, he began working as a correspondent for popular magazines covering labor relations in early twentieth-century Chicago and the tumultuous political situation in czarist Russia in 1905. After that reporting, he began contributing to those popular magazines as a short story writer. That work led to a career as a playwright and a novelist, his novel *His Family* becoming the first recipient of the Pulitzer Prize for Fiction in 1918. He published the follow-up to that work, *His Second Wife,* as a serial in *McClure's.*[7]

Poole died in January 1950, five months before Hillman killed his mother. His story, like that of Streeter, MacGrath, McCutcheon, and Beach, demonstrated a formula for popular American literary success. Men of privilege worked in journalism before moving on to short stories, novels, plays, and ultimately film to garner wealth and reputation. It was a model that Hillman would follow, one that many would-be writers would follow, but most moonlighting newspaper reporters, short story writers, and novelists would not have the financial success of the writers described here. Of course, McCutcheon, MacGrath, and even Poole never really developed work that was fundamental or canonical to American letters. That wasn't how authors gauged the success of their work in real time. Instead, they gauged it by media attention, prizes, and, ultimately, money. But even when canon status is removed from a historical evaluation of literary success, the vast majority of authors who published in popular magazines or wrote fiction while paying the bills stringing for newspapers never reached that bar. Hillman's story mirrors that of Streeter, Beach, and McCutcheon in many ways, but it is most representative of their less successful contemporaries.

One of his more successful contemporaries, meanwhile, was Katherine Anne Porter. Porter discussed submitting her first story to *Century* in 1923, its editor, Carl Van Doren, taking her under his wing, encouraging her gifts, and publishing the bulk of her stories in the magazine. Such, however, was not the beneficent fate of most magazine authors. Hillman and others submitted stories across magazines and genres in an effort to publish.[8]

Porter, like Hillman, worked as a journalist, and like Hillman used her experience to condition stories about the profession. Her short novel *Pale Horse, Pale Rider,* published in 1939, is about a female journalist in Denver, Colorado, during the 1918 influenza epidemic. She suffers from the flu, but her beloved contracts the disease while caring for her and dies. While the specific events themselves were fictitious, Porter had worked for the *Rocky Mountain News* during the epidemic and did contract influenza. Like Hillman, and at the same time as Hillman, Porter used her experience as a journalist to play on the cultural codes of the profession, to create a sense of reality and to analyze the role of newspapers in local communities. While history has remembered Porter and forgotten Hillman, and while Porter's story has greater depth and pathos than most of Hillman's, their newspaper office scenes are almost identical, demonstrating the role of experience in creating fiction and the near-ubiquitous magazine style of the day.[9]

Authors such as Hillman and Porter benefited from a growing readership for ephemeral publications, as education and literacy spurred both an audience more interested in reading such work and an economy that supplied the disposable income and free time for would-be middle-class readers to buy it. There were fewer than one hundred thousand U.S. high school graduates in the 1900 school term; in 1960, there were more than 1.8 million. While the percentage of students enrolled in college did not reflect that drastic change, university attendance did increase by roughly fifteen times during that same period.[10]

Such factors also facilitated the growth of the other principal form of ephemeral literature that dominated Hillman's life, the newspaper. Circulation of newspapers increased from just over fifteen million in 1900 to just under sixty million in 1962, pushed by a more educated populace and a product-heavy corporate culture looking to sell.[11]

And then there were the magazines. Commercial magazines "were inclined to perpetuate the ideological status quo," explains Theodore Peterson. The fiction featured in those magazines "tended to glorify the traditional values and goals and to sanction the conventional virtues." Short stories glorified a version of American success that not only emphasized the nuclear family and middle- and upper-class propriety but tied the measure of that success to the acquisition of the products advertised in the pages of the magazine itself. It was an aspirational fiction that assumed wealth as a given and presented proper social behavior as the principal means of keeping it. And that wealth and standing were presented as almost uniformly white. Those outside the bounds of upper-middle-class whiteness, when acknowledged at all, were relegated to stereotypical presentations that excluded them from those aspirations. In an idealized America, those who suffered the indignities of race, class, or caste only muddied what were supposed to be the pristine waters of lives where crises occurred within a decidedly circumscribed bubble.[12]

As Peterson has explained, mass-circulation magazines were "highly imitative. They were inclined to run with the pack." After an author demonstrated a version of popularity, "a number of magazines competed for his output." They discouraged literary experimentation and "became increasingly concerned with formula rather than form." That imitative nature ultimately created what Peterson termed

> a pseudoworld, a picture out of focus which readers sometimes confused with the real thing. The world was spun of both articles and fiction. It was a world of optimism and good works in which science worked only beneficent miracles, in which poverty was at worst a nuisance, in which anyone could do anything if he persevered, in which the most ill-matched couples would find marital happiness if they really tried, in which evil was justly punished, in which virtue and talent were inevitably recognized and reaped their due rewards, a world of golden light and few shadows.[13]

They were, as Joan Shelly Rubin has explained, part of the creation of a middlebrow culture. In that culture, in the conception of critic Margaret Widdemer, writing in 1933 during the prime of Hillman's literary career, if "highbrow" denoted cultivation and breeding, and "lowbrow" denoted a lack of any formal refinement, then "middlebrow" culture was somewhere between those two poles, "men and women, fairly civilized, fairly literate, who support the critics and lecturers and publishers by purchasing their wares." The middlebrow reader was "the majority reader." The framework of that definition survived through the run of Hillman's career, defining a literary space that included a group of magazines like *Liberty, American Magazine*, the *Saturday Evening Post, McCall's,* and others, which catered to an audience that was perhaps uninterested in more intellectual fare like that of the *Atlantic,* the *Nation,* or the *New Yorker* but was also uninterested in the pulp magazines of salacious adventure that catered to a lower-class, largely uneducated audience.[14]

Though they didn't even exist in the first half of the 1800s, magazines became the dominant form of episodic entertainment by the turn of the twentieth century, providing reading material for Rubin's "middlebrow" Americans. Richard Ohmann describes the early development of these magazines through "fiction to order," or "formula fiction," in which "some crisis tested and confirmed a known hero's qualities in predictably satisfying ways." It wasn't the only formula, but the fact that such formulas existed almost excluded a priori the writers of such fare from the status of literary legitimacy.[15] By the time of Hillman's arrival on the scene, the use of these formulas had abated somewhat, but many of his stories did fit that generic formula upon which the industry developed.

Hillman, for whatever formulas he was using, saw himself as writer of Porter's stature, a gift bequeathed to him by his mother. "Gordon Malherbe Hillman discovered early that he liked to write, began with poetry, then switched to stories which have occupied him ever since," went one of his autobiographical statements. "In between times, he is a music and drama critic. He was born in Illinois, but is equally at home in Chicago or Boston or New York."[16] In another such statement, he claimed that he "wrote poetry for a time, then turned to fiction. He has worked for movie companies in Hollywood, a place which he found 'pleasantly mad.'"[17] Hillman's sense of self, and his mother's sense of self, were outsized, often to the point of self-deception, a solipsism that would ultimately result in Hillman's murder of his mother.

That tragedy was fifty years in the making. The story begins in Chicago, before Hillman moved back East to Boston, where he spent most of the rest of his life. In an effort to introduce the life and times of Hillman, the circumstances of both the newspaper and magazine industries in the first half of the twentieth century, and the ephemeral magazine literature that was so much a part of Hillman's career, each of the following chapters includes three essential parts. A chronological biography of a part of Hillman's life opens each chapter. One of Hillman's stories that is illustrative of that portion of his life closes it. In between, analysis of the literary genre that the story and others like it represent will provide a transition from Hillman's life to Hillman's work. Chapter 1, for example, describes Hillman's parents, paying particular attention to his mother and the social and cultural circumstances at the time of his birth. The story that closes the chapter is one of a series of tales Hillman wrote in the 1940s that, as the transitional material makes clear, provide a glimpse of how he saw the woman who had loomed so large in his life. Subsequent chapters follow that pattern.

Chapter 2, for example, describes Hillman's time at boarding school and the stories that he wrote in his later life about the experience. In that effort, he followed a common trope of stories about the experience, probably made most famous by John Knowles's *A Separate Peace*, published in 1959. Thus while the chapters follow a chronological, biographical timeline, analyses of Hillman's stories related to the biographical subject of each chapter move in time and space across Hillman's life and the life of the given genre. The story in chapter 2 represents the large body of work Hillman produced about exclusive boys' schools.

Chapter 3 discusses the beginning of Hillman's work in the newspaper business, an industry that would sustain him for the rest of his life. It describes the history of the Boston journalism that supported him and the stories of the newspaper business that Hillman wrote and that became a phenomenon in the first half of the twentieth century. Still, despite Hillman's hard work in various roles at Boston newspapers, he was still a child of privilege. As a youth, he and his family spent summers on Cape Cod, and chapter 4 talks about that experience and the stories it later inspired, as well as the role of class in the creation of such stories, many of which were published during the heart of the Great Depression.

Chapter 5 describes the history of the magazine industry that sustained Hillman's writing career. Much of his writing was published by the popular magazines of the early century that fed the episodic entertainment of middlebrow life. Hillman's brush with Hollywood, as two of his stories were made into feature films, is discussed in chapter 6. He also witnessed the publication of his first novel, *Fortune's Cup*. Its success was temporary, however, and one that was representative of many writers of his caliber, as the movie industry used the profusion of short stories to generate treatments to sustain the constant demand for new films.

Hillman's success was as ephemeral as the media that sustained him, and the demands of a needy mother and a difficult decade ultimately led to the trouble in Room 519, the subject of chapter 7. The chapter also discusses matricide as a phenomenon, along with Hillman's spectral crime fiction, written for the pulps in the 1920s before he found his broader middlebrow style. Regardless, Hillman served only three years for his crime, and chapter 8 describes his later life, his marriage, and his continued work for Boston newspapers. His career as a fiction writer was done, but his life as a journalist and his life in general—his first real experience since boarding school away from his mother—was in many ways just beginning. His was the life of a reporter, critic, screenwriter, novelist, and poet, but his identity was chiefly associated with short stories, like Katherine Anne Porter, and so this book allows him to tell his own story in the way that would have suited him best, with his own fiction. In this final chapter, Hillman's story "The Wild Bunch," featured as an adapted television movie in the 1950s, concludes the volume.

It was the last national public display of Hillman's fiction, a fiction that was ubiquitous in the magazines of the first half of the twentieth century. A fiction written by an author who was almost famous. A fiction written by a journalist who followed in the literary and employment traditions of so many of his forebears and contemporaries. Who was representative of so many of the literary themes of the era, and so many of the real issues that the writers of that literature faced. And who, in desperation and psychosis, murdered his mother. This is the story of Gordon Malherbe Hillman, author and murderer, and of the literature, lifestyle, and employment he represents.

1. CHICAGO

Carolyn Piper was a child of New England. She was born in Concord, New Hampshire, on May 11, 1876, to Joseph Piper and his wife, Carolyn.[1] It was an auspicious time to grow up in New Hampshire. The Civil War decade saw the state's population decrease by 2.5 percent, from 326,073 to 318,300, the only decade in the century during which the area did not add population. It picked up again soon after, as the state benefited from the development of water power and improved transportation that gave New Hampshire a place in the Gilded Age Industrial Revolution. From 1873 to 1897, six new cities were incorporated as the rural state became slightly more urban. Its laws developed accordingly. In 1871, the state began compulsory primary education. In 1876, the constitutional convention removed the requirement that state officials had to be Protestant. Twenty years prior, such an effort had been rejected. In 1881, the legislature created a State Board of Health, and ten years later it created a library infrastructure. Such developments led to new immigration, particularly from Canada and Poland. By 1890, the state's population had increased substantially to 376,530.[2] It was, in other words, a state and state population that was small but aspirational, where anything seemed possible, and such was an attitude that would become a core part of Carolyn's outlook, to the point where her aspiration turned into delusions of grandeur. The foundations of those later reveries were built in Carolyn's youth, in a modernizing and urbanizing New Hampshire that was a constituent part of the Gilded Age economy, in which corporate growth and the robber barons who built it made the United States a global economic juggernaut even as they simultaneously created a new urban poverty. The worst horrors of the consequences of that economic blight, however, were happening far from Concord. Carolyn could become anything she wanted, just like the country, and the repercussions would be minimal.

And so Piper moved to New York for an acting career and was successful. It was there in the glow of her newfound fame that she met Frank, and in February 1899, she married him. Frank H. Hillman was an aspiring manager in the soap industry. He was an older man, born in New York in 1868, the youngest son of George and Mary Hillman, and thirty-one at the time of his marriage to the twenty-five-year-old Piper.[3]

Or such was the way that Carolyn liked to tell it. In a world where you could become anything you wanted, why not become a famous, successful actress? Such were the lessons of her Gilded Age New England upbringing, and her largesse would always be so much greater when filtered through her own imagination. From 1891 to 1895, for example, and against her own testimony, Piper was still in Concord teaching elocution and living with her father. By the time of her wedding to Frank, Carolyn had moved to the big city, but that city wasn't New York. She was living in Boston at the Hotel Oxford in the city's Back Bay near Copley Square—the same area where she would violently die fifty-five years later.[4]

Regardless of Carolyn's time on the stage and the level of success she achieved there, after her wedding in 1899 the new couple moved to Chicago, where Frank took a job as a private secretary for the N. K. Fairbank Soap Company. Though Fairbank's offices were housed in the Tribune Building in downtown Chicago, the Hillmans opted for a comfortable upper-middle-class life in the suburbs, moving around from Evanston to Oak Park to Des Plains and back as the first decade of the twentieth century passed. Soon after their first arrival in Evanston, on August 31, 1900, the couple had a child, Gordon Malherbe Hillman.[5]

Turn-of-the-century Chicago was a city adjusting to massive demographic upheaval. In 1850, Chicago had roughly fifty thousand residents. Thirty years later, it had five hundred thousand. In 1900, the city had 1.7 million residents, that growth built on eastern and southern European immigration and the development of industries reliant on the burgeoning post–Civil War railroad boom. At the end of the Civil War, there were 3,272 miles of railroad track west of the Mississippi River. By 1890, there were 72,473. The spread west of the railroads, combined with a growth in the mining and ranching businesses, expanded the country farther and farther west. And when the railroads came, the beef borne of that ranching could for the first time be efficiently transported back East. Cattle cars on railroads took cows to the intersecting points of the railroads, namely Chicago. It was this ranching boom that grew the infamous Chicago stockyards, making Chicago the meatpacking leader of the entire world and inspiring horror stories about the industry like Upton Sinclair's *The Jungle*. It was Chicago's growing meat industry, in turn, that prompted the 1870s innovation of refrigerated railroad cars, which could take the processed meat to retailers all over the country. That combination of railroad technology and electricity also helped Chicago develop a public transportation system that allowed its population to spread farther and farther from the city center. Immigrants and rural laborers coming to the city for work moved into cramped, stuffy tenement buildings, while white-collar businessmen and robber barons built giant homes and created the vision of excess that defined the Gilded Age.[6]

Those clear class lines, combined with the European origin of much of Chicago's working-class population, made the city a hub of labor radicalism. Low pay, on-the-job injuries, and other problems sparked the growth of unions throughout the country in the era. The principal labor organization of the 1880s, for example, was the Knights of Labor, founded in 1869 in Philadelphia. It was a largely conservative group by any modern or European standard. Some branches admitted women, some, African Americans, but most did not. The Knights of Labor was very reluctant to strike, but others weren't.[7]

In Chicago, in 1886, there were a variety of local labor organizations, made up largely of immigrants. Because of those immigrants, Chicago was the American hotbed of labor radicalism, and throughout the 1880s, anarchists infiltrated various unions in the city. On May 4, 1886, anarchists held a protest meeting at Haymarket Square in response to police violence against union organizing. The rally began peacefully, but when police showed up, someone in the crowd threw a bomb into the phalanx of police, and the police opened fire. The ensuing battle left fifty people wounded and ten dead.[8] Chicago responded to what became known as the Haymarket Riot by cracking down on labor and anarchism. Eight of the protesters were convicted (without evidence) of conspiracy to commit murder, and four of them were hanged. "I arrived in Chicago on an awfully hot July day," said Jessie Binford to Studs Terkel of her 1906 migration to the city. "Every other place was a saloon, the streets were dirty. The air was heavy. I had left the beautiful Iowa countryside, and I wondered if I hadn't made a mistake."[9] With the labor unrest, the poverty, and the resulting blight, the middle class responded by moving to the outskirts of town, creating suburban communities.

Evanston, for example, Hillman's birthplace, had been incorporated since 1863 but became a city in early 1892, just a few years before Hillman's birth. Oak Park, another suburban home of the Hillmans, grew from a population of five hundred in 1872 to one of almost two thousand in 1890 and almost ten thousand in 1900. By 1910, it had more than twenty thousand residents.[10]

They were cities modern in their construction, as the last quarter of the eighteenth century had been spent rebuilding from the Great Fire of 1871, which destroyed much of Chicago and left a third of its residents homeless. It was the city of Daniel Burnham and Frederick Law Olmsted, and despite its labor unrest, it was also the home of the 1893 World's Columbian Exhibition, held to celebrate the four-hundredth anniversary of Columbus's discovery of America. There were four hundred buildings across seven hundred acres on the south side of the city, home to many of those factories and tenements that had seen so much labor unrest. The exhibition grounds and buildings were known as the "White City," a neoclassical monstrosity that appeared far more European than American. The fair's Manufacturers and Liberal Arts Building was the world's largest and was simply an endless department store. It was a symbol of what the country and what Chicago was becoming. The largest building in the world, built to be temporary and torn down, was designed for nothing but commerce. Hovering over much of the event was a large wheel, 246 feet high. It had thirty-six cars that held sixty passengers each, more than 2,100 people when full.

The wheel, designed to outdo the Eiffel Tower from Paris's world's fair in the 1880s, was named after its inventor, a Pittsburgh bridge-builder named George W. Ferris. It did its job. When the exposition closed in November 1893, it had successfully announced America's full arrival on the world stage.[11]

And so despite the city's class conflict that helped create the suburbs where Hillman spent his early youth, its exponential Gilded Age growth, its European immigration, its success on the world stage, and the cloister of its suburban climes that allowed residents to avoid seeing the uglier working-class realities under the gilding made Chicago, too, an aspirational city, one that could open a world of possibility to a boy born in Evanston in 1900.

It could also be aspirational to an aspiring manager in the soap industry. The United States became a dominant soap-producing nation in the nineteenth century, led by British immigrants. In 1806, for example, William Colgate immigrated to New York from England, where he began producing soap and candles, and in the 1840s created a standardized bar soap that he sold nationwide. Meanwhile, Milwaukee's B. J. Johnson Company had produced a soap product combining palm oil and olive oil, naming their product Palmolive. It was so successful that the company took the name of its soap. At the same time, Procter and Gamble was founded by England's William Procter and Northern Ireland's James Gamble, brothers-in-law who founded a candle-and-soap company that flourished in the 1850s after it won a contract to provide soap to the Union army. In the 1880s, the company developed its Ivory soap bar, which floated in water, and their profits continued to grow. The craze for soap and candles in the Gilded Age prompted William Lant Carpenter to publish *A Treatise on the Manufacture of Soap and Candles* in the 1880s, a work so popular that a second edition appeared in 1895 despite the fact that Carpenter had died.[12]

N. K. Fairbank was one of the many soap manufacturers who thrived in the wake of such success. Fairbank began his career at Smedley, Peck & Co. "Although Mr. Fairbank's name did not appear[,] he was a potent factor in the concern," explained the *Chicago Tribune*, "as he furnished the necessary capital." After the company's plant burned in 1867, it reorganized as Fairbank, Peck & Co., and in 1885 incorporated officially as the N. K. Fairbank Company. What started as a small concern grew to a multinational corporation with offices around the country and in England and Germany.[13]

One of its signature products of the 1890s was Cottolene, a cooking shortening. "It is cheaper to use than lard or cooking butter and produces food that will cause distress to no one," claimed one advertisement, calling it "the most economical, most wholesome, *best* shortening that ever went into food." Another of its successful products was Gold Dust Washing Powder. It "makes the clothes white and clean without injury to the fabric in any way," the company said. "It does the work better than soap, requires only half the labor, and costs much less."[14]

The Fairbank company's offices were originally in the city's Fisher Building at Van Buren and Dearborn Streets, but it was a flawed home. In September 1900, for example, a passenger elevator broke, dropping four stories and injuring ten people, including several from Fairbank. When the new Tribune Building was completed early in 1902, Fairbank moved into the new edifice, "occupy[ing] the entire eleventh floor." It also created more space for the growing company.[15]

Such is not to say that problems didn't shadow Fairbank's success. In April 1900, residents of one Chicago neighborhood sued the company "on the ground that 6,000 barrels partly filled with oils, alkali, and other soap ingredients have made this neighborhood so noisome as to be almost unendurable." The complaint claimed that twenty-five local horses "have been killed by the odors and that scarlet and typhoid fever have been prevalent among the children."[16]

In 1901, representatives of Fairbank met in Chicago with representatives from Procter & Gamble, Colgate, and thirty-two other concerns to create the American Soap Manufacturing Association. James McMahon of Fairbank was made president of the new group and explained to the press that the organization was "simply for social purposes and mutual advantages. The association is not a trust in any sense of the term. We have formed in the manner that persons engaged in many other lines of business do." More than anything else, however, the association demonstrated the industry's coming-of-age.[17]

It also demonstrated that Hillman's father was a successful executive in a successful business. He was a rising member of the professional-managerial class that was so often a part of magazine fiction, a group whose values and ideals in many ways shaped the era. With an aspirational businessman father and an aspirational artist mother, it is no coincidence that Gordon Hillman would be prone to self-aggrandizing claims. The child was, as he later noted in 1920, "a descendent through Huguenot lines" of the sixteenth-century classicist poet and critic Francois Malherbe and seventeenth-century quietist mystic Madame Guyon. It was the kind of literary legacy in which both Gordon and Carolyn reveled, a birthright that validated both their writing and their sense of self. They were also fond of reporting that the Hillmans traced their American heritage back to the first Dutch settlers of Long Island. Such was the legacy of the Gilded Age: in the new, emerging America, you could be anything you wanted to be.[18]

What Hillman wanted to be was a writer, and as an adult many of his stories emphasized children living in this kind of aspirational privilege and their relationships with their mothers. Hillman often used his work to ruminate on the role of motherhood, as did many authors, but he also clearly drew on his mother's biography and personality in his stories. That emphasis illustrates the outsized role Hillman's mother, and her own outsized personality, played in his life, both in physical proximity and in the space her self-aggrandizing nature occupied in his mind.

The story that follows, "Broadway Doll," for example, describes a young actress who leaves her father in New York to travel to Illinois to stay with family, as her father, also in show business, is hurting for money. It was a culture shock for the cosmopolitan Doll. No one believed her when she nonchalantly explained that she knew the actors playing in the film at the local movie house. When she described their real lives and personalities, those around her were indignant. "Doll opened her mouth," the story explains. "Then shut it tight again. Miss Jimpson was a fan and she'd never known one before. Fans were worse than bobby-soxers." She feels a respite when she meets the native New Yorker who runs the theater: "He spoke to her as if she were his own age and she was used to that." Ultimately, she is forced to choose between her new life and "the shiny, hard, exciting one that was the Big Town with all its trumpets blowing." She chooses the new life, as did Hillman's actress mother, who maintained a similar worldly knowledge after her own time as an actress in the Big Town before settling for her life with the soap man and motherhood.

It isn't a biographical story, by any means. Carolyn Hillman moonlighted in the Big Town after a small-town upbringing, for example. But the story is clearly a portrait of her, cubist and fractured though it might be. In another of Hillman's stories that includes an approximate portrait of his mother, an overbearing actress comes to visit her son at his boarding school, wowing all of the students and faculty. Desperate for money, she finally decides to go to Hollywood. "And Mom was good," Hillman wrote. "She was awfully good. Mom was an artist, only no one knew it." Eventually, the son is able to convince his mother not to take the part she was offered in the movies: "Mom! Look, Mom! You're doing it all the wrong way. If you go out to Hollywood now, all they'll do is toss you around." Ultimately she decides to stay at the boarding school and teach theater to the students.[19] Again the cubism, the distorted portrait. Hillman long attended boarding school away from his mother, only to desperately crave her attention. In his fiction, he is able to get his way while describing a mother who turned down fortune in Hollywood for her son. In his fiction, his mother has a talent and demand that didn't actually exist, and his child protagonist had her proximity in a way that the young Hillman had not.

Such portraits remained a constant throughout his career, all playing on themes presented by his mother, and all published during a period when Carolyn was living with her son and posing a substantial financial burden for him. Stories like "Visitors from Vermont," "This Is Fair Warning," "Miss Baby Intervenes," and "For Your Own Good, Dear" all played on the tropes surrounding a modified portrait of Hillman's mother, and all were published between 1942 and 1948, later in his career as it began to devolve, as his relationship with his mother began to deteriorate.[20] They were signposts of an author attempting to come to terms with constant contact with his mother and, at the same time, a fracturing relationship with her, his finances, and his mental health. It was a cubist relationship and fed Hillman's literary distortions. The example presented here is "Broadway Doll."

BROADWAY DOLL

Published in *Collier's*, September 1948

SHE WAS GLAD Oliver Dale had come to the station with them because it was going to make things easier. For when you are leaving your father for the first time in your life, the last moments are apt to be pretty messy, particularly when you are only thirteen and your father is in the profession.

But here was Oliver, calm, plump, pink-cheeked, all of fourteen and with the infinitely knowing look of the theatrical child. Oliver was also in the money, which the Martins certainly weren't, for he was understudy for another juvenile who was playing a leprechaun in a long-run musical. So it was Oliver who guided Herbie and her through the echoing vastness of Grand Central.

"Track twenty-two," he said with immense wisdom. "Cleveland, Indianapolis, St. Louis."

"And not a good show town in the lot," Herbie put in gloomily.

Doll took a long look at Herbie because she wouldn't be seeing him again in a hurry. A tall man, her father, and eternally young with his bright gold hair with the thin streaks of dark in it, curling a trifle, and the chin that wasn't so firm as it might be. Herbie had on the glen plaid suit, which was not remarkable since it was the only suit he had; he was carrying his Malacca stick.

Oliver put his hands in his jacket pockets. "You got your money safe, Doll?"

"I've got it pinned to my pants."

"You got your ticket?" asked Herbie and you could tell he was an actor twenty yards away. If you were in the profession, you could also tell he was temporarily out of work.

Doll had her ticket in her hand. She also had copy of Variety and a box of chocolates Oliver had bought her. She had on her plaid shirt that had been purchased at the bargain on Fourteenth Street, she had on a blue hat, and her tan coat, that had been only slightly secondhand, was over her arm.

She had braided her soft dark hair about her head instead of leaving it in pigtails and she hoped she didn't look as if she were on her way to Sing Sing but that was certainly how she felt. She was a thin, sober-looking child, too tall for her age, much too old for her age, and her dark, slightly slanted eyes, her small, eager face, her serious mouth, made her oddly appealing.

"Your left sock's coming down," Oliver said critically.

Herbie's voice was shaky. "It won't be long, Doll. Honest it won't. Maybe a month."

Herbie actually believed that. Herbie believed that in thirty days he'd be working and have enough money saved to bring her back from Uncle Kimball's and Aunt Mae's out in Illinois. Herbie was kidding himself and he always would.

He now achieved a slight swagger. "I'll bet it won't he bad out there, either. You know, I wouldn't be a bit surprised if you had a simply swell time."

Oliver arose, "Listen, darling, you'd better be getting on that train."

She'd be having the shakes now if she weren't careful, for her father was stooping down to kiss her. "Goodbye, Dolly!"

Oliver simply shook hands. "Keep your tail up, kid!"

Herbie carelessly took a dollar from his pocket. "Here, porter, see my little girl safely aboard!"

He shouldn't have wasted all that money, Doll thought as she went doggedly through the gate. But then, as Oliver often said, Herbie *did* have a lot of ham in him. She sank down in her seat, somebody shouted, "Bo-oard!"; the station platform began sliding by. *And this was it.* This was the end of everything.

Doll was surely going to cry and Oliver always said that when you felt like that, you'd better start thinking like mad about something. Uncle Kimball and Aunt Mae. Aunt Mae was Doll's mother's sister and Mother had died five years ago. Mother had been an actress and she must have been pretty good because she was always working. They'd lived in the apartment up on Morningside and that had been quite nice.

Since then, things had been different. Herbie had a habit of getting into shows that looked wonderful in New Haven or Stamford and then took a terrible beating when they came to town. And then there'd be long, dry spells when he'd be doing nothing at all.

When they were in the money, they'd be living in those third-class hotels in the Forties that all look alike, inside and out. The next step was a tiny furniture apartment west of Broadway where at least there was a kitchenette to cook in. And finally, there was the furnished room where you really could get quite a good meal on an electric hot plate if you only knew how.

A life all ups and downs and a fine, free and easy life, too. Finest of all, right now in June with golden summertime glinting down the avenues. Hot, drowsy summer days when foolish people go out of town and the wise guys stay right where they are.

Plenty of splendid things to do, particularly if you have someone as sharp as Oliver to do them with, for the Staten Island ferry gave the best five-cent ocean voyage in the world. Or you can go swimming off the Palisades absolutely free.

But summer nights are better still— good and late when the shows are out— and you go sauntering up Broadway with Herbie and talking to whomever you meet. You stand on a street corner in your blue slacks with your shirttail out and everybody in the world comes along and stops to dish the dirt. Actors in jobs, actors out of jobs, the big blond who had grown old in the chorus of Oklahoma!, agents, stage managers, theater treasures, band boys, publicity men.

It certainly hadn't happened now, for the Martins were so down to rock bottom that though Doll wasn't very expensive to maintain she was still too much for Herbie to carry. So she was off to Illinois and Herbie was going to hole up for a while with Joe Edwards in Joe's room on 112th Street.

The train was going at quite a respectable speed now. A small darkish man was slumped down beside her with a fluff of hair under his under lip. Yes, a black instrument case in the rack overhead and a lot more of odd shapes and sizes in the rack near by.

"What band are you boys with?" Doll said comfortably.

"Dave Blanchard's." He nodded at the copy of Variety in her lap. "You in the profession?"

Doll felt entirely at ease. "No, but my father is. I'm going out to visit my aunt in Illinois."

The small man said, "Those peasants'll drive you nuts." He went on to say that his name was Steve and that the band was on its way to play a lousy date in a lousy hotel in Cleveland. He suddenly straightened up. "Come on back to the diner, kid, and tie it on."

Doll hesitated. "I'm pretty short."

"So what? Come on, baby. We got paid yesterday."

She had a most enjoyable dinner with three of the band boys who told her what sort of a guy Dave Blanchard was and how he'd flown out to Cleveland while they rode the cushions in a lousy day coach. She was doing fine and still had her five dollars.

THE BRAKEMAN snatched up her suitcase. "Come on, sis! This's Millfort." It was a squat, dingy station.

The brakeman said, "This is her, Ace," and handed her suitcase to a tall, lean old man whose hair was gray.

"Well, Dolly Martin!" said the lean old man.

"Are *you* my Uncle Kimball?"

"Nope. I'm Kim's father." He cupped his hands to shout, "Hey, Kim!"

Uncle Kimball, a round worried-looking man with a round face and big, round, rimmed glasses. Uncle Kimball, much more embarrassed than she.

"Well, well, Dolly!" He evidently couldn't make up his mind whether he should kiss her or not. "Mae meant to come meet you but she couldn't."

His father said calmly, "Did you have a good breakfast, Dolly?"

"Yes, sir. A traveling man bought it for me. He told me about his nerves. And last night the band boys gave me my dinner."

Uncle Kim looked quite shocked but his father said in a slow drawl, "Did all right for yourself, didn't you? Don't call me 'sir.' I'm not that old. I'll answer to 'Ace.'"

"All right, Ace."

The old man's eyes flickered with amusement. "Named me that when I was a river pilot."

Doll gave a little gasp. "Like Mark Twain?"

"Not much. River's not what it used to be. How do you know about Mark Twain?"

"In New York, you can get books out of the public library for free."

"That so?" The old man stood very straight and must have been six feet tall. "S'pose we mosey along uptown?"

They went down a wide, dusty street, a little like the Bronx but not much. Low brick building on either side and a hound dog asleep on the sidewalk. Big signs over small restaurants that said "HOT CAT."

Ace saw her alarmed look. "Fried catfish, honey."

A different air, a different feel to everything and even the wind was slow and warm and lazy. Not a bit like the Bronx now; tall old trees against bright blue sky and roses blooming.

A woman like a plump brown bird came running down a red brick walk in front of a big yellow house, "Dolly! Dolly Martin!"

Aunt Mae hugging and kissing her: Aunt Mae with her apron still on and her soft brown hair hanging down in strings. "I guess you're just about starved to death, Dolly."

Sitting in the dark dining room with more dishes set before her than you'd ever see in the Automat or Childs' or Schraft's. Fried chicken, an orange-colored yam split in half and drenched with butter, black-eyed peas.

"Have some hot cakes, honey," said Aunt Mae.

Across from her, Uncle Kim put down his fork in awe. "Good Godfrey, Mae, the child'll stuff herself to death."

"Don't mind him, honey. You just go on and eat."

She reached for her glass of milk and it was almost cream.

Ace sat back smiling. "Whoa there, Doll. Don't have to tank up against time. There'll be more tomorrow."

Her eyes went wide. "You mean you eat like this *every* day?"

Upstairs at last and a long, bright bedroom with a cool green paper and dark green blinds. A big four-poster bed, a green and white bureau, a dressing table with an enormous mirror—

"It's simply swell, Aunt Mae!"

Aunt Mae's eyes were brown velvet if you looked at them closely. "Do you want me to help you unpack, Doll?"

She looked at the suitcase and was ashamed. "There—there isn't much to unpack, Aunt Mae."

All alone now and she went to look out the window. A squat brick fire station across the street and the fireman sitting out in front in his shirt sleeves.

She knew what Herbie would say if he could see that. Herbie would say, "I told you it was a hick town!" Well, maybe it was but it was still pretty nice.

NICE, TOO, in the evening on the front porch with all the stars shining out of the hot dark and that strong, sweet smell was something they called honeysuckle.

Aunt Mae: "Nine o'clock, Doll. Don't you think you'd better go to bed?"

"Now? My gosh, it's awfully early."

Uncle Kim: "What time do you go to bed in New York, Doll?"

"Well, in the summer, maybe midnight—or later if it's terribly hot."

Uncle Kim looked as if he were about to say something and then didn't. No one said anything at all and the whole night was so silent it made your nerves jump.

"Gosh, is it always so quiet?"

A deep bass bellow lifted every hair on her head. *"What's that?"*

Ace began to chuckle. "Steamboat on the Ohio."

She lay back, laughing, for even if Ace were old, he and she understood each other. Her head dropped forward and she couldn't help it. "I guess you're right Aunt Mae. I guess I'd better go to bed." She rose, yawning. "I'm pretty well tired out." . . .

Doll had on her blue slacks with her shirttail hanging out and her face shone. She'd already seen the wonderful stove and was now running the vacuum.

"You don't have to help me, Doll," Aunt Mae said.

"But I like helping you, Aunt Mae."

"You certainly do know how to clean, Doll. I wouldn't have thought you'd done much of it in New York."

"Well, Herbie's a man and men are all sort of sloppy."

"I know. You like things neat."

Yes, Doll did. She'd never seen anything as spotless as Aunt Mae's house.

AUNT MAE said, "Sharon Fletcher's having a birthday party this afternoon and her mother's invited you to come."

She said doubtfully, "Is it just children?"

"Yes, dear. You'll have a lovely time and you'd better wear your best dress."

"I've only three dresses and I don't believe any of them is best."

Well, the party was simply terrible. She didn't know who anybody was and she hadn't the remotest idea what they were all chatting about. The fluttering little woman was Sharon's mother and she was mostly in the next room where there were going to be refreshments sometime. The tall angular woman with her was Miss Jimpson who had come in to help and Miss Jimpson looked just like the aunt in a Tom show.

When it came to the children, Doll simply gave up. There were so many of them and they all knew one another, and although they must be her own age, they were so *young*. She was an utter outsider and she'd better shut her head. She could feel the stiff little smile on her face and they'd turned the phonograph on and she danced with one boy after another.

The tallest one with the plump, self-satisfied, self-assured face cut in, and

Doll's mind said acidly, "Here's a big lug!" He held her, close, his cheek to hers and he kept crooning to the music.

"You going to high school in the fall?" he asked.

"Well, I don't know if I'll be here then."

"We've got a good gang. We're pretty careful who we take in. You have to be in a town like this."

Doll wondered why.

"I'm on the football team and I'm pretty fair if I do say so." Doll hadn't the least idea that all the boys at the party were fascinated by her and all the girls were jealous.

He held her closer still, "Say, you're a smooth dancer."

"I'm not very good. I was going to Ben White's dancing school but we got falling off the room rent so I had to stop."

"You got what?"

"We ran out of money."

His face told her that had been a mistake. Maybe out here it was a disgrace not to have money. It certainly wasn't in show business. She didn't notice the large blond girl glaring at her, and if she'd been told that the blond girl and her present partner were going together, it wouldn't have meant anything.

He began doing tricky steps. "Listen to that sweet sax! That's Benny Nolan's band. Gee, what a guy! I heard him up in St. Louis and I stood there so close to the platform I could have touched him. Was that something?"

Doll knew what Benny Nolan said about bobby-soxers who stood around and stared at him. "Benny's nice, only he hasn't much sense."

He stopped dead. "Say, do you *know* Benny Nolan?"

"Why, sure, I do."

He swung around and said in a shout, "Listen, everybody! *Dolly knows Benny Nolan!*"

The large blond girl came quite close, her lips twisting. "Does she? Well, Constance Curtis is playing in the movie down at the Bijou and I *suppose* she knows her, too!"

"Why, yes, I know Connie," Doll said.

She could see that no one in the whole room believed her.

She came home at last and Ace was sitting on the veranda, smoking his corncob pipe.

"Have a good time, Doll?"

"No. Lousy. Those kids don't know anything."

"So?" Ace pointed with his pipe. "Trouble's coming up the walk."

Miss Jimpson, looking more like Little Eve's aunt than ever, her cheeks fiery, her nose red. Miss Jimpson pounced on Aunt Mae in the parlor and you could hear her through the open window.

"I hate to tell you this, Miz' Stratton, but that child's untruthful. She tells fibs. She says she knows Miss Constance Curtis the film star. She actually up and said so."

Aunt Mae: "Did she? Doll, come here a minute, please."

Into the dim parlor and Aunt Mae asking crisp and cool, "Do you know Constance Curtis, Doll?"

"Sure. Why not? She isn't anybody."

Miss Jimpson bristled. "Miss Curtis is just about the biggest movie star there is and she comes of a *very* refined family from Kentucky."

"Like fun she does. Her father runs a delicatessen on Second Avenue."

Miss Jimpson began to shake. "Constance Curtis is a sweet, wholesome—"

Doll opened her mouth. Then shut it tight again. Miss Jimpson was a fan and she'd never known one before. Fans were worse than bobby-soxers.

Aunt Mae, so crisp she almost seemed to crackle: "If my niece says she knows anyone you can be certain she does. Dolly is a very reliable little girl. I wish you a good afternoon, Miss Jimpson."

The door slammed and Doll's eyes went wide. "Gosh, you didn't have to stand up for me, Aunt Mae."

"I certainly did. Why you're one of the family, Doll."

Ace fondled his pipe. "Been wonderin' what you were goin' to say to that hellcat, only you didn't."

"Just that Connie's a"—she sought about for a word that would be suitable for their ears—"a little tramp."

"Oh, dear," said Aunt Mae. "She shouldn't know about things like that."

"Might's well know 'em sooner as later." Ace put the pipe in his mouth.

The next afternoon everything went suddenly flat and stale. For the novelty'd worn off now and Millfort was only a stupid, dusty little place. She went walking downtown through the heat and there was no stir, no excitement; nothing to see, nothing to do.

She stopped before the Bijou theater and it was only a little hole in the wall.

"Hello, Broadway!"

She turned and the short, pudgy, red-cheeked man was smiling at her. "Pete Thurston. I'm manager of this flea bag. Come on in. How's the Big Town, sweetheart?"

Someone different, someone straight off Forty-second Street. He led her inside and it felt like a theater, it smelled like a theater.

"Want to see the show, Broadway?"

"It's a turkey, isn't it?"

"I'll say it is. It stinks the whole theater up."

"You got a pretty good house," she said professionally. "Much paper in it?"

"Nope. Mostly kids."

"Bobby-soxers?"

Pete shuddered. "Bubble-gummers. Come on up to the office."

A nice, small, cluttered, dusty, familiar place. Old copies of Variety and Billboard, press sheets, tattered stills, a typewriter with gray lint hanging from its one chair, her feet in another. "How come you're in this hick town, Pete?"

He spoke to her as if she were his own age and she was used to that. "Well, I'll tell you, Broadway. I was working for Lew's Neighborhood house over on the West Side. And I had a big bust-up. Nervous breakdown. The doctor said I had to keep nice and quiet. So they shot me out here."

"That's pretty tough going, Pete."

"Oh, it's not so bad when you get used to it. They tell me your father's an actor. How's he doing?"

"He isn't doing anything right now."

Pete nodded. "How'd he like to try the clam chowder circuit? Friend of mine's got a straw hat theater down on the Cape. I might shoot him a line. Not much dough but it's better than nothing."

Well, it wouldn't do any harm to try.

"If you'd put in a word for Herbie, Pete, that would be swell."

"Glad to." His eyes grew hungry. "Tell me all about the Big Town!"

It was ten days later when the letter from Oliver came. "—Herbie's got a job with a straw hat down on the Cape. I hear Rose Leonard's up there, too. You remember Rose—"

Doll stood there and bit her lip. She wasn't surprised that Oliver had written before Herbie did because Herbie always had a hard time with letters. Yes, she remembered Rose Leonard; a tall, rangy girl who thought she looked like Katharine Hepburn.

She had some luck in getting small parts and she was dead sure she was going to see her name up in lights. Rose was dead sure about everything. Rose was always right and people who didn't agree with her were wrong. Rose was coldly ambitious and though she wasn't a tramp or a heel, you had the feeling she was hard as nails inside.

It was silly, of course, but as Doll stood there, she had a dim feeling of disaster. When you started having the horrors, the thing to do was to go for a good long walk.

She went down Washington Street and the great trees, dusty with summer, almost met in arches overhead. Redbirds flashed against the blue glare of sky and it was steaming, sticky hot. She stopped by the tall green hedge.

THERE WAS a boy sitting just inside, deep in the shade of the sycamores. He was stretched out limp in a long wicker chair with an open book on his lap and his long face was very pale with the fair hair falling over his forehead. He might have been about twelve, and some quality about his eyes, a quick, sensitive keenness, reminded her of Oliver.

She pulled a handkerchief from the pocket of her shorts. "Whew, it's hot!"

He had a soft smile like Oliver's too. "It's cooler here in the shade. Come on in."

She sat gratefully down in the grass beside him and he was too old for his age as Oliver was. "You're the girl from New York, aren't you? I'm David Graham, I've been sick."

"You don't look very rugged, David."

He took up the book. "I've been reading David Copperfield."

Doll's eyes lighted up. "Where've you got to, now?"

"David's just coming to the old boat."

"Gosh! That's the very best of all."

His hands moved wearily. "Only I get so tired I have to stop."

"I'll read to you if you want, David."

Half an hour later, she'd put the volume down and they were so intent on each other they didn't see the tall, slim woman in shirt and jodhpurs come quietly across the grass.

"And you didn't have anything to eat *at all?*" David was saying.

"Well, not till I walked all the way up to 112th Street to borrow a buck from Joe Edwards."

"Company, David?" asked the tall woman.

"Yes, Mum. This is Dolly Martin and she's been telling me the most wonderful stories about New York."

Mrs. Graham was like something you sometimes see on the stage—maybe a little like Ina Claire—cool and quiet but with a radiance you sense even before she begins to speak. She held out her hand. "I'm glad you came, Dolly. David needs some company. Tired, David?"

"No, Mum. Dolly doesn't tire anyone." He looked up like a very small boy who wants something badly. "Mum. The Bijou's showing Great Expectations next week. I don't suppose I could go, could I?"

"No, I don't suppose you could. There'll be a big crowd and you're still pretty weak. You'd better come in the house now and Dolly'll want a cool drink."

It was a wonderful house inside and she was all alone with Mrs. Graham, and a Negro man in a white coat was actually bringing her a tall, frosted glass and a plate of cookies.

"I'll have a drink with you, Dolly." Even if Mrs. Graham's eyes were deep violet and her hair bright gold, she somehow made you feel right at home with her. "You see, David is a long time getting well and he frets about it. And when we have some of the other children over, they stay forever or are too noisy."

Doll nodded. "Sure, I know. When Jimmy Huston was sick, I used to stay with him when his father and mother had to go to the studio."

"Are those the Hustons we hear on the radio?"

"Yes. They had a tough time at first but they're in the money now."

Mrs. Graham smiled. "You know a lot about the world, don't you, Dolly? A lot more than I do." She held out her hand. "Come again, Dolly. Come often."

She went slowly down the walk and some odd words Ace had used came into her head. "Quality folks." Well, Mrs. Graham and David were. She'd never known any before. . . .

She came back up the walk at a hard run that next morning. She burst into the dining room and the sun was slanting there through the green blinds.

Mrs. Graham was such a lady that she didn't even look surprised.

"Look, Mrs. Graham, David could come down to see Great Expectations if there wasn't any crowd, couldn't he?"

David's face lighted up and even Mrs. Graham's soft voice sounded excited. "Why, what do you mean, Dolly?"

"Pete's running it off this morning so he can time it. There won't be anybody there but him and you and David and maybe me. You can have the whole house to yourself."

"Mum!" David's voice was bright.

Mrs. Graham was very quick. "You're sure we wouldn't be a bother? And would we have to hurry?"

"Gosh, no. Pete'll hold it till you get there. Take your time."

Mrs. Graham stood up. "Dolly, you must be a magician. I never felt so much like royalty in all my life."

Pete certainly did it up in style. Pete was out on the sidewalk waiting to swing the car door open. Pete said, "Good morning, Mrs. Graham. Good morning, David. I hope you'll like our little entertainment."

Pete ushering them into the empty theater. Pete putting David on the aisle. Pete called, "House lights!" and it all went dark. He called, "All right, Chad. Let her roll."

She could sense how excited David was and it was the right sort of excitement too: the kind you feel on an opening night when a show comes in cold and suddenly turns into a blazing success. She could feel his fingers touch hers and that was nice.

Well, holding hands like a bobby-soxer! How Oliver would grin if he could see her now. . . .

June slipping into July, July into early August. David was all well and growing very brown and they went swimming in the river.

She was weeding in the garden now and Aunt Mae slammed open the screen door.

"Special-delivery letter for you, Doll!"

Herbie's writing in a big scrawl and then she suddenly had to sit down on the back steps. Herbie married. Herbie married to Rose.

"Why what's the matter, Doll?"

Doll felt as if she'd been beaten. Herbie'd been going to send for her, first thing, as soon as he got into the money. He hadn't. He'd married Rose instead.

Aunt Mae took the letter from her.

Herbie had written: "It'll probably take us some time to get organized when we get back to New York in the fall. But when we do, you bet we'll send for you P.D.Q. You'll love Rose, baby. Rose will be a second mother to you. . . ."

Aunt Mae said, "That woman doesn't sound good to me." She said, "If you want to, Doll, you just stay right here and be our little girl."

She looked up. "Gee, you're nice, Aunt Mae. You're awfully nice." But Aunt Mae couldn't help her now. Maybe nobody could. "I got to go downtown. I got to talk to someone."

You feel lost when you've always counted on someone and now can't any more. When it's someone you've loved, it's worse. It gives you a nasty, sick, sweetish feeling.

For nothing would ever be the same in the Big Town again. Nothing ever the same between her and her father. Rose and she would never get on, no matter how hard they tried.

The old Herbie'd be gone too, and she had the dismal sense that maybe there'd never been an old Herbie, a fond, considerate father. Maybe that had all been in her mind.

BUT HERE was the pudgy little man standing in front of his theater. "Pete, can I talk to you, please?"

He took one look at her face. "Better come up to the office, Broadway."

She sat down, handed him the letter.

His eyes skimmed over it in a flash.

"I feel terrible, Pete."

"I know." He went over to the window. "I didn't tell you but when I came here, I was married. Bee was coming out too when I got settled. She didn't. She divorced me and got married to someone else."

Her eyes went dark. "But, Pete, people don't do things like that!"

"You know darned well they do, Broadway."

Yes, they did. Herbie had.

"I nearly went nuts," Pete was saying, "but after a while I started thinking. Bee never would have fitted in out here and we'd both been miserable. You want to cry, Broadway?"

"Only kids cry, Pete."

Pete's voice, very level: "You've got a lot of good friends, Broadway."

Yes, she had. Pete, himself, Aunt Mae, Ace, Uncle Kim, David, Mrs. Graham. And they all had one thing in common that Herbie hadn't: some hard core of honor. They'd keep their promises.

"Can you take a tough one, Broadway? I don't think your father wants you back too much. Not right now."

Yes, that was it. That was what made you bitter sick in your heart.

"Maybe you've had about enough of show business, Broadway."

There were two worlds before her and she'd have to choose: the shiny, hard, exciting one that was the Big Town with all its trumpets blowing; the neat, clean, quiet-to-dullness one that was Aunt Mae and Ace and Uncle Kim.

There was a third world, too: that of David and Mrs. Graham, and that was the best of all. Could she ever be like them? Could she ever be what Ace called "quality folks"? Probably not. But she could try.

"You know, Broadway," Pete was saying, "when things get different, you just can't go back and make them the way they were before."

"No," she said, and even if she lived a long time, she'd never feel as old as she did now. "No. You can't ever go back."

2. NOBLES

By 1909, that aspirational mind-set had become reality. At least for Frank. His profile had grown, and he took that prestige back to his wife's native New England, where he accepted a managerial job at a Boston soap company, the family moving into a Beacon Street apartment in Boston's Brookline suburb. The money was much better as a manager, and the Hillmans' greater prosperity allowed them to move to a nicer address on Columbia Street and send young Gordon to the prestigious Noble and Greenough School. Founded by George Washington Copp Noble in the aftermath of the Civil War in 1866, Nobles (as it was known) was an all-male preparatory school associated with Harvard.[1]

The Boston of Nobles was the Boston of James Russell Lowell, of Francis Parkman and Henry Adams, of Julia Ward Howe and Oliver Wendell Holmes, the intellectual hub of the country, the home of the Boston Brahmins, the *Atlantic Monthly*, and Houghton Mifflin. From the 1860s to the end of the century, as Nobles was developing into a city institution, Boston College, MIT, Emerson College, and Simmons all appeared, joining Harvard to further cement the city's intellectual reputation. At the same time, the city teemed with an abused working class who saw none of the hallowed halls of those universities, and a middle class that used Boston's burgeoning public transportation system to initiate the process of white flight to the suburbs.[2]

It was a mix that generated a penchant for social control unique to the city, as books, movies, and plays that officials thought to be immoral or salacious were censored or shut down completely, giving rise to the phrase "Banned in Boston," only exacerbating the city's reputation for intolerance across the country. It was a reputation cemented in 1927, when the city executed Nicola Sacco and Bartolomeo Vanzetti for murder and armed robbery in Braintree, one of Boston's growing middle-class suburbs. With conflicting and recanted testimony and little formal evidence, the defendants' conviction and execution seemed motivated by anti-immigrant bigotry more than objective standards of criminal guilt. And so Hillman's Boston was one with a grandiose intellectual heritage but also a stratified class system whose moralizing bigotry made the stakes for remaining ensconced among the elite incredibly high.[3]

Those stakes also made private schools like Nobles all the more important. Private education had existed in the country since the seventeenth century, but modern private education developed during the Gilded Age, a response to industrialization, its attendant immigration, and the broadening bureaucracy of public education. When combined with new money and an attendant Anglophilia, which romanticized schools like Eton, Harrow, and Rugby, the white educational flight to single-sex private institutions began in earnest. Nobles was part of that development.[4]

The school moved five different times in the nineteenth century, but in 1901 it moved to a property at 100 Beacon Street, where it would stay for the next twenty-one years. Hillman attended during its stay at Beacon Street. (In 1922, several years after Hillman's studies, the school moved again, this time to a one-hundred-acre property outside of the small town of Dedham, Massachusetts, just to the southwest of Boston. It remains on that property today.)[5]

Noble was the aged founder of the school, still around for Hillman's time at Nobles, as was his younger partner (and son-in-law), James Jay Greenough. Hillman was also a student at the school when Greenough unexpectedly died in April 1913. There was turmoil at the school. Noble was seventy-seven at the time. The school was experiencing financial difficulties. In response, a group of alumni and several outsiders associated with Harvard incorporated the school and created a Board of Trustees to govern it. They officially hired Noble as headmaster at an annual salary of three thousand dollars. The corporation also agreed to an annual $7,500 payment to Noble for the grounds and equipment of the school, which transferred into the hands of the Board.[6]

Noble was old, however, and would need help administering the school. Thus the Board named Albertus T. Dudley, a teacher at the school since 1896, assistant principal. Hillman spent much of his writing career reliving his life at Nobles, or what that life would have been had his career there lasted through graduation. He described prep school life at length in his short stories, and among his topics was such a search for a school administrator. In his story "Turn the Hour," published in *Good Housekeeping* in 1937, he described the plight of Mr. Douglas, a devoted teacher at a New England school like Nobles who was being considered by the Board of Trustees for the assistant headmastership because the headmaster's age was a hindrance to him doing all the work himself. Douglas wanted the job, and his students wanted him to get it, as well, and in the style of Hillman's stories, everything worked out in the end, with Douglas happily taking the job to the delight of the students. Dudley, however, was not so happy in the position in real life, preferring teaching to administering. In 1917, he retired, and the job went to George H. Fiske, a young faculty member who had arrived in 1912. Hillman would have been at the school for this transition, setting the scenario for his later story.[7]

It was also in 1917 when Nobles added students from one of its local rivals, Volkmann School, a formerly prosperous Newbury Street venture that had suffered under the weight of anti-German sentiment during the era of World War I. Boston was a hub of such sentiment: German books were pulled from library shelves; the city banned performances of Beethoven; and it fired the conductor of the Boston Symphony Orchestra because he was a German immigrant. The Volkmann School's founder was Arthur Volkmann, himself an immigrant from Danzig, Germany, and he would fall victim to the same sorts of rumors as would other German immigrants—that he was an enemy of the state, that he was un- or anti-American. In response, those sympathetic to Volkmann and his school helped engineer its merger with Nobles, bringing over its students, two members of its Board of Trustees, and two new teachers.[8]

"The boys, of course, were not conscious of these problems," asserts school historian Richard Flood. "To them, Mr. Noble was a symbol of their school." The class of 1918 dedicated their annual to him. By this time, however, the role of the octogenarian was largely ceremonial. "To the boys, Mr. Fiske was the real administrator of the school. They sometimes made fun of the way he manipulated his walrus mustache, but they appreciated his sincerity and interest. He was not a man to be feared, but to be accepted as working for their own interests."[9]

Gordon's high school years were filled with whispers about the war in Europe and what it might mean for the students at Nobles. The young man turned eighteen in 1918, and less than two weeks after his birthday, on September 12, he signed his draft card. In 1918, the Board created the Noble and Greenough Battalion, wherein the boys in the upper four classes paraded for two hours a week on the grounds of Dexter Field, the school's athletic area. Of course, registering for the draft so late in 1918 ensured that Gordon wouldn't have to fight. The armistice would occur two months later.[10]

Hillman, however, wouldn't be at Nobles to serve in the Noble and Greenough Battalion. The school's class of 1918, one class following Hillman's, produced R. Ammi Cutter, who would go on to become a justice of the Massachusetts Supreme Court. Ernest G. Henderson, later the president of Sheraton Corporation, graduated in 1914. Royal Little, later the president of Textron, graduated in 1915. Dwight P. Robinson, later the chairman of the Massachusetts Investors Trust, graduated in 1916. It was a distinguished lot, fitting the Hillmans' grandiose assessment of themselves, and attending a school that produced such a pantheon would help define the parameters of Gordon's life and imagination for decades.[11]

What made those parameters all the more bold is that Hillman's time at Nobles was relatively short. He entered the school as one of the "New Boys" in 1911 as part of the school's Sixth Class, the contemporary equivalent of Seventh Grade. He stayed for three years but kept a remarkably low profile while there, never becoming a part of any teams or clubs. His time prior to arriving at Nobles was spent being homeschooled, and he likely returned to that platform after his stint at prep school—if he returned to any official version of school at all. His early story thus mirrored that of Ernest Poole, himself born in the Chicago area, homeschooled in his younger days, then matriculating at Chicago's University School for Boys. Poole did not write as much about the passions of youth as did Hillman, but some of the influence of those times can be seen in his first novel, *The Harbor*, published in 1915. In book 1 of the novel, Billy, the protagonist, learns his love of art and culture from a doting mother before coming of age at school. The tone and language of *The Harbor* is similar to that of Hillman's later work and was almost certainly an influence. In his collegiate days, which take the patina of Hillman's boarding school stories, Billy makes a friend of a young man named Joe Kramer. "He belonged to no fraternity, and except on the athletic field he kept out of all our genial life," Billy explains. "And this life of ours, for all its thoughtlessness, was so rich in genuine friendships, so filled and bubbling over with the joy of being young, that we could not understand how any decent sort of chap could deliberately keep out of it." It was, in language and substance, a precursor to Hillman's tales of boarding school two decades later.[12]

The future author almost certainly read the popular *The Harbor*, but his actual schooling at Nobles would be interrupted by family tragedy. Frank Hillman would die two days after Christmas in December 1915, when Gordon was fourteen years old, leaving him and Carolyn to live at 2 Arlington Street in Cambridge. With his mother's grandiose vision of her own education and breeding, and the loss of Frank's paycheck to pay for another private school, the likelihood was that Carolyn took charge of her son's education, only further binding the two together and metastasizing their combined sense of self.[13]

In every autobiographical statement he made for the rest of his life, Hillman always mentioned Nobles as his school. In one such claim included in a poetry anthology in 1918, when he would have been just finishing high school, Hillman claimed that he was "educated at the Noble and Greenough School, preparing for Harvard College." He noted his work as a reporter and his interest in "short story writing, tennis, and 'going to college.'"[14] That was, of course, part of the self-delusion rather than any formal goal. It was actually the biography of Ernest Poole, one of his literary inheritors, who had finished prep school before attending Princeton, then going on to win the first Pulitzer Prize for Fiction, writing in a style that Hillman in many ways mimicked.

Still, in a life of self-delusion, the delusions themselves matter just as much as lived reality, and Hillman's obsession with prep school would dominate much of his magazine fiction over the next several decades. Hillman's time at Nobles was short, but it loomed as the educational lodestone of his life, both in his autobiographical author statements and in the stories that the author produced. Nobles, when Hillman attended, was still ensconced on a Boston street corner, had yet to make its move to the campus at Dedham, but when he wrote about prep school, Hillman wrote about a campus like that of Nobles at Dedham. Depending on when he was writing, the school he described throughout his writing career was either known as Dunstable School or Somerset School, but they were unmistakably the same place. In one story, Hillman described the school as founded by Reverend Peter Dunstable during the presidency of James Monroe, a "school for the sons of gentlemen." In another, it was founded by Reverend Peter Somerset during the presidency of James Monroe, an "academy for the sons of gentlemen."[15]

Either way, it was a school with a campus like the later, not the former, Nobles. The Chapel Tower loomed over the campus, its Chapel Clock chiming the hour. "As you come up the hill to the School, the first thing you see is Chapel's white-topped tower there among the trees," Hillman described in "Day to Remember," published in *McCall's* in 1940 and featured at the end of this chapter.[16] Dormitories like Wingate House and Ames House accompanied academic buildings like Forsythe and Hall, situated around a quadrangle known as The Yard. The structures were Georgian in design, overlooking natural landmarks like Little River, which ran through campus, and man-made ones, like a war memorial that featured war dead from the school beginning in 1863. When students sought to escape the cloister of campus, they went into town, an activity referred to as "going down to the vill." While such descriptions clearly fit the newer Nobles rather than the old, there were still vestiges of the school as Hillman knew it as a student. Coventry, for example, was the institution where the School would send its reprobates, surely a crib of premerger Volkmann.

Regardless, these details demonstrated a devotion to place, spread as it was across the breadth of Hillman's stories about boarding school. The fictional School's unquestioned leader was known to the students as Fuzzy. He was Francis Pierce Adams, one of the country's foremost classicists. In early stories he was the school's assistant headmaster, later its headmaster. Fuzzy was "M.A., Litt.D., and fellow of half a dozen learned and obscure societies"—demonstrating that the adult Hillman felt the progression of the characters in his stories in real time.[17] Adams, for example, was also the father of Sally, who began in Hillman's stories as a relatively young girl but would, as the years passed, grow up. Some students at the school did the same, returning through various stories. One, known as Merry during some early stories, returned to the school as a teacher, Mr. Merriam, in a story called "Schoolboy's Return." Merriam, in that story, ultimately marries Sally, cementing a romance that was budding through several of Hillman's earlier school stories.[18] The story "Turn the Hour," published in *Good Housekeeping* in 1937, tells the story of Mr. Douglas, a teacher at the school hoping to become assistant headmaster (just as had happened at Nobles in actuality during Hillman's youth). Douglas was a legacy, like Merriam, a former student who had gone to Harvard and returned to teach at the school: "It didn't seem as if the School could ever change, as if anything about it would ever change, but it could."[19]

Students with names like Manning, Steens, McReynolds, and Fairfield continued in school, waiting until they would attend Harvard. But their loyalty was always to the School. The students sang "Auld Lang Syne" at Chapel, joined clubs and played sports. One of the school's societies was Owls, a group of juniors chosen by seniors, who entered junior boys' rooms and silently tapped them on the shoulder to let them know they had been chosen: "It was a very silly sort of society, Robbie explained loftily. None of the best boys bothered with it at all."[20]

Still, despite the sylvan setting and developed academic Yoknapatawpha, the stories belied a conflicted author working through his childhood relationship with his own school experience. "Gentleman's Estate," for example, published in *American Magazine* in 1937, describes the loneliness of a young boy away at school, whose mother is an actress and whose father was distant and aloof. "He wasn't even a good father," the story explained. But at least the boy had his school: "The School would look after young Austin. For that was the way the School did. In all the world, the School was the only thing that didn't let you down."

It was another of Hillman's semi-biographical efforts writ into his fiction, demonstrating that, to Hillman, with a flighty, self-aggrandizing mother and a businessman father, Nobles, "the School," really did matter, as his autobiographical statements also demonstrated.[21]

That said, not all of Hillman's characters agreed. In an early story in which Fuzzy still served as assistant headmaster, Mr. Sandringham, "who was no ordinary headmaster and never took himself seriously, had always contended that the school was founded and conducted on a series of bad jokes." That particular tale told the story of a relatively poor country boy who invites a rich New York boy home for summer because he has again been abandoned by his parents. He's worried about it, but the wealthy friend is impressed: "Joel thinks I'm a little tin god. He thinks he's nobody. Matter of fact, people really like him better than they do me. And what he doesn't see at all is that he's the best friend I ever had."[22]

That sense of lack of belonging was a common theme. In "Nine Lives to Love," another 1937 story published in *McCall's*, a boy who lives next to the School wants desperately to attend but seems to have no hope, seems totally separated from that world until an incident with a cat, a rescue that demonstrated compassion and convinced his aunt to let him attend: "You only had to look over the wall to be in Paradise. There was Chapel tower, a straight shaft of red and white against the sky with the gold hands of its clock ticking the slow hours away; there were old Georgian buildings so dreaming in the sun; there was the school." It was the stark display of aspirational storytelling in microcosm:[23] "It was sheer magic to stare out his study window and see the red shaft of Chapel's white-tipped tower and the crisp green of Forsythe hedge and the long lawns and the old copper beech tree." Being at the School "was just like waking to a great golden dream every single day—a dream that never dawned at all." In one story, a legacy student, whose father attended in the class of 1917 (Hillman's class), discovers, through an act of childhood cruelty, that he is adopted, but his father, one of the Old Boys from the class of 1917, comes and makes everything okay. In another, one student is struggling with his guardian to stay at the School, while another one, visiting for the day with his senator father, hates the one he attended, "that dingy school in the dingy grey city block where they crammed you with facts that always seemed grey and dingy, too." When the visiting boy enters the gate of the School, he "had the odd impression that what he felt, what he thought, suddenly wasn't so important any more. And that was because, through all the long years, so many boys had gone in the gate with their youth strong upon them like a golden shield."[24] It was, in a sense, a story of Nobles' transition told through a tale of two boys hoping to stay at the stand-in for Nobles' Dedham campus.

Another of Hillman's school stories told the story of a former student whose son has died, and who was thus never able to attend the School. He returns to see Fuzzy and the grounds and to find solace. He was a student in the early 1910s and remembers his friends who died in World War I. It is a rumination on the generational meaning of institutions like the School, the importance they have in the lives of boys and the men they become, a story all the more prescient because Hillman himself only attended the School for a couple of years. While the returning student is back on campus he donates money to help a student whose financial problems were going to force him to leave before his senior year, a symbolic salvation for Hillman's own school career.[25]

It is worth noting that parents are rare on Hillman's fictional campus. When they appear, it is for brief visits, and their appearing in the story is to demonstrate that they will not be returning for their children over holiday break. It is a liminal space where parents are loved and revered, where their occasional appearance is appreciated, but where life, freedom, and the most meaningful parts of growing up happen without them: "What they [parents] never seemed to understand was that School was another world—a little world all by itself."[26]

Another story that otherwise tells the tale of a bully who reforms his ways at School includes a reference to a student from Austria who left in 1914, never to return, a casualty of World War I. Hillman's school always supported both World War efforts. "The Sound of Trumpets," a later story in the genre published in *Liberty* in 1941, told the story of a worried mother trying to use School officials to help keep an older son, a former student there, out of the military, before learning her lesson about sacrifice and necessity in war. It was a tale that surely relied on Hillman's own conversations with his mother after signing his draft card for World War I.[27]

In "From Now On," Hillman combined his common themes, describing one student's embarrassment at his family's behavior and another's worry that his poor grades would force him to leave School. In true Hillman fashion, everything worked out well, the embarrassed senior made a tutor for the failing junior, but that theme of fear of not belonging, whether through family or aptitude, remained vitally present. It was a fitting subject for an author who had not attended college, who had not finished his diploma at his exclusive prep school, and for an author whose writing provided a living but never provided the Pulitzer Prize and accolades of Ernest Poole.[28]

It was also a fitting subject for a series of stories written entirely during the Great Depression, providing a succession of aspirational narratives for a population suffering under economic collapse and recovery. Much of the popular writing of the Depression era depicted the hopelessness that so many felt. James T. Farrell's Studs Lonigan trilogy of novels, for example, published from 1932 to 1935, were exemplary of that strain. In another decade, Studs Lonigan probably would have risen from poverty to become successful and rich. But in Farrell's novels, the hero cannot overcome his harsh environment and dies young, poor, and alone. Robert Elliott Burns's *I Am a Fugitive from a Georgia Chain Gang*, published in 1932, described a war hero who returned from Europe to sink into poverty and crime and a miserable life. The film based on the novel won an Academy Award. Perhaps most emblematic of this line was John Steinbeck's *The Grapes of Wrath*, the story of an Oklahoma family's fortitude in surviving eviction from their land, migrating west, and suffering exploitation in what was supposed to be the promised land of California. It was the bestselling novel of 1939.[29]

But *The Grapes of Wrath* was also a story of aspiration and hope, bridging the other dominant theme of Depression-era literature. Tales of an aspirational nature appeared regularly. It was the decade of Dale Carnegie's *How to Win Friends and Influence People*, published in 1936. At the other end of the literary spectrum, it was the decade of Zora

Neale Hurston's *Their Eyes Were Watching God*, published in 1937, of Stella Gibbons's *Cold Comfort Farm*, published in 1932, and F. Scott Fitzgerald's *Tender Is the Night*, published two years later, all of them aspirational in either setting, content, or voice.[30] Hillman was no Fitzgerald, no Hurston or Steinbeck or Gibbons, but those books, combined with the preparatory work of earlier authors like Ernest Poole, laid the ground for the acceptance and readership of authors like Hillman, telling aspirational magazine stories of an exclusive boys' school in the heart of an economic collapse.

Hillman's school stories were open examinations of his own fraught experience with education. At the same time, they also fit into the linear development of such fiction, which began with the 1857 publication of *Tom Brown's School Days*, by Thomas Hughes, a story of England's Rugby School told by an author who attended. It was an influential novel that led to many similar examinations, like Alec Waugh's 1917 *The Loom of Youth*, which told the story of Sherbourne School. Such tales were far more critical of their subjects, their authors willing, unlike Hillman, to take on the darker side of prep school. Waugh's novel was incredibly controversial, for example, because he described homosexual activity at the academy. After Hillman's era, such stories would come to full flower in 1959 with John Knowles's *A Separate Peace*, a coming-of-age narrative set at a prep school called Devon, which was itself a stand-in for Knowles's own alma mater, Phillips Exeter. It, too, had homoerotic overtones. It, too, was a story that concentrated on the legitimate fears of schoolboys worried about the onset of a world war.[31]

What Hillman's tales did not have was the fraught nuance and dark tragedy of such stories that appeared before and after them. His academic stories demonstrated a longing for the simpler days of his school experience, but they were also part of the aspirational formula stories of popular magazines of the era. His inability to write critically about his experience or to move beyond the expectations of interwar magazine readers could have served as a barrier to his larger authorial ambitions. The stories were, however, just as able to describe the school experience, just as able to act as catharsis for an author coming to terms with his educational life. They recapitulated the mixture of shame, dependence, and hope that was Hillman's own school career, however brief, and gave it the long life that it was never able to have in the real world. It was a phenomenon demonstrated well by his 1940 story "Day to Remember."

DAY TO REMEMBER

Published in *McCall's*, June 1940

As you come up the hill to the School, the first thing you see is Chapel's white-topped tower there among the trees.

Crosby knew that his father would say something as soon as he saw it for it seemed as if his father was always saying things at the least excuse ever since he'd become a senator. And before the day was over, he'd have made his same old speech. For that was what they'd come for.

The Senator fingered the white piping on his waistcoat. The Senator said in that important voice, that sounded so pompous if you had to hear it often, "There's the School, son. It's a very old school. And I've heard that it's a very good one."

Crosby knew that the Senator wasn't saying that to him at all. He was saying it to the man who drove the station taxi and to the tall dark woman in the smart black coat. For Crosby's father always had to have an audience nowadays.

The tall woman was quite young and her face was sharp and alert and a little troubled somehow. She said shortly, "It's a very queer sort of school. And a very odd old man runs it."

Crosby stared at her and it was strange how grim and determined she looked for she was quite pretty really even if she did try to be brisk and efficient.

The Senator looked more pink and white and pompous than ever. He said smoothly, "You have a son here?"

She said, and her voice was sheer acid, "I've a nephew in school. I shan't have long."

The taxi stopped by the great school gate and Crosby's face was dull with boredom. It was just another school and all schools were alike. He'd seen a good many of them, for his father frequently took him with him when he went to make speeches to squirming and unhappy boys, just as he was taking him now.

And Crosby'd hate this school but it wouldn't matter for they'd only be here for a few hours. He'd hate it just as he hated the school where he went now: that school in the dingy grey city block where they crammed you with facts that always seemed grey and dingy, too.

THEY ALL got out of the taxi and went in the gate and Crosby had the odd impression that what he felt, what he thought, suddenly wasn't so important any more. And that was because, through all the long years, so many boys had gone in this gate with their youth strong upon them like a golden shield. But Crosby couldn't know that.

All he knew was that the sun was slanting down on the long green level of the Yard, the warm red brick of the old Georgian buildings, and that the big copper beech tree was swaying softly in the wind. He didn't know that he was seeing the School just as boys had seen it for a hundred years or more. And if he'd known, he wouldn't have cared, for after all it was just a place where his father was going to make a dull speech, that speech that spoke of "the playing fields of Eton," that speech that warned against wasting the fleeting hours, that speech that bade boys drive straight and steadfast toward their goal, for, as his father would never fail to say just before he sat down to a spatter of polite applause, "There isn't much time left."

Crosby had heard the speech so often that he nearly knew it by heart. And he hated it just as much as the boys would.

He hated his father's voice too, that voice was so smooth and unctuous as the Senator said, "I wonder where the headmaster's house is. He's a Mr. Adams, I believe."

The tall woman said, and she seemed to be angry all over, "I'm going there myself."

She walked across the grass as if she wanted to tramp it under foot, as if she wanted to tramp the whole school underfoot, as if anger was a rising flame within her, a flame that made her cheeks blaze and her eyes snap. And Crosby wondered who her nephew was and what on earth he'd done.

The headmaster's house was quite small there among the trees; the whole school seemed small and a trifle shabby. It wasn't half as impressive as some of the schools he'd seen.

The tall woman knocked on the door and it opened. A freckled-faced girl stood there in a boy's shirt and old boots and breeches.

The tall woman said, "Is Mr. Adams in? I'm Miss Elkins."

"He's expecting you." Crosby could tell she was troubled about something. She was looking at his father, "You're Senator Crosby, I'm sure. Won't you come in?"

An old man was coming toward them and he was so tall and thin he looked a little like a rusty sort of stork.

He held out his hand and said, "I'm glad to see you, Miss Elkins. I'm glad you've come." He said, "How do you do, Senator Crosby. I'm afraid I'll have to ask you to wait a minute. It's something rather important about one of my boys."

It didn't seem possible that this frail old man could be the headmaster. But he was. And he was worried about something. The girl was worried, too, and she ushered Crosby and her father into a small room.

Crosby looked up at his father, who was so plump and pink and white, and he could see his father was angry. He was angry at having been shoved aside into this room. He sat there like a statute of offended dignity.

The girl said softly, "Father's very much upset. You see—"

Miss Elkins voice came sharply from the next room, "It's an outrageous thing to do. Roger's much brighter than boys of his own age."

Then the headmaster's voice and there was still that little worried note in it. "He's a very bright boy. One of our best boys. But he has to work too hard to keep up. I've thought it all over quite carefully, Mrs. Elkins, and I've decided to set him down a class."

CROSBY SAT up straight. For the old man was fighting for something; something he thought was right. He was fighting for one of his boys. Crosby couldn't quite tell how he knew that, but he did. It was all in the old man's voice somehow. And he knew too that the old man had always stood up for his boys.

He was saying now, "You see, Miss Elkins, Roger isn't getting what he should from the school. Under the circumstances, he really can't—"

Miss Elkins' voice seemed to cut clear through the room. "Mr. Adams, if Roger is put into a lower class, I shall take him out of school. That's exactly what I wrote you; that's exactly what I meant, I shall take him away today."

Crosby knew that the old man was losing his fight. And he felt badly about it somehow; almost as badly as the freckled-faced girl did.

She was looking at him now, she was saying, "It's a shame. He's such a nice boy and his aunt wants him rushed through school—"

The Senator said, "Ha-rumph!" and blew his nose. And Crosby knew he didn't understand at all. He was only angry because he had to wait. And he wished his father was like other fathers and not a Senator at all, not just dull and pompous, not always making speeches that were dull and pompous, too.

They could hear the headmaster's voice again. They could hear him say, "I'm sorry, Miss Elkins. But it doesn't do just to cram a boy with facts." He said softly, "He's very young."

Miss Elkins said, "He's to enter college when he's seventeen. I shall place him in a school where that can be done. Will you send for him?"

Crosby was suddenly angry. He was angry that the tall woman should talk that way about a boy. He was so angry that his rather squarish face flushed and he ran his fingers through his close cropped hair. For the headmaster knew all about boys and what they wanted and Miss Elkins didn't know at all.

THE GIRL said, "I'll have to go tell Roger." She walked slowly toward the door as if something in her had gone limp, as if she hated injustice just as much as Crosby did, as if she couldn't do a single thing about it.

Crosby looked up at his father and his father hadn't sensed anything at all.

Mr. Adams came into the room and he looked old and worn. He looked as if he'd lost one of his boys. He said, "I'm sorry to keep you waiting, Senator." He said, "I think you've already met Miss Elkins. She's taking her nephew away."

The Senator said, "Shake hands with Mr. Adams, Donald." He said sententiously, "Mr. Adams is not only headmaster here; he's a most eminent classical scholar."

But he didn't have to say any of that at all. For Crosby was shaking hands with the old man. He was saying, "I'm glad to meet you, sir." He was trying to tell Mr. Adams how much he liked him.

Miss Elkins broke in. She said, "Has anyone been sent for Roger?"

The old man stood up very straight. He said, "My daughter's gone for him, I think." He said, "It'll take him a little time to pack, Miss Elkins." He stared out the window as if he were seeing a small shadow going out the great gate, a small boy who wasn't coming back. He said softly, "I hope, Miss Elkins, you can stay to hear Senator Crosby's address in Chapel tonight."

Crosby looked at his father and he seemed to swell as if he were adding importance every second. He said, "I hope you will, Miss Elkins. I hope you will, indeed. And then we could have your company on the train."

It was queer how his father impressed people, Crosby thought. He was impressing the tall woman now, he was making her do something she didn't want to do. For she was saying, "Well, I suppose I could. After all, it's a much faster train."

Mr. Adams had his hands shoved deep in his pockets. Mr. Adams was saying, "Perhaps we'd all be more comfortable in the library."

The first thing that Crosby saw when he stepped into the long, low room was the boys. There they were, in faded photographs on the walls; class photographs with dates that went back a long time.

And yet you could almost see them in this quiet room that looked out on the long green Yard, you could almost hear them talk. For they'd left something of themselves here and that was their youth.

Crosby couldn't quite understand all that; he could only feel it. He was still looking at the pictures when Mr. Adams spoke to him. Mr. Adams said, "They were all here once. They're all gone now," and Crosby knew he was thinking of Elkins, for in a few hours Elkins would be gone, too. Mr. Adams would hate that; just as he hated to see any of his boys go, just as he'd always hated it.

"Yes, sir," Crosby said. "You've been here a long time, sir, haven't you?" and then the door was opening and someone was coming in.

It was a small boy with heavy horn-rimmed glasses across his face and his shoulders stooped as if he'd spent long hours bent over a desk, staring at Latin and Greek and Mathematics through the thick lenses. His face was dark and sober.

He said, and his voice was utterly lifeless, "Hello, Aunt Kate."

He looked at Crosby and his father with no curiosity at all and the room was suddenly very still.

Miss Elkins' voice cut through that stillness. Miss Elkins said, "I'm taking you away, Roger. You'd better get your things packed."

Elkins just stood there and his face didn't change at all. He said dully, "Yes, Aunt Kate," as if it were something he'd been expecting for a long time.

Mr. Adams was moving toward him and saying, "I'm sorry, Elkins. I'm sorry to have you go."

Elkins face twitched as he stared up at the gaunt old man. He said, "I'm sorry, too, sir," and all he wasn't saying was suddenly in his voice, that young voice that had grown so sober and so old.

Mr. Adams fingered the wisp of whisker on his chin. He said, "Suppose you take young Crosby over to Wingate with you and introduce him to some of the boys. It would be rather dull for him here, I'm afraid."

Elkins looked at Crosby and Crosby could see his eyes behind the heavy glasses. They were young eyes, frightened eyes, eyes that had a hurt look in them. "All right, sir," he said and you could see he was holding himself in tightly.

Mr. Adams smiled at Crosby. "Would you like that?" he said.

"Yes, sir. Very much, sir," Crosby said, for he suddenly knew that Elkins wanted someone with him, that he didn't want to be alone, that he didn't want to just keep dully saying over and over to himself, "I've got to go. I've got to go."

"My daughter'll show Miss Elkins and your father around," Mr. Adams was saying and then Crosby and Elkins were going down the steps in the sharp sun.

They were cutting across the Yard and boys were shouting there and Elkins looked as if he didn't see or hear anything at all and he was an odd, old, stooped, sallow little figure there in the sun.

Crosby said, "I'll bet you'll be glad to get out of school."

Elkins looked up at Chapel's red and white tower but he didn't seem to be seeing it. He said slowly, "No, I won't. I won't be glad." He said dully, "I can show you around. I've got to pack."

He was so tense it hurt just to hear him, just to wonder what he was thinking deep down inside. It hurt because he didn't show a single thing he felt; he wasn't going to. "Gosh," Crosby said, "that's all right." He said, "I hate the school I go to."

Elkins looked at him sharply. He said, "You wouldn't hate it here," and then they were going in Wingate's dark door and up the stairs. They were going into a study where the sunlight made little dancing shadows all across the walls. On one side of the study, bats and balls and tennis rackets and a baseball glove were stacked in a corner; on the other side, there were none of those.

Elkins stood by the window, staring out at the School. He stared for quite a long time. He said dully, "You see, Fuzzy—I mean Mr. Adams—wanted to set me down a class but my aunt wouldn't have it. She—she's sending me through school."

Crosby looked out the window, too, but he couldn't quite see what Elkins was staring at. For there was nothing there but the School.

Elkins was still speaking, as if he were talking to himself, as if he were trying to make it all seem right. "You see, my father and mother haven't any money at all. You see, my aunt's in business for herself. She's awfully smart. She wants me to get ahead. She made Fuzzy put me in the Fourth class though he didn't want to." He brushed his hand across his eyes. "I've got to pack."

IT WAS queer but Crosby could suddenly see it all. It was queer he could see it so sharply for he hadn't thought about anyone but himself for a long time. He could see Elkins trying to keep up in a class that was just a little ahead of him; he could see him trying so hard he didn't have much time for anything else. He could see the lamp burning quite late and Elkins hunched over his books and all the other boys making fun of him.

He put his hands in his pockets and said, "Gosh! I guess all your friends'll be sorry to see you go."

Elkins pulled out an old trunk and lifted the lid. He said, "I haven't any friends. Nobody that is but Hathaway and he's my roommate."

He took out the trunk tray. He bent over so Crosby couldn't see his face. He said, "All the fellows—all the fellows call me the Greasy Grind." He straightened again and said defiantly. "Nobody'll care whether I go or not. Nobody'll care a bit."

It was true. Crosby knew. Nobody'd care what happened to the Greasy Grind; the sallow boy who was always bending over his books, the boy who didn't have time to go shouting through the Yard or run across the green playing fields. They'd all just think he was queer; they'd be a little glad when he was gone. It was always that way with Greasy Grinds, wherever they were.

There was a knock on the door and a boy came in. He was quite a small boy with yellow hair and bright blue eyes. He said, all in a rush, "Gee, Elks, I just heard. Have you really got to go away?"

Elkins looked surprised. He said, "I've got to go." He said, "Austin, this is Crosby. His father's going to talk in Chapel tonight."

It was funny how Austin's face showed just what he felt. It showed he was upset just as Fuzzy and his daughter had been, upset about Elkins. He was saying to Crosby, "Your father's a Senator, isn't he?," but he wasn't thinking about that at all. He was thinking how the Greasy Grind would hate to go away.

He said, "Gosh, Elks, I'm sorry." He looked at all Elkins' books heaped up there underneath the lamp. He said, "I guess we could have had some good times together."

He was telling Elkins something without saying it in words to all; he was telling him he didn't think he was just a Greasy Grind, that he was sorry he'd got to go away, that the whole School was sorry, too. He hadn't had to come to tell Elkins that but he had. For he knew just how Elkins felt.

He stretched out his hand and said, "I've got a class. Goodbye, Elks."

Elkins' glasses had a little haze on them now. He said and his voice suddenly was fresh and young. "Thanks, Austin. Thanks a lot."

And Crosby knew that Elkins wouldn't think of himself as just a Greasy Grind any more; he wouldn't because Austin had been so kind.

Crosby could feel that so sharply that he said, "That Austin, he's a swell guy."

Elkins bent over his trunk. He said, "Of course he is." He turned to pick up a pile of clothes. He said, and his voice was muffled, "He's one of the scrubs. I—I never knew him much."

Crosby stared at the stooped figure there by the trunk. And he knew that Elkins wasn't just packing clothes away. He was putting in all the things he wished he'd said, all the things he wished he'd done, all the great golden things he'd wanted to do when he was a boy in school. All the things he'd dreamed of, all the things he'd lost, all the things he hadn't had; laughter and friendship and the long, sunny days of school, all the shimmering hours he'd somehow missed. They were all there in the trunk—all the keen feel of early Fall—all the soft green glory of the Spring—and all the people, too, all the teachers he'd liked, all the boys he'd never really known, all the boys he'd wanted to know. They were all there and soon he'd shut down the lid upon them. And when he unpacked, they wouldn't be there. There'd be nothing but loneliness and the Greasy Grind starting in a new, strange school.

Elkins' hands shook and fumbled and a sweater fell on the floor.

Someone said, "I've got it, Elks," and a dark boy had stooped and picked the sweater up. The dark boy was tall and oddly handsome with bright spots of color burning in his cheeks. He said, "I just heard you were going. I thought maybe there'd be something I could do."

Elkins looked up as if he couldn't quite believe it. He said, "Gee! Oh Gee, Manning!"

You could see by his eyes what an honor it was to have Manning come; you could see it was an honor because Manning was a junior and he'd be one of the best liked boys in school.

Manning said in that soft, warm voice of his, "You're making an awful mess of things, Elks. Let me straighten it out."

He was talking to Elkins as if Elkins was someone beside just a Greasy Grind.

He smiled at Crosby and said, "You're the Senator's son, aren't you?" And then he turned to Elkins again. He'd pushed Elkins away from the trunk and he was talking as he packed. He was saying, "It's a shame you've got to go, Elks. I guess, in the Spring, you could have gone out for coxswain on the crew." He put a pile of books into the trunk and said, "I bet you'd have been pretty good."

"Gosh, sir! D'you think so, sir?" Elkins said. He stood there, blinking, and he looked a little like a bug. But you didn't want to laugh at him.

Somewhere a bell began to ring and Manning jumped up. He said, "That's History II. I'll be late." He held out his hand and said, "Goodbye, Elks, and good luck."

Elkins stood there and he didn't seem so tense. For he had two fine things to take with him now when he went: quick kindness and friendship. He'd remember them all his life, he'd remember just how Manning stood, just how Manning looked.

Chapel bell stopped ringing and footsteps thudded on the stairs. They were the quick, light footsteps of someone who was happy, and a boy burst into the room. He was about Crosby's age with a tanned face, dark eyes that seemed to dance, and short black curly hair.

His whole face shone and he said in a shout, "Hi, Elks! My father's come! My father's come again!"

He saw Elkins' half-packed trunk and all the vividness seemed to drain from his face. He said, almost in a whisper, "She—she's making you go away?"

Elkins nodded and his voice was quite harsh. He said, "I've got to go." He turned and said, "This is Crosby. Would—would you take him out, Hathaway, and show him around?" He said in a desperate rush of words, "I've got to pack. I've got lots to do."

Crosby stood up for he knew that Hathaway was Elkins' best friend. And Elkins didn't want to say goodbye to him just yet. When he said that he wanted to turn and go quite quickly. And now he wanted to be alone; to hear the soft tones of Chapel bell, to stare out at the School as the dim twilight shut down, for he saw something there that Crosby couldn't quite see yet—something he'd had once, something he'd never have again.

Hathaway fumbled in the corner for a football. He said, "Come on, Crosby." He said, "Your father's going to give us a good going over in Chapel tonight, isn't he?" He said, just as if nothing were wrong at all, "So long, Elks. See you later!"

They went down the stairs and out into the Yard and they were both silent till Hathaway said, "Poor old Elks! I guess he never did have much fun." He tucked the football closer under his arm. "I guess he never will."

Crosby looked up and you could tell just by seeing Hathaway that he'd always had a good time, that he always would, that he'd go through life with his eyes dancing just the way they'd be dancing in a second now.

They came to the wide playing field, all golden in the last sharp sun, and a tall man was standing there with a knot of small boys about him. He looked just like Hathaway and his dark eyes were dancing, too.

"Hi, Dad!" Hathaway called. "Here's Crosby. His father's going to make a speech tonight."

The tall man looked down and smiled. He said to Crosby, "Are you a little scared about it?"

Crosby said, "Yes, sir." For the tall man knew just how he felt, he knew he was afraid his father was going to make a fool of himself so that all the boys would be laughing at him, laughing because he was so pink and pompous, laughing because of the dull, stupid things he'd say.

Hathaway was whispering something to his father and it must have been about Elkins for his father's face changed. He said, "I don't suppose there's anything we can do about it, son."

Hathaway shook his head and his father called, "Want to help catch punts, Crosby?"

THIS WAS the way life should always be, Crosby thought, as he turned and ran and the football thudded against his ribs and he held it fast. There should always be a bright wind blowing and the golden sun going down there just behind Chapel tower, soft green turf for your feet to tread and all the other boys shouting there as the first faint twilight closed in. And it would be just this if you only had such a gay, gallant father as Hathaway had, a father who wasn't afraid to take off his coat and kick a football for the boys, a father who'd stayed bronzed and young and always would, a father who loved his son so well he'd often come up to school to see him.

He could see how close they were there in the twilight, Hathaway and his father, how they smiled at each other, how they seemed to have hidden secrets together and all those secrets would be gay and golden and glorious. It was a shame his own father couldn't be like that, Crosby thought, and then he was running after the ball till his face was red and his wind was gone but he was so happy he didn't mind.

It was darkening fast now, across the fields, across the school, and little lights were sparkling out in the buildings. Hathaway's father laughed and shouted, "Time!" He shouted, "It's too dark and you young devils have gotten me all out of breath, anyway." He said, "Come on, son! Dinner bell'll ring in a minute."

Crosby looked up and he could see his own father, stiffly standing there in the thickening shadows. Mr. Hathaway was going up to him, saying, "You're Senator Crosby, of course. I've already met your son."

The Senator said something and he was smiling in that expansive, half-patronizing way of his but Mr. Hathaway didn't seem to mind. Mr. Hathaway was saying, "You're seeing the School at a bad time, Senator. Of course you've already heard about Elkins and his aunt taking him away." He said and his voice had a sharp edge, "It's a shame. I'd like to wring that woman's neck."

The Senator cleared his throat. He said, "I've seen something of Miss Elkins this afternoon. She's a rather remarkable woman."

That was just the sort of thing his father would say, Crosby thought, and then they were all walking down the path together and all before them, the School lay dreaming in the quiet dusk. It seemed to Crosby as if he'd seen it all before somehow, as if he'd keep on seeing it for a long time. But of course that was silly.

Mr. Hathaway was staring at the School too. He was saying, "It seems good to be back here again." He said quite softly, "You see, Mrs. Hathaway died this Summer." He stared deep into the darkening shadows. He said, "Somehow it seems to make it easier for both of us if I come up to School sometimes. I was here, myself, a long time ago."

CROSBY LOOKED down at Mr. Hathaway's sleeve and there was a black band upon it. And he was afraid his father would say something resounding and sententious. And he shouldn't.

The Senator looked different somehow but perhaps that was only the dying light. He said simply, "Of course." He said, "I've been talking to the headmaster. He's an astonishing man."

All the vividness flooded back into Mr. Hathaway's face again. "Isn't he?" he said. He looked as if he were staring straight into some lost and happy land he'd known long ago. He said slowly, "Fuzzy was here when I was a boy in school. And he's here still. The School wouldn't be the same without him."

From far above them Chapel bell rang out just as it had rung when Mr. Hathaway had been a boy in school. And that must have been a long time ago.

Hathaway caught his father's arm. He called, "Hurry, Dad. That's dinner bell," and then the two of them were going deep into the dusk.

It made Crosby feel queer somehow to watch them. For the secret they shared wasn't golden or glorious at all. But they'd never let anyone know that for there was something gallant about them both.

It made him feel so strange that he was talking to his father as he never had before. He was telling him in a sudden burst, all about Elkins and how he thought he hadn't any friends and then found he had, he was telling him how

THE TROUBLE IN ROOM 519

hard it would be for Elkins to leave the school. But he felt he wasn't telling it very well.

He wasn't for the Senator was shaking his head. The Senator was saying, "It's too bad, son. But that's the way life is. And it's all the worse when you can't change it, when you can't do anything about it at all."

They were coming up to the high steps of Hall and Fuzzy was standing there. He said, "Wouldn't you rather have dinner with the boys than sit with us?"

It was funny how Fuzzy always seemed to know what a boy would like. Crosby said, "Yes, sir. You bet, sir!," and then he was suddenly sitting at Wingate table with Elkins by his side.

Elkins' face was flushed and you could tell how miserable he felt. But all the other boys wouldn't let him. They were talking to him. They were saying, "What do you think, Elks? Isn't that so, Elks?" They weren't giving him any time to think, any time to know that in a short hour he'd have to leave them all.

And suddenly Crosby felt all limp and hollow inside. For he'd never see these laughing boys again either, he'd never see Fuzzy again or all the little lights sparkling through the School as the dusk drove down. He felt as if he was losing something; something he'd never really had, something he'd always wanted although he'd never known it until now.

The teacher at the head of the table was standing up. He was saying, "Everybody over to Chapel. Senator Crosby's going to speak."

THEN THEY were all going across the Yard—all the boys—and their voices were young and eager in the dusk. And Crosby felt sick inside. His father didn't have a single thing to say to them, a single thing they'd want to hear. He couldn't even say a thing that would stop Elkins from feeling lost and alone, just as he was feeling now as he went up Chapel steps.

For Crosby's father would only be pink-faced and pompous and dull. He couldn't be anything else, really.

Chapel seemed filled with a soft warm friendly light as Crosby filed into a row with all the boys of Wingate House. He looked up and he could see Elkins' aunt and Fuzzy's freckled-faced daughter sitting a little to one side. He looked up and he could see his father and Fuzzy together on the platform.

Fuzzy got up and he looked older and more frail than ever. He said, and it was surprising how far his thin, cracked voice carried, "We have a very distinguished guest tonight, who is going to speak to us. I know you'll all enjoy hearing him." He bowed and said, "Senator Crosby!"

The Senator came forward and he looked smaller as if he'd shrunk a little. He didn't look half so pink and white and pompous as he had.

And in a minute, Crosby knew, that deep voice would begin to boom out, "They say that the battles of England were won on the playing fields of Eton! I want to impress upon you—"

Crosby's hands clenched tightly for he didn't want to hear it; he didn't want to hear those windy words.

The Senator started to speak. He said, "It's a strange thing but ever since I've been here I've wished I was a boy in school myself." He said, and suddenly he wasn't just a stout and pompous man but a little pathetic somehow, "I never went away to school. I wish I had."

Crosby sat up quite straight. For this wasn't the old speech; these weren't the old windy words. This wasn't even the Senator's usual voice. It wasn't the Senator at all; it was just a father quietly talking to other fathers' sons.

Chapel was very quiet now and Crosby's father was talking on. He was saying, "I've always thought before that what boys learned out of books was the most important thing. I know it isn't now. It's the friends you make and the things you say and the things you do outside of class that really count. It's all the fun you have and all the little things you'll remember long after you are gone."

Crosby knew what his father was doing now and his heart jumped. For his father wasn't looking at the boys or really talking to them at all. He was staring straight at Elkins' aunt as she sat there so straight and stiff by Chapel's shadowed wall.

He could hear his father's voice and it made you see things that weren't there at all; the sun slipping down a reddening sky and the river all agleam as the crews came by and the coxswains shouted, "Hit it up there! Stroke! Stroke! Stroke!"; all the warmth of June stealing through the land and the grass green on the playing fields, the crisp crack of bat on ball and a boy running there through the dust with the light all golden on his head; then something else, deeper, quieter, perhaps, a boy lying lazy on the grass with his knees hunched up, a boy reading a book.

His father was saying, "It's just the same when you see Eton or Winchester or Charterhouse; you wish you were a boy again and in school there. But you're too old then."

He swung around so he faced all the boys again. He said and his voice rose, "But you're young! You're having your best time now; the best time you'll ever have here in the old School. There'll never be such a great, golden time for any of you again." He said softly, "But only a few of you know that. Only a few of you know that now. You won't know it really until you've grown up and grown old and gone away. And then you'll know."

Crosby's father took out a handkerchief and mopped his face. He said, and he seemed tired, "I've talked too much. I'm a tiresome old man." And then he sat down.

He was tired, Crosby knew. He was tired because he'd tried so hard to make Miss Elkins—crisp, hard, efficient Miss Elkins—see what it meant to be a boy in school. And now he knew it hadn't been any use.

There was a sharp sound all along the rows and all the boys were clapping. Crosby looked down at his own hands and they were clapping too. He couldn't help it for he'd never think of his father as pink and white and pompous again. That was just a shield his father wore against the world—only he'd never known it until now, never known what a quiet, kindly man his father really was.

And now it seemed that everybody knew.

Fuzzy stood up and he looked pleased. He said, "I shan't say anything about Senator Crosby's speech for you've all said it for me." He suddenly seemed old and worn again and his voice cracked a little. He said, "I have to announce that Roger Elkins is leaving school. We've all known him and all liked him—" He stopped and just stood there and he seemed to be waiting for something.

Hathaway jumped up. Hathaway's face twisted oddly. He said, and he was embarrassed at standing there before all the school, "Suppose we give three cheers for old Elks: just to show him we were glad he was here and we'll be sorry when he's gone!"

There was a second's silence and Hathaway's face went a dull red. And then all the boys stood up and began to shout: the long school cheer and then "Elkins! Elkins! Elkins!"

Crosby turned and Elkins didn't look like a bug any more. He didn't because his face was buried in his hands and his shoulders shook.

Someone was coming down the aisle; someone was coming toward them quite quickly. Crosby looked up and it was the freckled-faced girl, Fuzzy's daughter, Sally.

She stooped down and touched Elkins' shoulder. "Come on, Elks! Come on out of here." She smiled. "You've got an awful lot of unpacking to do tonight. Your aunt's decided to make you stay in school."

Elkins looked up and his glasses were so badly blurred he had to take them off. His lips moved but he couldn't seem to say anything.

Sally said, "You'll have to get some new books, too. You aren't in the Fourth Class any more."

Elkins stumbled in his feet and Crosby knew he couldn't quite realize it yet.

It seemed a long time after that when Crosby was standing in the hall of the headmaster's house and putting on his coat. It seemed a long time because so much had happened.

Elkins' aunt came in the door and she looked different. She looked glowing and lovely and young. She said, "I've just been over to see Roger. He's so happy." She blew her nose quite hard. She said slowly, "I never knew anyone could be as happy as that."

She held out her hand to Fuzzy and he looked younger, too. He looked that way because he wasn't going to lose one of his boys now. She said, "I'm afraid I made a fool of myself, Mr. Adams."

Fuzzy's voice was very kind. "You're fond of the boy, Miss Elkins. You wanted to see him get ahead."

And Crosby knew it was true. For Elkins' aunt wasn't harsh or hard at all. She'd only seemed that way because she didn't understand.

She was talking to his father now and her cheeks flushed and her eyes shone. She said, "Congratulations on your speech, Senator. I'm glad I stayed to hear it."

It was time to go and Crosby was holding out his hand to Fuzzy. He was saying, "Goodbye, sir. I've had a great time, sir," and he didn't want to say it at all. He didn't want to turn and go.

And Fuzzy must have known that for he was saying, "Come up again some time, Crosby. We'll all be glad to see you."

The Senator said, "Ha-rumph!" and suddenly he looked pinker and whiter and more pompous than ever. He said, "Do you like that school where you are, son?"

"No, sir," Crosby said. "Not very much."

His father wasn't looking at him at all, his father was saying in an odd, shy voice, "Well, how'd you like to come up here, then?"

And Crosby's voice was shy, too, as if they'd suddenly found each other, he and his father, and didn't want anyone else to know it. "Gee, Dad! You bet I would, Dad!"

EVERYTHING SEEMED a little hazy in the hall somehow but that was only himself. For it was such a swell school. And they were all such swell guys there—all of them—small Austin and tall Manning and Hathaway with his dark, dancing eyes, and Elkins, even if he did look a bit like a bug. And his father was a swell guy, too. And that seemed the most important thing of all.

Fuzzy was saying, "We'll be glad to have him, Senator. We'll be glad to have him here."

The Senator said severely, "It'll be a relief to get him settled for four or five years. He's an annoying sort of boy." The Senator smiled and his voice dropped to a dim whisper, "I sometimes suspect him of knowing I'm not a great man."

3. THE *TRANSCRIPT*

Gordon had always shown a propensity for writing in high school, and Nobles provided many opportunities to develop it. The school newspaper, *The Nobleman*, first appeared in 1911, and two years later the first "class book," or annual, appeared. No evidence survives to demonstrate that Hillman was on staff at the paper, but it would have been the one extracurricular activity that aligned with his interests.[1]

In emphasizing writing as his avocation and, soon after, his vocation, Hillman was taking after his mother, a budding poet herself, one of her many artistic endeavors. He was, in fact, already publishing soon after his brief time at Nobles, joining the newspaper industry either during his second stint as a homeschooler or, more likely, in lieu of that stint. And it was, in fact, the newspaper industry that served as his entrée into his literary endeavors. Gordon worked with the *Boston American,* the *Boston Record,* the *Boston Advertiser,* and the *Boston Evening Transcript,* among others, bouncing around the incestuous world of the city's print media.

It was an auspicious place for such a career. Boston was considered the birthplace of American journalism, the home of the first colonial newspaper in 1690. Its press dominated the thought of the colonies through the eighteenth century and continued into the early national period. In 1813, the *Boston Daily Advertiser* was founded, a paper that would later employ Hillman and one described by journalism historian Manny Paraschos as "the first successful New England paper catering to the interests of the elite." Seventeen years later, in 1830, another such paper appeared, the *Boston Transcript*, "a stodgy, literary paper, which served the city's gentry." In 1842, Cornelia Wells Walker took the reigns of the *Transcript*, becoming the nation's first female editor of a major newspaper. She and her fellow editors of the glut of Boston periodicals situated themselves on Washington Street, creating the city's famous Newspaper Row, a journalism district in downtown Boston. "The air," claimed Joseph Edgar Chamberlin, "seemed to quiver with new dailies."[2]

The following century, in 1920, T. S. Eliot wrote a poem about the *Transcript*:

> The readers of the *Boston Evening Transcript*
> Sway in the wind like a field of ripe corn.
>
> When evening quickens faintly in the street,
> Wakening the appetites of life in some
> And to others bringing the *Boston Evening Transcript*,
> I mount the steps and ring the bell, turning
> Wearily, as one would turn to nod good-bye to Rochefoucauld,
> If the street were time and he at the end of the street,
> And I say, "Cousin Harriet, here is the *Boston Evening Transcript*."[3]

By the time of Eliot's celebration, the *Boston Globe* had appeared in the city in 1872, the *Boston Record* in 1884. William Randolph Hearst had founded his *Boston American* in 1904 and purchased the *Advertiser* in 1917.[4] And Hillman had left Nobles and had begun his journalism career as a stringer for the *Transcript*, a constituent part of the paper that Eliot so carefully carried to his Cousin Harriet.

The newspaper business that Hillman entered had undergone a series of transformations since the mid-nineteenth century. In the Gilded Age, newspapers largely divorced themselves from the political factions whose mouthpieces they had been, proclaiming their independence and groping toward what would eventually become the practices of objectivity. When combined with the creation of the Associated Press in 1848, news became a national industry. Syndication became common in the period, and "journalism began to emerge as a profession." As Richard Ohman has explained, one of the most influential transformations of American newspapers occurred in the 1930s. Not only did papers drop the prices of the product to encourage circulation and greater advertising, but they started devoting more attention to reporters and reporting. Newspapers began "to keep track of crime and high society, to acknowledge the daily life of the city." Nowhere was this trend more pronounced than in New York, but so too was it felt in Boston, which considered itself the birthplace of American journalism and prided itself on being a leader in revolutionary trends.[5]

While the *Transcript* took part in some of the revolutionary journalistic activity that had taken place in the nineteenth century, it was not a penny daily and did not play to a working-class audience. It was a newspaper always heavily grounded in the fine arts, housed as it was in a city so grounded in them. The *Transcript* developed an official department for music and dramatic criticism in 1881, only formalizing a tradition that dated to the paper's inception. The same was true of its book department. As early as 1843, the *Transcript*'s Cornelia Walker took aim at poet Nathaniel Willis, who "was a good writer, but had not force enough either of mind or matter to appear well as a public speaker." That kind of attack created controversy in both Boston and New York and demonstrated the personal nature of antebellum literary criticism, though Willis would reconcile with the paper after Walker's reign as editor and even write for the *Transcript* at times. That willingness to engage passionately on literary subjects and insert itself into the narrative of cultural value in Boston and the nation demonstrated its vested interest in American letters, but the paper did not have an official literary editor until 1875, when Charles E. Hurd took the post. His successor, Edwin Francis Edgett, created the paper's "Book Section," devoting even more space to the endeavor. Similarly, the early twentieth century saw more and more room in the paper's pages for the "Dramatic Department." Such was the calling card of Boston, and it was the calling card of its "stodgy, literary" representative.[6]

But the *Transcript* could be stodgy in other ways, as well. In September 1919, for example, Boston's police went on strike for better pay and working conditions against a recalcitrant police commissioner and a Massachusetts governor, Calvin Coolidge, who was largely unsympathetic. Whereas most papers in Boston sided with the police, urging a compromise that would lead to a resolution, the *Transcript* sided with the police commissioner, decrying even the notion of a police union as a threat to public safety.[7]

Historian Joseph Edgar Chamberlin described a decided "moral tone" in the paper as it existed in the decade following the Great War. As of 1925, the *Transcript*'s editor was Henry Turner Claus, who argued: "We do not believe those who subscribe to the *Transcript* want the lurid or sordid emphasized. In other words, they prefer that we keep a true sense of values." Those values would combine with the paper's emphasis on dramatic and literary criticism to make its reputation.[8]

And the *Transcript* would be Hillman's home for much of his career. In that he followed the path trod by authors like Harold MacGrath, Edward Streeter, George Barr McCutcheon, and Ernest Poole. MacGrath worked for the *Syracuse Herald*, Streeter for the *Buffalo Express*. Poole's work as a journalist led him to groundbreaking coverage of Chicago's meatpacking industry, as well as analyses of the Russian Revolution of 1905. Most didn't have Poole's journalistic impact, foreign and domestic, but fiction authors often made their livings by working in journalism. Perhaps most famously, naturalist writers like Frank Norris and Theodore Dreiser supplemented their incomes from works like *McTeague* and *An American Tragedy* with newspaper work. While the murder in Dreiser's *An American Tragedy* is sparked by reading a newspaper account, the fictional stories of these journalists tended not to emphasize the inner workings of the newspaper itself.[9]

Hillman, however, was not alone in depicting newspaper life. The most famous such effort during Hillman's writing years probably came from British novelist Evelyn Waugh's 1938 novel *Scoop*, which tells the story of William Boot, a foreign correspondent for the fictional *Daily Beast* who is sent to eastern Africa to cover an uprising. Before Boot, however, there was Jasper Milvain, a fictional young newspaperman navigating the world of London journalism in George Gissing's 1891 *New Grub Street*. In between those two poles, as Hillman was getting his start, Sherwood Anderson's *Winesburg, Ohio* told the story of George Willard, who reported for the fictional *Winesburg Eagle*, recording the stories of the town's denizens. A decade later, in 1828, Ben Hecht and Charles MacArthur's *The Front Page* premiered on Broadway. The comedy presented the Chicago newsroom of the fictional *Examiner*, following reporters covering the story of a nearby prison escape. So stories depicting the press weren't absent from the fictional realm, but they were not a dominant theme, despite the fact that so many fiction writers spent much of their days working for newspapers.[10]

Unlike others, Hillman's time at the *Boston Transcript* dramatically imprinted itself on his fiction. Whereas his boarding school stories largely occurred during one lone decade, his tales of newspaper life ran the gamut of his literary career. It was a demonstration of the impact his time at the *Transcript* had on his imaginative mind.[11]

The paper and the life it provided would become the setting for much of Hillman's fiction, wherein he proved his affinity for the business. The setting for the bulk of Hillman's newspaper stories was the fictional *Courier*, with Big Ed as city editor and a gruff man known simply as the Top as news editor, a former artillery sergeant who "had never gotten over the effects, either physical or mental."[12] The bulk of the action took place in the City Room, a long open-floor office with a bank of desks lined by a bank of telephone booths from which reporters called in stories. On one wall was a long bench where office boys read comic books and waited to be of use. "The windows hadn't been washed and newspapers still lay on the floor where the staff had flung them," went one description. "A gray haze of cigarette smoke hung over everything, and it might have been the identical haze that had been there before he went away. Disorder reigned in the long room, and it always had, and it was deceptive, for the very disorder had an ordered purpose."[13]

The hierarchy in such a place was clear. "The Big Jump in the newspaper business is from copy boy to apprentice reporter," one of Hillman's characters explained, describing his own rise in the business without the credential of formal education. "After that if you're any good at all you're all right."[14] Making that rise did have its privileges. In another story, Hillman described a reporter named Stephen Jackson, "large and plump, with a choice sprinkling of reddish freckles and nearly no hair," who "was turning out something for Sensational Detective Stories on the company's time." It was again the stuff of autobiography, as Hillman would spend the bulk of his life moonlighting as a short story writer while his job at the newspaper provided a base salary. As such, the newspaper was a place to be revered. "In this echoing place, great men walked like gods," Hillman wrote of the fictional *Courier*. "Wisdom abode in them and they were the elect of the world."[15]

In "Tough Guy," published in *McCall's* in 1935, Hillman tells the story of a fire that destroys the local Argyle Club. What had originally seemed a dull evening on duty at the newspaper became far more exciting. The Top ordered the original front page scrapped in favor of the incoming new story. The office moved from stasis to chaos in a matter of moments, as even the office boys moved frantically in and out for information. One in particular was distraught because his mother had been at the Argyle at the time of the fire. As more and more victims were discovered dead or arrived at the hospital, his concern grew greater and greater. He asked to go home, but Big Ed kept him at the office, assuring him that it was the paper that would have the first news of her whereabouts, that there was no better place for him in a time of tragedy. Eventually the woman arrived at the hospital with minor wounds, much to the office boy's relief. The story's message, however, was clear: the newspaper itself was its own version of family, a reliable source not only of information but of stability. It was a common theme of Hillman's stories of the newspaper business. The chaos was, itself, a creator of order, an order that Hillman surely relied on for much of his adult life.[16]

"Lead All, Baby," published a decade later in *Liberty* in 1947, tells the story of Tim, a boy who worked at the *Courier* after school. He had only worked there a few weeks, "but he was sure he'd stay there all the rest of his life." He lived in a South Bay tenement with his Aunt Doris, a young, stylish woman. "It always seemed queer to call Doris 'Aunt.'" Doris had a young baby, and when the baby became sick and Tim was late to the paper, he knew he would be fired. Instead, however, the paper got behind Tim, saw a potential story in the tragedy, and paid to airlift the child to Children's Hospital in New York to be treated by a specialist. The baby was saved, the *Courier* got both the scoop and the appearance of magnanimity, and Tim's devotion to the business only blossomed. One hard-beaten editor, realizing that Tim's Aunt Doris was in New York with the baby, even offered to take him home and give him a place to stay. The reporters and editors in such stories were jaded, they were heavy drinkers, but they had a moral core and the influence that allowed them to use it. Newspapers were more than the Fourth Estate; in Hillman's hands, they were the conscience of a community. His veneration of the business remained constant throughout his newspaper stories.[17]

Many other stories coursed with this theme of journalists acting with a moral compass. In another of Hillman's efforts, a reporter uses his information connections to find a local Italian shoemaker's brother, locked in a World War II prison camp. "After all," the story claimed, "newspapermen did do remarkable things." In another, a reporter wrote a story about a lonely girl in the hospital on her birthday, prompting scores of readers to send her presents: "You couldn't imagine a room so stuffed with presents. You'd never believe three quarters of a column in the Bulletin could do all that." The reporter demurred: "Oh, the Bulletin didn't do it all. They're good-hearted people in this town. We just gave them a little nudge."[18]

In another story with a similar message, a *Courier* reporter covering a ship caught in a gale off of Cape Cod sent a reporter to the home of the ship's captain. She interviewed the captain's wife and talked to her children. Ultimately the ship weathered the storm, and when she received the news, the captain's wife broke down in tears. When the reporter sought to comfort her, she replied: "It isn't that. It's just because you've all been so kind. I never knew newspaper people could be so kind."[19]

Such is not to say that Hillman was unwilling to be critical of the business of journalism. In "The Unhappy Union Boss," published in *Liberty* in 1946, the president of the copyeditors' union harangues his colleagues, "You're always complaining that you don't get paid enough, and three quarters of you don't ever do an honest day's work for an honest day's pay." The staff "claim to be newspapermen and there aren't half a dozen good newspapermen among you."[20]

In "A Happy Man," published three months later in the same magazine, two young stringers for the *Courier* visit the small town of Statesville, where Claire, one of the stringers, is from. The local paper, the *Evening Banner*, treats her homecoming as big news, noting that "Miss Stratton, who began her journalistic career on the *Banner*, is now one of the best-known newspaperwomen in the East." She was not, of course, one of the best-known newspaperwomen in the East, but her airs suited her sense of self on her return home. Her traveling companion, Steve, was more honest about his role at the *Courier*, and about his appreciation for Claire's hometown. To Claire's consternation, Steve decides to stay, taking a job as city editor of the *Evening Banner*. At the *Courier*, or in New York, Steve argued: "I'd be buried there. Too many other pretty good newspapermen." Working for the small-town paper would allow him to stand out. If he stayed in the East, he'd grow "to be an untidy old man sitting on the rim of the copy desk and boring everybody by telling how good I used to be." It seemed a grim future: "Six days a week I'd read other people's lousy copy, and on the seventh I'd go out and get drunk." That Hillman never opted for such a small-town option, that he stayed ensconced in Boston journalism his entire career, gives the story an air of regret that it might not have to many reading the story as a celebration of Middle America. But that regret is undeniably there.[21]

Also significant is that stories with such complaints were written and published in the late 1940s, as Hillman's finances began to falter, his dependent mother becoming more of a burden. His stories prior to the late 1940s looked at Hillman's day job through rose-colored glasses, but these later stories deal with some of the warts of the business that became clearer to the author as his own fortunes and finances disabused him of his earlier notions. In all of the stories, however, as in those about the prestigious boys' school, the common theme was working to create some measure of legitimacy in a field that judged success by time served, by experience, and gauged it through a hierarchy that could be intimidating to those just entering the business. It created a different kind of liminality than that manifested in the class privilege of boarding schools, but it was liminality nonetheless, one that would appear across all of the varied subjects of Hillman's stories.

Still, Hillman owed much to his time at the big-city paper. It was at the *Transcript* where "Ace," as Hillman was known to his newspaper colleagues, made the acquaintance of one of the paper's star literary editors, William Stanley Braithwaite. The *Transcript* was known for its relatively highbrow literary appeal. That being the case, it was a place where both Hillman and Braithwaite would thrive.[22]

William Stanley Beaumont Braithwaite was the son of a British immigrant and spent his early childhood in the relative cloister of the Anglophile's homeschooling. He first experienced public school after the death of his father but soon dropped out, at age twelve in 1890, to take various jobs to help support his family. He finally landed as an apprentice for the publisher Ginn and Company, and it was there that his real education began. Braithwaite developed a love and knowledge of publishing, poetry, and books. In 1904, the now-twenty-six-year-old published his first volume of poetry. He began writing criticism, as well. The *North American Review*, *Scribner's*, and *Atlantic Monthly* all featured his work, which led to a job offer from the *Transcript*, where he worked as a literary critic and, eventually, a literary editor. At the same time, he began a broad program of anthologizing poetry of all kinds, his most influential work being his annual compilation of influential American poems and poets. He was also a publisher, creating, with his friend Walter Reid, the Cornhill Company, a modest Boston vanity press that published all kinds of literature but emphasized poetry in particular. Much of Braithwaite's legacy comes from his devotion to many poets of the Harlem Renaissance, and his inclusion of the works of Sterling Brown, Claude McKay, Langston Hughes, Countee Cullen, and others in his anthologies. His Cornhill Company published James Weldon Johnson's first book of poetry. It published works by Joseph S. Cotter and Georgia Douglas Johnson and became a home in the late 1910s and early 1920s for lesser-known Black authors to publish books. Braithwaite, however, was also a friend to lesser-known white authors, and his acquaintance with the Hillmans soon began landing them in his anthologies. In 1913, he published his first annual anthology of American magazine poetry, which he would continue publishing until 1929. It was, for W. E. B. Du Bois, "an annual bible of American poetry. No one who wishes to follow the outpouring and striving of the American spirit can be without this volume."[23]

Braithwaite's anthologies ultimately spawned similar collections of fiction and drama. Mary Lamberton Becker called them "a national institution." In the annual editions, Hillman found his work next to that of Robert Frost, John Gould Fletcher, Edgar Lee Masters, Vachel Lindsay, Robert Penn Warren, Wallace Stevens, Edna St. Vincent Millay,

Hart Crane, and Lola Ridge, among so many others. "The world of letters owes William Stanley Braithwaite a tremendous debt," explained Margaret Haley Carpenter. "No literary history of our country is complete without reference to the impressive and dedicated service which he performed for both poets and poetry." Hillman, too, owed a debt to Braithwaite, his aspirations stoked by proximity to greatness.[24]

The anthologies grew from Braithwaite's original survey of poetry in an edition of the *Transcript* in 1906. He described being "challenged by the counting-room" for the effort, the paper's leaders originally assuming that poetry was not a paying endeavor. The *New York Times Book Review*, however, also started paying attention to poetry, and the momentum ultimately led to the founding of the Poetry Society of America in 1910. Then the first poetry magazines followed, creating a revival in the country's appreciation of poetry and setting the stage for Braithwaite's anthologies.[25]

It was a period of poetry dominated in one way or another by the free verse of the Imagists like Amy Lowell and others, writers either falling in line or actively reacting against the new trends, all of which made collections and anthologies that much more difficult as editors like Braithwaite sought to balance the competing ethics of modern and classical styles without demonstrating an overt favoritism. Then there was the concurrent rivalry of New York and New England, the latter long serving as the country's literary capital but declining at the turn of the century. The assumption that New England had been used up, both as ideology and subject, permeated below the region's southern border. "At the beginning of this century," wrote Braithwaite, "any treatment of New England life and character, no matter how skillful, whether in prose or verse, was shunned by the New York magazine editors and publishers." It created another bridge for Braithwaite to cross. It also put writers like Hillman, who eschewed modernist free verse and wrote lovingly of New England, at a decided disadvantage, making his success through the years of the Depression all the more remarkable.[26]

It was a success fostered by Braithwaite and his anthologies. Hillman first appeared in one of the editor's collections in 1918, when he was at the age when most were graduating high school. He claimed in his author biography that he was a graduate of Noble and Greenough and that he was planning to attend Harvard, but such was another of Hillman's fictions, another paean to Ernest Poole. The poem in that first Braithwaite collection had originally been published in the *Transcript*, where Hillman had worked long enough to earn the right to publish his poetry. He hadn't graduated high school, and he wasn't going to Harvard. He was a newspaperman and used his newfound vocation as an entrée into his avocation.[27]

His first anthologized effort was a dialect piece, its last stanza representative of the whole.

> The king, 'is a ruler, the queen she is his wife,
> The general's a rubber doll wot's sudden come to life.
> A 'ero is a 'erg, a-wearin' of 'is cross,
> But you'll find a hero's missus alius is 'is boss![28]

His work again appeared in a Braithwaite collection in 1920, a poem called "The Tankers" originally published in *Contemporary Verse*. "Thrashing through a tearing gale with a dark green sea ahead," went one representative stanza,

> While the funnel clews sing madly against a sky of red,
> Foam choked and wave choked, scarred by battered gear,
> The long brown decks are whirling seas where silver combers rear.[29]

Such was not free verse, nor was it Imagism, nor was it Robert Frost, Vachel Lindsay, Edna St. Vincent Millay, or Lola Ridge. Hillman's poetry was not his strongest work, but he was young and yet to fully develop as an author. Had he been a random high school dropout with no literary connections, such work would most likely have never made it into print. But he was a high school dropout with a job at the *Boston Transcript*, which fostered his newspaper career and simultaneously helped launch his creative writing endeavors by publishing his early poetry, connecting him to Braithwaite, and providing the setting for stories that he would continue to write throughout his career. It was a series of intertwined relationships that would continue to bear fruit. One of the later stories in this genre, titled "Lead All—Baby," appeared in 1947.

LEAD ALL—BABY

Published in *Liberty*, June 1947

IN THIS echoing place, great men walked like gods. Wisdom abode in them and they were the elect of the world.

The new boy, Tim O'Brien, was sure of that as he hurried in with the papers, a long lock of straw-colored hair hanging over his thin forehead and the big clock at quarter of six in the city room of the Daily Courier.

Four first editions, so fresh that they still smelled of the press, for Mr. Arthur Dale, and he was assistant managing editor: a red-faced wiry little man with a temper that often flared into fire.

Four to be slipped on the big desk before Myles McAndrew, the city editor, large, thick set, and looking rather like a judge, with dark hair receding from his broad brow and a quick intelligence lurking in his deep-set eyes.

"OK, Tim. You've got your good night after you finish handing the papers around."

Myles was a great man—a very great man—but he still wasn't Tim's choice among all the people—the wonderful people—who tenanted this noisy, confused, cluttered room and almost casually got the paper out.

One first edition for Dolly Knap. She looked up with her swift darting smile. "Thanks, Tim. How'd it go today?"

There wasn't another woman in the world like Dolly, who might almost have been a little girl with her short black hair, her round dimpled face, her fire-red blouse and her blue skirt. They said she was the best newspaperman in town.

One paper for Harry Blair, and Harry was all Tim ever hoped to be, only, of course, he never could. Harry was tall and slim and dashing with his curly brown hair and mustache. He was slipping into his smoky-blue topcoat now. Harry's tanned face was all alive with fun and maybe a little malice too, and he knew everything worth knowing and was a first-rate rewrite man besides. Some said that Harry was hard and conceited and cynical, but of course that simply wasn't so.

If it had been, Tim wouldn't have dropped his papers to be helping Harry on with his coat, as he was so proudly doing now.

"Thanks, Tim." Harry picked up his pipe and put it in his mouth. He snatched a paper and walked rakishly up to the desk to get his good night.

Tim wondered what Harry was going to do this evening and was sure it was something marvelous.

The day side were all slipping out now and the night side coming in. All the little lights winked on above the desks and the room slid deep into six-o'clock quiet. Tim stuffed his own paper into his pocket and left this enchanted kingdom with regret. For to him, in two short weeks, the Courier had become the whole world.

He worked for it, actually, only a few hours after school, but he was sure he'd stay there all the rest of his life. It was a brave future to look forward to as he went up the dim stairs of the dingy tenement house in South Bay. He'd lived there with Aunt Doris ever since his father and mother'd died. He and Aunt Doris and the quiet baby lived there all alone now, for Aunt Doris' husband was away in the navy.

It ALWAYS seemed queer to call Doris "Aunt" because she wasn't very old, really. It was hard to think she ever would be when you saw her bright golden hair, her jet-black eyebrows, and her almost violet eyes behind her long lashes. Only tonight the eyes had a dull, listless look as she stirred something on the stove.

"Here's the paper, Aunt Doris. It's a swell paper tonight."

The woman smiled. "And all absolutely free, too," she said.

He hardly dared ask the question: "How's Julie?"

Aunt Doris stirred harder. "Just the same."

"Did Dr. Peruzzi come over?"

"He did." She stirred harder still.

"Aunt Doris, did—did he say anything different?"

"Only that—" She kept her head turned away from him. "Look, Timmy. Go in and stay with her, will you, while I get the supper ready?"

He went into the bedroom with the red cabbage roses rioting on the moss-green carpet. He bent over the white crib. Julie was lying on her back, quiet, as always. She was small for a year and a half and she would have been a pretty baby if it hadn't been for that old, old look she had. Her face and arms and hands were almost colorless.

She'd looked old ever since she'd been born, and Dr. Peruzzi had fussed and fussed over her. Finally, two weeks ago, he'd brought over another doctor from City Hospital and they'd given Julie's illness a long Latin name. They'd said it was quite an uncommon thing and that a man in New York named Gerrish was an expert on it.

Tim leaned far over the crib. He never could tell whether Julie knew him or not. He was so close to her now he could hear her faint labored breathing, and he had a sudden sure sense of what Dr. Peruzzi had said today. He'd said she wouldn't get well.

He straightened up with that knowledge hard and cold in his head. She was such a good baby; she nearly never cried. Perhaps it would have been easier if she had.

"Come on, Tim," Aunt Doris was calling. "Supper's ready."

He sat down at the table and began talking away furiously. He told Aunt Doris all about the people on the paper.

HE AWOKE with a startled jerk, and Aunt Doris was standing at the foot of his bed in her white nightdress.

"Timmy, go down to the store and phone Dr. Peruzzi. Get Dr. Peruzzi as quick as you can. Tell him—" she put both hands up to her face. *"You'd better get Father Barry too!"*

HE CAME into the Courier city room very late that afternoon. He knew what was going to happen and it did.

Myles swung angrily around at the desk. "You boy, come here! Tim, you're paid to be here on time. What do you think this is, anyway, a newspaper or a charity school?"

Myles was quite right. When you work on a paper, the first thing you learn is that the paper's got to come out every day on schedule no matter what happens.

In a second, now, Myles would fire him.

He stood there, suddenly weak at the thought of that. "I'm very sorry, sir, but she's so sick. She's so awfully sick. They—they don't think she'll last much longer."

Myles hooked a chair with his foot. "Sit down, Tim. Who's so sick?"

"Julie. The baby. Aunt Doris' baby. And Dr. Peruzzi says nobody can do her any good but a Dr. Gerrish over at Children's Hospital in New York. She's such a good baby, Mr. McAndrew. She never cries."

"Hey! Take it easy!" Myles' thick eyebrows seemed to come closer together. "What's the matter with her?"

Tim felt a sea of helplessness flooding over him. "It's some long Latin name." And then he began telling the big man all about it.

Myles took up the shears and began to tap on the green desk blotter. He said suddenly, "What's this Dr. Peruzzi's number?" Tim never would have believed Myles could be so quick. He'd snatched up the phone and he was talking to Dr. Peruzzi. "City editor of the Daily Courier, doctor. We're interested in this Julie Lydon baby you're looking after. What's the story on her? . . . No, I don't get it . . . You'll have to spell it out . . . All right, what's the nature of it?"

Tim sat there and the wire machines were whirring, the typewriters going, the fire tapper counting off an alarm in its corner.

MYLES WAS still talking at the telephone, low and clear. "Could this Gerrish guy really do anything for her? . . . No, I know they haven't got any money . . . It would have to be quick, would it? How quick?"

You could hear Dr. Peruzzi's excited voice through the receiver.

Myles said a perfectly absurd thing: "Listen, doc. Could the kid fly to New York?"

Tim still sat there and nothing made sense. Myles' voice had a driving quality now. "Look, doc, I want you to drop everything and go straight down to

C Street and stay with that kid. The paper'll pay for it."

You could hear Dr. Peruzzi's angry sputter quite plainly.

Myles swung around. "Tim, they're calling for a boy down in Sports. And keep your tail up. Maybe we can do something."

They couldn't, of course. Nobody could. But when Tim came back by the city desk, Myles was still at the phone.

"This the chief of staff at City Hospital? Courier desk calling. You went over to see that Lydon baby on C Street, didn't you? ... Sure, I know it's a rare case ... Yes, you bet we're interested ..."

"BOY!" said Mr. Dale in a shout, and Tim had to go running over.

He had to go down to the composing room too, and when he came back, Myles had pulled his chair over to Mr. Dale's desk and was talking to him, sharp and quick.

Tim could only hear snatches, and those were very strange. "You checked it with City?" Mr. Dale was asking. "And Father Barry said it was all straight? If Father Barry says anything, you can bank on it." He drew the day's dummies toward him. "All right. Go ahead. Spend some money on it. Build it up. We need a human-interest story in this paper." He swung around angrily. "BOY! Keep that wire copy coming!"

Tim ran down to the machines that were pounding out all the news of the world on long strips of white and yellow paper, and when he came back, the whole city desk was caught up in a strange new tension.

"Here's Al Hines on the New York Star," Myles' assistant was saying.

Myles' voice was even sharper now. "Al, we've got a pretty good story shaping up here." There was so much noise in the room that Tim couldn't hear for a minute and then could again. "Yeah. Gerrish. Dr. John Gerrish. We're putting the kid on a plane, and I want the doctor at Children's Hospital the minute the baby gets there. Yeah, it's a good yarn on your end too."

He put down the phone, ripped open his shirt collar, then caught up the phone again. "Get me Chet O'Donnell in South Bay. Chet, get over to 323 C Street in the hell of a hurry. See Mrs. Doris Lydon. Baby's desperately sick over there. Get everything you can for a color story ..."

"BOY!"

TIM HAD to run out to Reference and wait there while they hunted up pictures, and when he came back at last, the Western Union operator was waving a yellow slip at him.

"Take it up to the city desk."

As he ran, he read the wire and it was very odd: "Got Gerrish. Will be at Children's when your kid gets there. Will have police escort LaGuardia Field to hospital. Pls give us full story your end. Al Hines."

He put the slip down on the big desk and then everything seemed to happen at once.

Myles' voice was a steady roar: "Get Jim Brady at Airlines! PHOTO! Two cameras out here in a hurry. DOLLY! Ready to go! Call Johnny Sullivan at police headquarters! Harry Blair, drop what you're doing."

You would never believe things could move so fast. Two photographers coming toward the desk with their hats and coats on. Dolly snubbing out her cigarette and snatching up her handbag. Harry Blair tearing something out of his typewriter.

Myles at the phone: "Jim Brady? I've got to get a sick baby, her mother, a reporter, and a cameraman on your next New York plane . . . Well, bump somebody off, then. This is emergency . . . You will? Listen! You may have to hold that plane a few minutes. Yeah, you'll know when you hear those sirens coming."

Myles swinging around. "Dolly! You're flying to New York with a sick baby. Take Robbie with you for pictures."

Myles at the phone again: "Johnny Sullivan? I want a City Hospital ambulance and a police escort at 323 C Street as fast as you can get 'em there. HARRY BLAIR! Take Chet O'Donnell off twenty-two and then I'll talk to you. TIM O'BRIEN!"

H E STOOD at the desk, shaken and confused, and Myles smiled at him. "I guess you know it without my telling you, Tim. We're flying your aunt and Julie to New York. They'll be very comfortable all the way and Dr. Gerrish will be at Children's Hospital when they get there. Dolly and Robbie are with them, so there's nothing to worry about."

It wasn't real, any of it. It couldn't be. Poor people don't have planes held for them, nor policemen on motorcycles racing before them with shrieking sirens and everything else getting out of the way. And a great man like Dr. Gerrish isn't waiting for a quiet baby from South Bay.

"Pick up that phone!" said Myles.

An infinitely unhurried voice said in Tim's ear, "Johnny Sullivan. Tell Myles his police escort is on the way."

H ARRY BLAIR had gotten very tired of listening to Chet O'Donnell in South Bay. He hung up his phone, stared at his notes and, as Myles walked over to his desk, asked in utter disgust, "What's this stuff all about?"

Myles brushed back his dark hair. "It's quite a story. We're flying this baby to New York to save its life—I hope."

Harry felt listless and bored and a bit irritated too. When city editors dreamed up a stunt like this, they always thought it was wonderful. That went with being a city editor, he supposed. If you couldn't summon up that flaming enthusiasm, you wouldn't be much good at the big desk.

So he said wearily, "One of those things?"

Myles nodded. "We're going to lead the paper with it. The sick kid's a cousin of Tim O'Brien, the copy boy."

Harry yawned. "The one who's always going around with his mouth open, admiring everybody?"

"Yeah. You'd better take some more notes. The baby has some sort of obscure circulatory ailment. I'll spell its name out for you. . . ."

Harry's pencil moved automatically and he looked up at the clock. He'd have to write this story in a hurry. And it was deadly stuff to do.

"You'd better make it lead to come," Myles said finally. "We'll slap on a two-paragraph precede when we actually get them started on the plane. It's a story that'll sell a lot of papers, so give it all you've got."

Harry grinned acidly. He sawed his hand across his opposite arm as if bowing a phantom violin. "Hearts and flowers?"

Myles rose. "Sure. Don't be so damned cynical. Get going."

Harry stared savagely at his typewriter. He'd write a baby story to end all baby stories. He'd let himself go. He'd do a stinker.

His fingers began to tap the keys, slowly at first, and then very fast. It didn't matter much whether the baby died or not, the thought. Maybe it would be better if she did. For little girls don't have much of a chance when they grow up in a South Bay slum. They live in a bitter, vicious world and few of them have the sense to be hard-boiled about it.

You have to be hard-boiled, Harry knew, for he hadn't had an easy life himself. You have to see things clear and sharp—just as they are; not as you'd like them to be.

When you're young, you're sure you'll amount to something. When you're thirty-five, you find yourself tied to a typewriter and turning out mush like this for a lousy tabloid.

He suddenly sensed that the story he was writing was getting out of hand. It wasn't shaping up as he'd meant it to. Stories did that sometimes, and he began to type faster still.

"Swell stuff, Harry," Myles called down from the desk.

He said "Nuts," under his breath, loosened his tie, and lit another cigarette. For he'd got caught now in the old, old way that good newspapermen do. He didn't see the city room at all but another room altogether: a room somewhere in South Bay, a room with a quiet baby in it, a baby who didn't cry.

"Start your lead!" said Myles in a shout. "They're off on the plane."

"LEAD ALL—BABY."

THERE! DONE at last, and Arthur Dale dashing down to the composing room, and pretty soon the papers would come up, and then he'd get his good night and go out and get drunk. He didn't very often, but now he'd set it down in words, he couldn't get that damned tenement room or that dreadful baby out of his head. He could even see the awful rug O'Donnell had described, with the red roses on it.

Myles came slowly toward him and he looked tired. "I'm sorry, Harry, but I guess you'd better stick with the story. I'm going to hang around too."

Of course that was the way it would be. Writing new leads all night long. Crying over a baby who didn't have a chance.

"Oh, Lord, Myles! Anybody on the night side can turn out this tripe."

"No, they can't," the big man said. "Because it isn't tripe."

Tim didn't hear them. And he still couldn't make any of it real. Aunt Doris and Julie weren't on a plane soaring through the skies. If he went home to the dingy house on C Street, he'd find them still there.

"TIM O'BRIEN!"

"Yes, Mr. McAndrew."

"Pick up that phone and read Harry's story to a rewrite man on the New York Star."

The sheets of soiled copy paper lay before him and he began to read. And suddenly he could see Aunt Doris sitting in the plane and the baby wrapped in a light-blue blanket in her arms. He could see it, because Harry'd seen it so sharply, because Harry'd seen it all just as it was. He'd even known about the moss-green rug with the wonderful red roses on it . . .

"Hey," said New York, "keep your voice up. I can't hear you."

He hung up at last. Until now he'd felt frozen tight inside. Since he'd read Harry's story, he wanted to cry.

Myles looked at him as if he saw how he felt. Myles said, "I can use you, if you want to work tonight."

Myles knew that he wouldn't leave this dark room where all the echoing winds of news blew in from the whole world, that he couldn't leave. The people on the paper were wonderful. They knew everything. First edition up and the headlines huge and black on the front page:

STRICKEN BABY
IN PLANE RACE
AGAINST DEATH

First edition up and Harry Blair laid his down on the desk. It was cheap, awfully cheap, the way the whole thing had been handled. Why couldn't they let the poor sick kid die in peace?

THE NIGHT side were coming in now and the night city editor sat down to read the paper. He got up and went over to the water cooler.

"Who wrote the baby story?"

The head of the copy desk said over his shoulder, "Harry Blair."

The night city editor took a long, deep drink. "I didn't know Harry was so softhearted." He blew his nose with some vigor. "I didn't know I was, either."

Harry supposed he might as well eat. "BOY!"

Tim O'Brien, of course, with those bright blue eyes blazing in that thin pale face.

Tim O'Brien with words stumbling out of his mouth so fast they fell over each other. "Gee, Mr. Blair, what you wrote about Julie—honest, Mr. Blair—gosh, I wish Aunt Doris could see it!"

Harry felt faintly sick because the kid had that shining look of having visions that only the very young and innocent can know: of seeing everyone and everything forever bright and fair.

So he said quite sharply, "Hop across the street and get me some coffee and a ham and cheese on rye." His voice seemed to be going on of its own volition: "Treat yourself to the same."

He stood staring out the window so hard he didn't notice that the city desk switchboard was a sparkle of lights, nor how busy the night side were at the phones.

"Courier desk . . . No, madam, nothing new on the baby yet."

"Courier desk . . . Certainly. If you send it care of the paper, we'll see the mother gets it."

"Courier desk . . ."

Tim O'Brien back again with a tall paper bag and words bubbling from his lips. "Gee, Mr. Blair, the elevator man asked me about Julie, and the janitor too." He began laying things out on the desk. "Gosh, Mr. McAndrew and Mr. Dale and everybody have been awfully good to us."

The poor stupid kid, Harry thought, he doesn't know they didn't do it to save the baby's life, which they probably won't. He doesn't know they wouldn't have done it at all if they hadn't needed a human interest story. Oh, hell, he concluded, why spoil it for him?

"Come on," he said. "Pull up a chair and we'll eat together."

The phone rang at his elbow.

"This is Joe Kane, the mayor's secretary. His Honor wants to know how the little girl's getting along."

Yes, Harry thought. His Honor keeps a pretty close eye on the South Bay vote now it's near election time.

Still, there was no harm in keeping Tim's spirits up. "That was the mayor's office. They were asking about Julie."

"*Gee!*"

"BOY!" called the picture editor.

He tossed a glossy print at Tim. "Tell the art department first page for this edition and hurry it!"

He was halfway down the hall before he looked at the picture. The baby was in Aunt Doris' arms and a stewardess was helping them into a huge plane.

Harry was on the last of his sandwich when Myles came to his desk. "You'd better start writing the fund story."

"What fund?"

"The one for the baby. Hell, people have been calling the desk for hours and wanting to give money. We've got five hundred dollars promised so far and we didn't even ask for any."

Harry said, "Oh, nuts!" and reached for copy paper.

Myles grinned, "Your own fault, wise guy. It's your story that's doing it."

Fund stories were rotten things to write, and Harry was having heavy going when four men came warily into the room. Three of them fanned out beside the fourth as if they were watching over him. They all kept their hands in their pockets.

The fourth was burly and broken-nosed in a livid green suit, green hat, green tie, and Myles was bringing him over.

Myles said, "You know Knocko Dineen, Harry."

Knocko was a particularly repellent racketeer, and Harry looked at him lazily.

"Why the army, Knocko?"

The ugly man's voice rasped: "A couple of guys don't like me, so I bring the boys along. Listen. This piece in the paper about the sick kid—" He rubbed his nose. "I ain't got no kids myself. Oh, hell! Buy the baby something, will you?"

Myles stood watching the four go out. "Just a sentimental sap!" he said.

"Sentimental, hell. He'd wrap a lead pipe around his mother's neck for a nickel."

Myles picked a crumpled piece of paper from the desk. "I guess you don't know a hundred-dollar bill when you see it, Harry."

Harry tried to put his mind on the fund story.

Myles called down, "That was Father Barry on the phone. He wants to know right away when we get any word."

Harry started to say, "Oh nuts!" and then stopped. The trouble was he could see Father Barry too plainly: the poor overworked parish priest who'd never get any further in the Church; who'd know how bad South Bay was and wear his life out trying to make it better. You see a lot of Father Barrys when you're on a paper.

He'd finished the fund story and took it up to the desk. Myles sat there, a phone still dangling from his hand. He was swearing in a low, steady stream, and he never did that.

He didn't even look up. "The plane can't land at LaGuardia. It's hitting fog."

He rose and started pacing to and fro, his hands jammed into his pockets. "Maybe I was just too damned smart."

That's the way it is when you try to balloon a story, Harry thought. You try to play God and then you get into trouble.

But he said, "Take it easy, Myles. There are plenty of airports."

He went to the window and a thin rain was driving down with a whining wind behind it. There was a strong smell of old stale liquor somewhere, and he turned around. Katie had come in with her pail and her mop. Katie was a night scrubwoman, stringy, white-haired, bleary-eyed, and very often a fountain of screeching profanity. She forever had a gin bottle hidden somewhere about her.

"Mister Harry, has the little girl got there yet?"

"She has not. There's a thick fog and the plane can't land."

"The poor baby!" Katie put down her pail with a clang. "I guess I'll slip around to St. Ann's and light a candle."

SHE WENT away, and Tim came trotting into the room, that trusting look still on his face. He wouldn't know yet about the plane being in trouble, but somebody'd be sure to tell him.

Harry fumbled about in the bottom drawer of Dolly's desk.

"Hey, Tim, how about a game of checkers?"

"I don't play very well, Mr. Blair."

Harry set the pieces out on the board. "Neither do I. Which'll you have, red or black?"

At the desk, Myles had a phone at his ear. He said slowly, "That's good. Thanks."

He came toward them and all his muscles seemed to sag. "Plane's down safe at Newark. New Jersey state troopers are escorting them in. Give me four fast paragraphs for this time, Harry."

Four paragraphs fast while they held edition for them.

"Gee," Tim was saying in utter unbelief, "they got the cops out way down in Jersey—just for Julie!"

Harry was beginning to feel quite queer and it must be because his day had been so long. "Sure. Sure. Let's start this game. You take red." The queerness was still in his mind, and it was often that way when you'd been dead wrong about something. For he'd been superior and scornful about the story all-along. And Myles and Arthur Dale, the assistant managing editor, had been far wiser than he. They'd known that if you get people excited, if you stir them, touch their emotions, you can sometimes accomplish the impossible.

OVER IN South Bay, Father Barry would have known that almost all his life.

He wouldn't care what the paper said or did, as long as it helped the child. And while they might have started it just to get a sensational story, it hadn't worked out that way. It had turned into something nearly as fine and shining as Tim thought it was.

For the sick baby, the very small baby, was actually a far bigger thing than any story could be.

"Your move, Mr. Blair," said Tim.

Harry was excited now and he hadn't thought he would be. He was caught in a tight tension, as you sometimes are when a story is unfolding before your eyes and you can't tell yet how it's going to turn out.

Those Jersey troopers would get them to the hospital pretty fast: through the tunnel and up the West Side Highway with the sirens screaming.

He looked up at the clock—that same clock that had been droning off the minutes one dull Sunday afternoon when a lethargic office boy had casually laid a torn piece of wire copy down on Arthur Dale's desk:

ATTN ALL EDITORS—FLASH—JAPANESE PLANES ATTACK PEARL HARBOR.

Arthur Dale hadn't looked down at his desk for a little while. When he finally did, he'd gone, for a few minutes, quite quietly mad.

And now the clock was still ticking, as calm as the spinning Fates. It simply didn't give a damn.

"Your move, Tim."

Twenty minutes—thirty—the three quarters—the hour.

"Gee, that's three games I've beat you, Mr. Blair!"

"HARRY BLAIR! Take Dolly off twenty-two!"

He could hear the checkers go clattering on the floor as he snatched at his phone.

"Harry? I'm calling from the hospital. Dr. Gerrish has just finished his preliminary examination. He gives Julie a better than fifty-fifty chance. And, Harry—"

"Yes, Dolly."

"She's such a sweet baby—so quiet—she didn't cry a bit all the way over. Let me talk to Tim, will you, Harry?"

He pushed the phone over. He pawed around his desk. No carbons, of course; no copy paper, and the clock was racing like mad now, as it always did when last edition was going in.

Tim set the phone back in its cradle. "Gee, Mr. Blair, that doctor's going to get Julie well. *I know he's going to get Julie well!*"

Yes, the doctor probably would, Harry thought. And he'd always thought that faith was a lot of nonsense before, but it was a quality Tim certainly had; faith in Myles and Arthur, faith in everyone and everything, faith even in someone called Harry Blair who was quite unworthy of any such thing. "Hey," he said in a shout, "get me some carbons! Make me up some books. Shake that lead out of your pants. We've got to get this story in the paper!"

Two o'clock in the morning and he was so tired he could hardly put his coat on: tired of the story and the paper and everyone on it. Tired most of all of Tim and his doglike adoration. Oh, well, in twenty minutes he'd be treating himself to a good stiff drink.

TIM WAS hunched on the office boys' bench, and he looked up at Harry as if there wasn't anyone to equal him in the whole world. "Good night, sir. Gee, sir—"

Oh, hell! Harry thought. Somebody's got to look after him.

He bent over the bench most unwillingly. "There won't be anybody left over at your place now, will there, Tim? Be sort of lonesome, won't it?"

The kid was so done in he could hardly talk. "No, sir. Yes, sir."

"Better come home with me, then. There's plenty of room."

"Won't—won't I be a bother, sir?"

You bet you'll be a bother, Harry thought. I can't even get tight if you're there.

He slapped Tim on the shoulder. "No, you won't be any trouble. Matter of fact, I could do with some company. Hurry up. Get your hat."

4. THE CAPE

Braithwaite's press was just as friendly to the Hillmans as were his anthologies, and in the months after the armistice, in 1919, Gordon and his mother published a collection of their poetry, *Rhymes Grave and Gay*, with Braithwaite's Cornhill Company. They dedicated the book "to one who is no longer with us," a reference to Gordon's father, and in an opening poem that served as a second epigraph, mother and son eulogized the fallen soap manager.

AROUND THE YEAR

We sometimes think he must return
Ere yet the May-time passes,
In summer-time we do not yearn;
He rests beneath the grasses.

But in the spring, each tender tint
Each new moon birth is telling
Of here, once more upon the earth,
His gentle spirit dwelling.

In later year, when skies are gray
Or snow is heaped in masses
Again from us he wends his way,
Again his brave soul passes.

The volume contained sections dealing with wartime, with country life, with Nantucket, and finally with "Visions, Voices, and Vagaries." It was not the kind of work that would appear in the American canon, but it was well received by the Boston press, the *Globe* claiming that the work was "written in a most graceful and pleasing way."[1] With its publication, Gordon's writing career had officially begun.

Hillman wrote lovingly in the collection of his time on Massachusetts's Cape Cod, describing both the visitors and the locals with equal care. "I could see when I looked out from my window," went a poem called "Harbor Lights" in *Rhymes Grave and Gay*,

> The great white ships a-sailing off to sea,
> As on and on and on they went a-fairing,
> Past the lighthouse at Brant Point on the lee.
>
> And there was one old squat tub of a steamer
> That tramped and wallowed all the way to town,
> To New Bedford, where she docked, and snorted
> When her captain brought her in and laid her down.
>
> I loved to ride on that old white steamer,
> But far better still I loved to sail
> Up the harbor on the dingy packet
> That carried the brown canvas bags of mail . . .
>
> But best of all, I loved to go a-fishing
> For the bluefish, away off on the rips,
> With my dear old brown wigged landlord captain,
> Who sails the sea no more in man-made ships.[2]

The poetry itself is maudlin, formulaic, but it is more than anything else autobiographical. When the family returned from Evanston and the elder Hillman began making an even better salary, not only was the younger Hillman sent to prestigious Nobles, but the family began spending summers at Cape Cod, the fashionable retreat of Boston's upper class. "Harbor Lights" describes the famous lighthouse at Brant

Point, just north of downtown Nantucket, and the ride across the bay to nearby New Bedford, providing a lived geography of the summers of Hillman's youth and the wistful memories he still carried of sailing with his father, that "dear old brown wigged landlord captain / Who sails the sea no more in man-made ships." Those summers and the powerful memories they held for Hillman ensured that his time at Nantucket and the Cape would become settings for his stories, settings that were, in fact, characters in and of themselves, exerting themselves on the characters as they had on the memory of Hillman's youth.

His fictional space for that particular realm of his personal biography was Good Harbor, a fishing town "founded in 1623 by Thomas Craven, Samuel Shepherd, and forty farmers and fishermen from Dorchester in England."[3] It was a town whose church was known as Our Lady of Good Voyage, a seaport that had become a summer haven for the wealthy of Boston but whose most influential organization was still the Master Mariners' Association. It was a town in transition to a vacation economy, and many of Hillman's stories of the Cape and of Good Harbor were about the misunderstandings generated from contact between the town's permanent residents and its summer ones.

In one such story, "Tides of Memory," published in *American Magazine* in 1936, a descendant of Craven finds herself on hard times, struggling in that liminal space of an economy in transition. She made do clerking in a dry-goods store, making fudge, and cutting flowers. Her monetary need came because she was taking care of Captain Thatcher, an old sea captain in decline who ultimately died. His passing was symbolic of the town's old identity, as it moved into the modern era. A series of his colleagues testified at his estate hearing, demonstrating that fishing and seafaring in general were not completely absent from the community, but its best days, like those of Captain Thatcher, had long passed. Good Harbor now belonged, in a sense, to vacationers like the Hillmans who would keep its economy afloat.[4]

"As Long As You Want Me," another *American Magazine* story from 1942, tells the story of David, who "was a Cape boy, a village boy, and he'd never be anything else." He entered a star-crossed relationship with Cecily Carpenter: "The Carpenters were summer people and Uncle Ben said they were poison rich." Such was the other clear division between the two groups at the Cape. The temporary residents not only had a lesser stake in the town and its survival; they also had a wealth that served as its own barrier to less-than-formal contact. The story ends, in Hillman fashion, with Cecily and David's love solidifying around the fact that Cecily was actually a Cape person at heart: "When you'd been hurt, you always came home—home to the Cape and the sea and the big house and Uncle Ben—just as he had done, himself. He saw now it had always been home to Cecily, too. She'd really told him so a long time ago, only he'd been too stupid to understand."[5] The message of the story, however, was that Cecily was the exception, that there was a largely unbridgeable divide between the visitors and permanent residents.

It was a common theme for Hillman, seemingly representative of his own experiences growing up as a visitor on the Cape. And it was a continuation of the dominant theme of all of Hillman's work. In his stories of Nobles, his stories of journalism, and his stories of the Cape, the conflict inherent in occupying the liminal space between legitimacy and outsiderism, in traducing the line between visiting and permanence. It was there in the status of privilege of Hillman's boarding school stories. It was there in the experience and hierarchy of his newsroom stories. But it was perhaps most pronounced in Hillman's stories of the Cape, demonstrating his own feelings as an outsider through the various stages of his life, but in particular in his time as a youth, seeing the Cape as his own, but knowing that others who lived there year-round saw his family as interlopers.

In another story, a desperate sixteen-year-old summer resident of Good Harbor, Johnny, finds himself in love with his friend Bonnie, who also spends her summers in the Cape town. But Bonnie develops an infatuation with a local painter, Mr. Marshall, who is using her as a model. Johnny's worry about the relationship is misplaced, as the adult Marshall is not even aware of Bonnie's fawning. Ultimately, Marshall breaks her heart, and she sees that her fellow summer resident was her true love all along.[6]

"My Fair Lady," again from *American Magazine*, this time in 1943, tells the story of a boy and his careless mother in another of Hillman's summer vacation tales. "Ma's housekeeping habits had been greatly disturbed by her being a big he-woman" who spent the day riding horses, "in fact, they could hardly be said to be housekeeping habits at all." It puts her son Donald in a position of de facto caretaker, particularly in her romantic endeavors. "Rupert was about to gyp Ma," Donald assumes at one point in her most recent relationship, "as all gentlemen did and always had since Pa had died eight years ago." It was more autobiography, and more fretting about belonging and legitimacy.[7]

In another of his Good Harbor stories, for example, a rich summer resident loses all his money but is saved by the beneficence of a wealthy local sea captain at their resort home. Meanwhile, in the style of that particular genre, his daughter finds a local love. Though "Storm Song" was published in January 1937, well before Hillman's later troubles, it foreshadowed the wishful thinking that he surely felt in his darker moments, the old summer Cape resident wanting love and salvation from his crippling financial trouble.[8]

In his analysis of an 1895 *Munsey's* story, Richard Ohmann had emphasized the role class played in such aspirational narratives. The plot's "benign fulfillment confers ideological blessings not only on a vague doctrine of progress and a new economic order, but more specifically on the project and prospects of an emergent class."[9] It was a reality inherent in Hillman's stories of the Cape, as it was in his stories of boarding school. The problems of the characters are ones foreign to those in poverty, demonstrating hope not only in the efforts of the protagonist but also in the broader conceit that wealth or proximity to wealth can create a catalogue of crises that are, by the standards of the audience of mass-circulation magazines, almost impossible to imagine. They are relatable, in that the problems of human interaction are always relatable, but they also serve as problem-as-goal for so many seeking a life where struggling to make ends meet was not the overarching shadow covering relational differences.

One of the common themes in both the Cape stories and in a selection of those concerning boarding school was a dominant, overly demonstrative mother figure. The vacation stories in particular were family tales wherein the relationship between adolescent boys and their mothers plays a prominent role. The clear tension between mother and child in the scenes from Cape Cod provided some of that relatability for readers who would never be able to take such vacations, and the tension in the stories was built on Hillman's fraught relationship with his mother.

In 1935, Gordon and Carolyn returned to the Cape and spent the summer at the Colonial Inn in the South Bay town of Scituate.[10] Their relationship was a complicated one, filled not only with a false sense of grandiosity but also a devotion or codependence that verged on relationships like the one featured in the 1975 documentary *Grey Gardens*, where Edith Beale and her mother live a secluded life filled with delusions of grandeur in the Hamptons. Hillman's fraught relationship with his mother, with whom he spent the first fifty years of his life virtually without interruption, did feature in many of his stories. In tales like "For Your Own Good, Dear," and "This Is Fair Warning," Hillman featured domineering mother figures who controlled the behavior of their families with schemes and manipulation. Stories like "Miss Baby Intervenes" and "Broadway Doll" featured actress mothers whose outsized sense of self was the core of their personalities. In "Woman Power," an actress mother comes to visit her son at boarding school, embarrassing him (because of his own fear) until she proves herself incredibly popular with all of his friends, thereby redeeming herself in the eyes of her son.[11]

That theme of family redemption continued in "Visitors from Vermont," wherein a family afraid that their northern New England relatives would embarrass them (Carolyn was from nearby New Hampshire) discover that there is wisdom and value in people from such climes. Such might be the kind of story that one would expect from an author seeking to defend his mother's exaggerated sense of self, but the relationship and its representation were even more fraught. Stories like "Roman Holiday" and "New Love for Freddy," for example, feature relationships between young men and older women, relationships that bear no specific relation to Hillman and his mother but stand as unique signposts nonetheless in a domestic partnership that lasted half a century.[12]

Both Gordon and his mother benefited from their association with vanity publishers like William Stanley Braithwaite, but they also did their best to run in broader literary circles, again searching for the legitimacy with which the younger Hillman dealt in his stories. In the summer of 1920, Gordon developed a fast friendship with Leighton Rollins, a fellow poet and general assistant to the director of the Repertory Theater of Boston. By that time, Gordon had become the photoplay editor of the *Transcript* and spent his time away from movies reading, playing tennis, and writing short stories. It was a life of relative overindulgence, with Gordon and Carolyn living dually at hotels in Wellesley and on Beacon Street. Built by Charles Norton Taylor in 1912, the Waban Hotel replaced the preexisting Waban Hall after a fire destroyed the original structure and served the Wellesley community in relative luxury. But the Hillmans also lived at Stanford White's Boston Hotel Buckminster, moving there after World War I from a posh apartment at 2 Arlington Street in Cambridge. They were there in the Buckminster in September 1919, for example, when Chicago White Sox first baseman Chick Gandil met the gambler Joseph "Sport" Sullivan in the hotel and made a deal for Chicago to throw the World Series, the beginning of what would become the infamous Black Sox scandal.[13]

While Gordon served as photoplay editor at the *Transcript*, his mother was working as a critic for Mary Baker Eddy's *Christian Science Monitor*. She, too, became close to Braithwaite, and she, too, cultivated a literary crowd. She became close to Katharine Lee Bates, the Wellesley professor, poet, and composer of, among other songs, "America the Beautiful." She also cultivated a relationship with Harriet Monroe, founder of *Poetry: A Magazine of Verse*, which helped popularize poetry in the early century and provided a publishing outlet for hundreds of poets who otherwise might have gone wanting.[14] It was the sort of contact that would only enhance Carolyn's outsized sense of self. The woman who claimed to be a famous actress, who saw herself as a suitable substitute for Noble and Greenough, would also, for example, claim later that she, too, was a Wellesley professor. (She was never a Wellesley professor.)[15]

Gordon did not develop a connection with Monroe and *Poetry*, but he did play on his mother's relationship with the *Monitor*. Beginning in 1919 and lasting through much of the following decade, he published dozens of stories and poems in the newspaper. "Upon our barn so very high," went one such poem,

> A gold ship sails against the sky,
> With golden spires and decks and rails
> In rain and sun and winds and gales.
> It goes due West with all its might
> Then turns about some time at night—
> Then sails around to South again.
> It is, you see, our weather vane.[16]

Hillman's poetry was not the stuff of the American canon, but many of the early poems cowritten with his mother and featured in *Rhymes Grave and Gay* first appeared in the *Monitor*. That work led to the publication of other poems like "Weather Vane," which ultimately led to Hillman getting more page space in the paper for full-length short stories. It was the praxis of aspirational narcissism writ onto actual lives, and it was successful. Hillman was a legitimate part of the journalistic and literary realm of intellectual Boston—and, through national magazine publications, the nation.[17]

This kind of generic success, combined with contact with people like Braithwaite, created in Gordon and Carolyn the expectation of a certain lifestyle, which would ultimately lead to their later financial troubles, and at the same time fostered in Carolyn a certain vanity that had been there since her time as an "actress," since her development in Gilded Age New Hampshire, typified by the fact that the 1930 census lists her as Gordon's sister, rather than his mother, and reverses her age, noting that she was forty-five instead of the actual fifty-four. That vanity then created more financial need, beginning a vicious cycle that would create calamity when Hillman's stories stopped selling and the money disappeared.[18]

Before calamity came, however, there was the Cape. A representative story in the genre was "A Ship Comes In," first published in 1935.

A SHIP COMES IN

Published in *Fiction Parade*, July 1935

It was a bathing-suit as blue as the sea, a bright, bright blue. It was a brief bathing-suit. Above it, tendrils of gray hair blew from a tight rubber cap. Grandma Spain, at seventy, was as straight as an arrow.

A window went up in the long house that stood among the rustling roses.

"Grandma oughtn't to wear that thing," said the girl at the window. She was tall and blond with fiery red cheeks and eyes that glistened now blue, now green.

"Don't make such a fuss, Doris," her sister told her softly. "Grandma spent more than an hour buying it."

"It makes her look so silly!" protested Doris.

"But it doesn't," said Mary Spain. She was an absurdly small girl, absurdly tiny, absurdly brown. In a brown shirt and sailor trousers, she seemed like an infinitely merry small boy.

"Mary Spain," said Doris pityingly, "you'll never grow up!"

"Never!" called Mary Spain and ran out on the lawn.

It was so long a lawn that it ran from twisting street to sharp cliff edge, and the house, added to, improved, enlarged a dozen times, ran with it. It was the only house on the cliff that was lived in, season in, season out.

The Spains had lived here since their fortunes had failed and Grandma had sold the old Spain house at the other end of the Island. And here Grandma had surveyed the ways of the summer women and found them good. That was why she wore the bathing-suit.

She was shamelessly sprawled in the sun now. "Needn't tell me," she said. "This rig shocks Doris."

"Well, she doesn't like it much," Mary said.

"She's afraid of what people will say," said Grandma Spain. "Wants to fix me up in a lace cap and mitts. Won't do it. The Spains don't."

She stared at a tanker's smoke against the sky. "About time for Bill," she droned. "About time for Bill to propose, I think. He'll look funny when he does."

Mary lazed contentedly in the soft wind and sun. "How'd Grandpa do it?" she asked.

"He never did it properly," said Grandma Spain. "What he said was, 'I've only a sixth share in the ship. That's not much.' And I said, 'It's enough.'"

Mary knew the rest of the story. After Grandma Spain was married and her husband had gone to sea.

Three days of wind, three days of

fog, three days of storm . . . all long, long ago.

Then the knocker going like mad on the broad front door, voices in the mist, and the mist beating down on Grandma Spain's bonnet and shawl as she ran blindly toward the sea. Limp black figures waiting for a ship, and the fog before them like a gray wall. And Grandma Spain with her back against a bollard, her young face set smooth as milk, and only her heels tap-tapping against the planks and her heart a steady thunder within her.

Through the fog then, an old Spanish bell in one of the Island churches had begun to toll and the black bowsprit of a ship showed in the mist.

Mary could hear the bell too, could hear it pealing triumphantly as lights blazed through the gray smother, and Grandma Spain went swinging up the street with her shoulder against a seaman's rough blue coat.

"Mary! Mary!" Doris was shouting from the doorstep, "Bill's here!"

It was all over, it was all gone, all the tall ships and tarry seamen, all the Island's golden glory. Island girls no longer watched and waited, and Island men were all like Bill.

He stood now beside his motor car, fussing because the seconds were spinning out in the sun. He stood there, thick set, with a square face and his hair brushed back into black smoothness.

Doris stood beside him, and Mary noticed that all the glint of green had left her eyes. They were soft blue now.

"We ought to hurry," said Bill. "I want you to look at a spot for a house."

He stared disapprovingly at Mary's wide trousers.

"Then there's no time to change," said Mary quickly and climbed into the car.

Behind them, the white pillar of the lighthouse dwindled and the sea's roar dimmed. Hedges went by and odd little houses, half hidden in roses.

One of them was white with blue blinds.

"That's cunning," said Mary.

"But it won't rent," Bill told her. "Too far from the water."

She wondered if he thought of the whole Island in terms of houses that would or wouldn't rent. She wondered if the sea meant to him only an added attraction for summer visitors. She supposed it did, for he sold real estate.

She had known him now for three years and each year he had come more often to loll on the long, narrow verandah. It was appallingly evident that he would soon ask her to marry him.

If she did, they would live on the Island in the summer and sell real estate. They would live near New York in the winter and sell real estate. And soon enough Bill would be thoroughly successful.

It was silly, she knew, sometimes to wish that instead of being an exceedingly nice, exceedingly solid young man, he was of a hard-bitten, salt-water breed. There were no men like that left on the Island now.

"I wonder what's the matter with Doris?" Bill was saying. "She acts queer."

"Perhaps it's Grandma," Mary suggested. "That new bathing-suit provokes Doris nearly to death. She's always afraid of what other people are going to say."

"It's a pretty bright bathing-suit for an old lady," Bill agreed. "Well, here it is."

Beside them a green meadow sloped to the grayness of the moors. Dwarf pines stood upon it and there were buttercups. There were no houses on the meadow, but across the road, half a dozen, shamelessly new, stood in a long line.

Mary stretched her arms to the wind and sun. "Wouldn't it be nice," she cried, "if all those houses weren't there?"

"Why?" Bill asked her. "They're well built. I sold two of them, myself."

She had said the wrong thing. She was always saying the wrong things to Bill. She tried again.

"What I was really thinking," she said, "was that the Island was better in the old days, the very old days."

Bill looked puzzled. "What's the matter with it now?" he asked.

She changed the subject. "I should think this was a fine place to build."

"It is pretty," he admitted. "But I don't want to be in too much of a hurry. There are other sites that are as good. I'll have to think it over. Pays to be safe."

It did pay to be safe, Mary knew, as the motor car went roaring down the moor road. But none of the Spains had been safe, sane people. None of them.

In a moment or two, Bill would ask her to marry him, she thought. She could almost sense his brain considering it. And she wondered what she would say. She had always liked Bill, she had liked him a great deal. But now that a proposal was in prospect, she was listless.

"Gee," said Bill suddenly, "I forgot. I've got to see a man in town. It's really important. I'm awfully sorry."

She should have been indignant, she knew, but she was merely relieved.

"That's all right," she said briskly. "Let me out anywhere."

By chance, he parked his car on Orange Street and she was left staring at the brown squareness of the old Spain house. Summer people owned it now. High above its roof, sun swept the captain's walk, and something told her she should be standing there, watching for some sailor's ship to break that circle of blue sea.

"That's silly," she told herself. "Where'd I get a sailor?"

She wandered up the wide main street with its cobblestones, its constant tide of motor cars, its bright stores of red brick, its green benches set on the sidewalk. Sailors were there certainly—sun-dried men from the seiners and draggers. Most were Portuguese, few were young.

There was a steady tide, too, of bronzed young men in wide white slacks and yachting shirts. And they all looked somewhat alike. Most of them looked a little like Bill.

The sweet wind lured her on past the old red houses, through the crooked streets, till at last she came to the top of a hill where stone gateposts were embellished by long, black tassels of iron.

It should have been a dismal place, but it never was. She paused by a stone that leaned seaward in the long grass, and the inscription was dim through the moss:

CAPT. LEONIDAS SPAIN.
BORN IN NANTUCKET

He was not there, this Captain Leonidas; he had turned to coral long ago on a southern shoal. And all the captains, whose names were on the stones about him, were as far away. They all slept in strange seas to which their last dark adventures had driven them before the storm.

SHE STILL had half an hour to wait for Bill and she drifted down to the long wharf. All about her the town was decaying, the town was dying like the Spains. Now it was only a playground for the summer folk.

There were a crowd of them looking down at a long flight of steps and a white float and she went to stand beside them.

A boy bumped into her and cried, "Excuse me. The plane's coming in!"

He was no more than fifteen and his hair hung down in a long lock over his forehead. She wondered what made him so excited.

"Here she comes!" he called to her as he hurried down the steps. "Sandy's bringing her in! Don't stand up there! You can't see anything."

The boy's excitement must have been infectious for she ran down the steps to the float. Far above the harbor the plane was swooping down like a great red bird. It struck the water in a cloud of spray, it slowed and swung toward the landing.

A young man in shirtsleeves, a white and blue cap on one side of his head, crawled out upon one of the pontoons. He was amazingly young, his face was narrow and ruddy and alive; sunlight struck sparks of gold from his hair.

The boy caught at one of the plane's pontoons and missed. The young man flung a rope's end and shouted at Mary: "Hi, kid! Catch it!"

She caught it expertly, she wound its loop about a post. She was suddenly without a thought in the world save that she must do the young man's bidding.

The young man leaped to the float and pulled open the cabin door.

"Now, sir," he said, "if you'll please step out. Be careful, please. Just a moment, madam."

Then he turned to Mary and his face went red with embarrassment. "I'm sorry," he said jerkily. "When I threw that rope, I thought you were a boy."

Mary smiled up at him. "Well, I caught the rope all right, didn't I?"

The boy, Roger, smiled too. "Pretty good for a girl," he said excitedly. "Say, Sandy! Father's going to let me learn to fly!"

"Fine!" said Sandy and struggled into a gray coat. It was old and worn and spotted, but all the oldness and the spots seemed to make him look even more distinguished. A red-faced man came down the steps, and Sandy said hesitantly:

"On time again, Mr. Sturgis."

Mr. Sturgis scowled. "Well, don't let that swell your head, Hathaway!" he growled unpleasantly.

They left him glaring at the plane, and Roger hissed as they went up the steps, "I'd like to punch his face!"

"Doesn't mean anything by it," said Sandy. He stared curiously at Mary. "Come on over to the yacht club, sister, and I'll buy you a bottle of pop."

Mary grinned. He thought she was a friend of young Roger's. He thought she was about fifteen.

But Roger didn't. He caught at his idol's sleeve. "Sandy!" he cried. "She isn't—you shouldn't—she's a grown-up young lady!"

Sandy's neck was dyed a deep red. He was horribly embarrassed. "I didn't know," he told her uncertainly. "I thought you were only a kid, I beg your pardon."

Mary laughed, "I'm all of nineteen," she said, "and I'm not a bit insulted. But I *was* invited to go to the yacht club and have a drink. May I?"

Sandy was too embarrassed to do more than nod.

She had a curious sense that, at this moment, as she walked into the gray yacht club, life was quickening, life was hastening like the turn of a boiling tide.

She sat on a tall stool, drinking ginger ale, and Sandy muttered, "I don't suppose this is any way to treat a young lady. You see, I don't know much about girls."

Roger seized her arm. "There's father!" he cried. "Let's go see him."

Roger's father sat facing the sea. He was gray-haired without being old, ruddy without being red-faced. He had little puckers of merriment at the corners of his eyes, as if he found all life amusing.

"Father," said Roger, suddenly becoming very solemn, "this is Miss— Miss—"

"Spain," Mary told him.

"Miss Spain," Roger repeated. "And though she looks very young, she's quite a grown-up young lady, you see."

"I see," said Roger's father. "Sit down, Miss Spain, and talk to me. It'll be a relief from my son's eternal gabble about flying."

He was nice, Mary thought. He made her feel almost at home in this world of mahogany express cruisers and sailboats that were like glittering toys.

"Been here long?" he was asking her.

"I live on the Island," she told him.

"Of course you do," he said. "Spain's an Island name. There's a Captain Leonidas Spain up on the hill, or rather there's a stone to him."

"My grandfather," Mary told him. "My grandmother's still alive. So much alive that she refuses to grow old. We all live together over on the other end of the Island."

Roger's father waved his hand at the yachts and yachtsmen. "All this must seem quite silly and amateurish to an Island girl," he said.

"I don't know," Mary confessed. "I've never been in the club before. I wouldn't be now if Roger hadn't dragged me in."

Roger's father smiled. "Then you haven't my son's fine scorn of it all. He scorns everybody but flying men. And he adores young Sandy. He'll be adoring you before you know it. I hope you won't mind."

"I won't a bit," Mary told him, "and I can see why he likes Sandy."

"Now there's a remarkable young man," said Roger's father easily. "I can see you think so too. He's the youngest pilot on the line and he reminds me of those old portraits you see here on the Island. Boys who went to sea at fourteen—"

Sandy was standing behind them. "I'm glad you're going to let Roger fly, sir," he was saying. "He's so keen on it."

"Wants to be a second edition of you," said Roger's father dryly. "He's a regular hero-worshipper."

A clock chimed somewhere, and Mary leaped to her feet. "I didn't know it was so late," she cried. "I've got to meet someone in town."

Sandy stood hesitant. "Might—might I escort you?" he said a little stiffly, and she nodded.

"Goodbye, Miss Spain," called Roger's father. "I hope that you'll let me come and see your grandmother some day soon. I like to hear the old Island stories."

Her eyes widened as they hurried through the town. She had never seen the streets lie so golden in the sun, the salt wind had never blown so sweet. All about her the old town was neither dead nor decaying: it was alive and stirring.

When they came to Orange Street and the car, Bill was hunched grumpily at the wheel. She could almost see Bill bristle when she introduced Sandy and he said irritably:

"I ought to be over at the other end of the Island now. Wherever have you been?"

The car started with a roar and Mary shouted to Sandy, "When do you fly back?"

"Half an hour," he told her.

The car was moving and she had to shout more loudly still:

"Come over and see us!"

She could not help looking back to see the slim, tall figure striding down the street with its white cap perked over one ear. Sandy looked, she thought, like some ghost of the old golden days going down a street of dream. But Bill didn't. "That kid," he said bitterly; "they should never trust him with a plane."

"Why, he's one of the best pilots on the line!" Mary flared.

"What if he is," Bill asked savagely. "You can bet you wouldn't catch me being a flier! Where'd he take you?"

"To the yacht club," said Mary indifferently.

"Mary," he said with immense dignity, "you're not the kind of girl to be dazzled by some fool flier. You want—"

A dim drone came to her ears and she sat suddenly erect. "I wonder if that's Sandy's ship!" she said.

She had forgotten entirely that Bill might be about to make a proposal. And he had made none at all when he irritably left her at her rose-twined gate.

Grandma Spain, still in the blue bathing-suit, was watering the lawn. "Well, well," she said wickedly, "was it a nice young man you met?"

Mary hugged her. "You're an old devil!" she cried. "Do you know everything?"

"Most everything," Grandma admitted. "You looked like a sleepy doll when you left: now someone's woken you up. Will I like him?"

"You'll have to," cried Mary and ran into the house.

DORIS WAS waiting for her, curled up on the sofa with a suspiciously damp handkerchief by her side.

"Look here, Mary Spain," she said roughly, "did Bill ask you to marry him?"

Mary stared and shook her head.

Doris stood up and her hands twitched. "Are you going to marry him?"

Mary said, "No." She said it without thinking.

Doris' eyes blazed. "Well, I am, if he'll have me," she said huskily. "I don't care if people say you threw him over and I was only second best."

Mary stared at her sister as if she was a stranger.

"I thought you cared awfully about what people said," she told Doris.

"I don't now," Doris cried. "I don't care about anything."

Her eyes were like blue sparks and Mary hugged her. "You fool sister!" she said. "Why didn't you tell me long ago?"

Mary went upstairs, whistling. Even the house seemed gay and reckless now.

The sea wind was blowing strong next day when a motor roared in the drive, and she could see Roger's father standing on the cliff edge, chatting to Grandma Spain for all the world like an old friend. Grandma's bathing-suit was as blue as ever and she was laughing.

She half started to her feet in the living room as Sandy came in, cap in hand.

"Hullo," he said. "Your Grandma told me you'd be here. Isn't she great!"

"Immense," Mary told him. "You don't think, do you, that her bathing-suit's too bright?"

"Of course not," said Sandy. "Makes her look like a girl. Isn't this fine?"

He sprawled luxuriously in the easiest chair and lit a pipe. His voice was a soft drawl and he looked, Mary thought, as if he had been lounging forever in the long room. He seemed as much a part of it as the dark-daubed portraits of the old Spains upon the wall.

She felt as if the house, the room, the pictures had been waiting for him for a long time, that their pattern had been incomplete before he came.

"It's an awfully homelike room," he sighed, and his eyes roved toward the old Spains. Who were they, he wanted to know, and what had they done?

She was just beginning to tell him when the telephone jangled.

"It's Sturgis," an angry voice roared at the other end of the line. "Is that lazy, useless Hathaway kid over there? Tell him I want him! Burns is sick and he's got to take the two o'clock plane out. Hurry up!"

Mary's voice was curt and crisp. "If you can't have any better manners, Mr. Sturgis, I won't tell him at all."

Mr. Sturgis gurgled. "All right, Miss Spitfire! Will you please tell my distinguished junior pilot that I need him? Thank you."

Sandy had his cap in his hand when she came back. "I'm awfully sorry," he said shyly. "I really have to go. But might I come back—some time?"

"Of course you may," said Mary Spain.

As she stood waving at the big car, she could hear Grandma grumbling at her elbow: "Just like a Spain to get a dratted man she can only see in snatches. You're as bad as I was. Worse."

Yet even if Mary did see Sandy in snatches, it was surprising how many times he managed to tumble into the old house, only to tumble out again because his time was up and he must be flying again.

It was equally surprising how many times Mary rattled over to town in her shabby old car and parked it on the long wharf. These visits always occurred when the plane was due, and oddly enough, she made a friend in Mr. Sturgis, the Island agent of the airplane line. She would sit on a shelf in his cubicle while he smiled at her and described Sandy as a "tow-headed ruffian" and a "swollen-headed little mutt."

Grandma Spain never called Sandy anything of the sort. She knew all about him at once, knew that his parents had died in a train wreck when he was fourteen, knew that he had put himself through Technology and that he had a hard time making a living.

"Ho, hum," she would say whenever Mary made one of her sudden starts for town. "I spent most of my life waitin' on a wharf and now you're doin' the same. All the Spains are fools."

It was on a certain Saturday that Sandy sprinted up the steps from the plane in double-quick time. "Mary Spain," he cried, "I'm staying on the

Island tonight. There's a dance in town. Could—could you come?"

"Of course I'd like to come," Mary said.

"I didn't know," Sandy stammered. "There's no reason why you should. I'm just a tramp pilot and—"

"—At times an awfully shy and difficult young man," said Mary Spain.

But the dance was a dismal, flat failure. It was atrociously hot in the rooms over the long line of stores; drums and saxophones beat brazenly in their ears; awkward couples collided with them.

They circled dully in the noise and the heat. They were silent. All talk had gone dead between them.

"Mary Spain," Sandy said suddenly, "let's get out of here!"

Beyond the broad windows, a soft wind was whistling down the main street and little lights were dim among the trees.

"Let's!" cried Mary.

They went down the stairs like two truants from school. They went running into the soft sweet night and the sea wind was cool upon their faces.

"Wasn't that simply terrible!" cried Mary Spain.

"Awful!" said Sandy.

There was no constraint between them now; they were like two children laughing in the dark. They swung toward the wharf where the seiners lay and the harbor was a broad black mirror.

They sat on the wharf's edge and let their legs dangle and the golden moon came out of the sea. There was soft magic in the sea wind and they were silent for a long time.

It was Sandy who spoke first. "Of course," he said, "I don't make much money—"

"It's enough," said Mary Spain and drew his face down to hers. All about them the moonlight was a golden flood.

All the gold had gone to gray next afternoon as she sat in the long room where the old Spains smiled stiffly down from the wall. Outside, flecks of high fog flung by, the sea pounded dully, the very windows rattled in their frames.

There was a leaping fire on the hearth and in its light she could see Doris and Bill, side by side. Bill had a blueprint on his lap but Doris was as intent upon it as if it had been a plan for Paradise.

Mary smiled at the old Spains and the old Spains smiled back. Soon they would be staring down at Sandy with that same warm smile. He was so much like them he might almost have been a Spain himself. The fog came thicker now; she could scarcely see from the west window.

A little quiver of dull dread ran through her, and her knuckle tapped on the window pane.

On the verandah there was a crash as a chair went over. The fog was blind now; it was groping among the houses. Through it came the thunder of the rising sea.

"Don't look so worried, Mary," Doris was saying. "Don't—"

The telephone rang and Grandma's voice answered it, a voice that was sharp, even against the storm.

It was sharper still when she came into the room, her hands fumbling at a battered hat. Her face was grim and white and set.

"Mary Spain," she said. "Get your coat!"

The room whirled about her, a gust of wind drowned the fire to a dead blackness. She seemed always to have been standing by the gray window, always to have seen Bill looming helplessly above her, always to have been jerking her arm into a yellow oilskin coat.

Grandma flung open the side door, and the wind and the rain beat in.

"Mary Spain," she said. "Come on."

The storm tore at them as they staggered to the car. The surf was roaring in a steady thunder, the thin line of trees were whipped half over by the wind.

Automatically, Mary crept beside the wheel of the battered old car.

"Sandy," she said dully. "Did he—is he?"

Grandma bent to button her coat. "Sandy's plane left the mainland at noon," she said. "It hasn't been heard from. Start the car, child."

THEY SWUNG down the driveway and the rain beat upon them. It rattled on the roof, it stung their faces. The lights made little golden paths through the mist. There were lights in the houses, too, that went swinging by so crazily. But then the lights all died away and they were out on the moors with the wind shrieking in their ears.

Somewhere off the coast Sandy had been flying in a bright red plane, flying into fog and a screaming storm.

"He's quite alone," said Grandma Spain.

Sandy was quite alone in a dim, dull smother, alone with the sky and the sea and the wind. Mary's foot pressed down, and the old car rattled and roared.

It rattled and roared through the streets of the town, and those streets were strewn with broken branches. On the wharf, all the lights were staring through the fog and the harbor was a dull gray pit of wreathing mist as they jerked to a stop and Roger's father, tall in oilers, came running up.

"I heard about Mary and Sandy yesterday," he told Grandma, "and I knew she'd want to come."

The door to the office stood open wide; the office itself was a golden circle of light. Roger was hunched on a desk and his face was a white fury.

Mr. Sturgis, his coat unbuttoned, a dead cigarette between his lips, was endlessly fiddling with a pencil, his ear to a telephone. "Can't you get through?" he was saying dully. "Coast guard base! Coast guard base!"

He only nodded as Mary came in, and shoved the telephone away.

"The lousy little fool," he droned and the cigarette dropped from his lips.

Roger came erect, wild-eyed and snarling. His voice screamed into the log. "You filthy pig! You hated him!"

Roger's hands were over his face. He was sobbing. He shook. He half fell against Mary Spain and she sat down in a chair. Roger's knees buckled. His head was in her lap.

"Don't cry, Roger," she said. She could not believe it was her own voice, she could not believe she was sitting in this circle of light with the sea beating like a blind thing against the shivering wharf outside.

She did not seem to be there at all; she was out in the fog where a red plane rolled and the sharp waves tore at its wings.

Mr. Sturgis' eyes were dull and dead. "Cheest," he said. "There's so much fog. And that big bum out there all alone!"

Grandma Spain sat on a desk, a shriveled little figure with her heels tapping. "You're fond of him, aren't you?" she said.

Mr. Sturgis writhed in his chair. "Aw!" he droned. "Aw, hell, no!"

Roger's father tapped at Mary's arm. "The coast guard's out looking," he said. "A cutter and a picket boat. There's nothing to worry about . . ."

Mary slowly shook her head. She sat erect as wind screamed through the open door and rain made a darkening pool on the floor. Outside it was dusk, and that seemed strange, for in her mind, time seemed to have stopped dead still. It was not possible that it would ever go on again, it was not possible that the fog would lift or that the sea would ever stop its roar.

She would be here always, slumped in a great chair, endlessly stroking the head of a sobbing boy while a red plane splintered and sank and a gay white and blue cap went bobbing on the gray waves.

Yet she knew suddenly, sharply, that it would not be so. The fog would lift: life would go on. Roger would grow older, grow up—forget.

But she would never forget: she would always see Sandy as she had seen him once, a slim, tall figure, endlessly going down a golden street of dream.

Mr. Sturgis rose. He rose because he could not stand those dark eyes smoldering in that set white face.

"Got to see a guy—" he mumbled. "Steamboat office—can't tell—got to do something."

Behind him the door crashed shut in the wind, but Grandma Spain's heels never stopped their tap-tapping on the desk.

There was only dull emptiness in Mary's head now, a conviction that Roger must be soothed and comforted, that he must not cry so terribly, Sandy wouldn't like Roger to cry so. And Sandy—

A great sea crashed and the whole wharf shook. Then, through the fog, an old Spanish bell in one of the Island churches began to toll.

Feet came running across the planks, the door slammed open, Mr. Sturgis crashed into the room.

"He's coming in!" he shouted. "He's coming in! The steamer picked him up! They just radioed."

Mary Spain couldn't see him any more. She couldn't see any of them. They were all in a mist. For she was crying very quietly.

Grandma Spain was stroking her shoulder. Roger's father was helping her to her feet.

And Mr. Sturgis was saying over and over again: "Now, sister! Now, sister! He's safe! He's safe! He's only got a busted arm."

Suddenly, they were standing in the mist—mist so heavy that the lights bleared through and the dusk came down. They stood in a long line on the wharf with the fog before them like a great gray wall.

Mary's back was against a bollard and her heart was a steady thunder within her. Through the fog, the old Spanish bell was still tolling, and soon a ship was coming in.

5. THE MAGAZINES

The literary life of culture and art was part of the aspirational project in which Carolyn had been engaged since the nineteenth century, and it would drive the life of her son, as well, but it was Gordon's newspaper work that kept paychecks coming and allowed for the steady income that facilitated his participation in the literary life. Even in that newspaper effort, however, Hillman was part of the artistic milieu. His theater and film reviews kept him in the public eye, even for those not interested in ephemeral fiction, as local movie advertisements often included his positive comments on their pictures to lure in new viewers. Through the late 1920s, he wrote for the *Advertiser*, before moving to the *Daily Record* in 1930. Whether for the *Advertiser* or the *Record*, however, Hillman's reviews were filled with the kinds of gauche superlatives that made them quotable in film advertisements. *Cavalcade* (1933), for example, was "the finest film ever made in the English language." *Becky Sharp* (1935) was "the best color film ever produced."[1] In between such efforts, however, Gordon began focusing intently on short stories as his artistic medium of choice.

Magazines had been a part of American life from the colonial era, the first founded in February 1741. Neither Andrew Bradford's *American Magazine* nor Benjamin Franklin's *General Magazine* had long lives, but they served as precedent documents for the genre. In 1787, the year of the Constitutional Convention, Noah Webster published New York's first monthly periodical, also called the *American Magazine*. As historian James Playsted Wood has noted, the country's early magazines "were an important sign of America's dawning cultural as well as political independence." George Washington observed that such publications were "more happily calculated than any other, to preserve the liberty, stimulate the industry and meliorate the morals of an enlightened and free people."[2]

In 1815, the *North American Review* became the first periodical to attempt a broader national scope. Six years after that, the *Saturday Evening Post* was founded, and nine years later, *Godey's Lady's Book*, which, according to Wood, "became an American institution in the nineteenth century. It affected the manners, morals, tastes, fashions in clothes, homes, and diet of generations of American readers." Just prior to the Civil War, *Harper's* was founded in 1850, the *Atlantic Monthly* in 1857.[3]

The modern version of the national magazine developed in the Gilded Age following Reconstruction. The Civil War had laid bare sectional animosities, and the government realized the necessity of disseminating national information sources as a vehicle of national unity. In 1879, the federal government reduced the price of mailing periodicals. In 1893, affordable, popular magazines like *Munsey's* and *McClure's* catered to a national readership. Several years later, Cyrus H. K. Curtis purchased a struggling *Saturday Evening Post* and began reviving its relevance. From that point, magazines developed with relative alacrity into a national phenomenon.[4]

Matthew Schneirov's study of turn-of-the-twentieth-century popular magazines asserts that such magazines redefined the meaning of national culture. "Instead of a link to the past, a source of reassurance, a repository of timeless and permanent virtues," argues Schneirov, "'culture' was associated with a series of future projects or 'dreams.' The new culture sought not permanence but possibility, not character but desire." It was an aspirational culture, and it would come to dominate the American mind: "The dreams of abundance, social control, and social justice became the cornerstones of a post-Victorian mass culture and through the pages of popular magazines attained a legitimacy and a national audience." In the same vein, Daniel A. Clark has claimed that such magazines "challenged American beliefs about work, leisure, and identity."[5]

Educated readers in the Gilded Age flocked to what stood as highbrow fare, *Century*, *Harper's*, *Scribner's*, *North American Review*, the *Atlantic*, all propagating a form of literature known as genteel, a saccharine attempt to denude the more troubling aspects of the era, eliminating vice and urbanization in favor of a better model of society. (The label "genteel" came from George Santayana and was originally an epithet for a fictional output that refused to push boundaries and thus break new ground.)[6]

Frank Munsey, S. S. McClure, and others saw that such vanilla, highbrow fare left room in the market for magazines with more universal appeal. Along with an unserved readership, the shift to an urban industrial economy also created a need for ephemeral media that could bring advertising messages to national markets. Low-cost general-interest magazines fit both bills. The development of rotary presses and mass production models that replaced the slower and more work-intensive flatbed presses also facilitated such growth. Magazine production, writes Tom Pendergast, "shifted the terms of success for American magazines and immersed them in a commercial marketplace in ways that they had never been before."[7]

McClure had not been able to read magazines in college because the cost was prohibitive, and the resulting frustration convinced him to create an inexpensive popular magazine. Founded in 1893, *McClure's* cost fifteen cents, down from the usual price of between twenty-five and thirty-five cents. At roughly the same time, iron-mining magnate John Brisben Walker bought the struggling *Cosmopolitan* magazine in 1889 and revived it using the same model, cutting the price of an issue (in an annual subscription) from twenty-five cents to twelve and a half cents by 1893. The final step in the evolution came later that year when *Munsey's* reduced its price to only ten cents, and its annual subscription price from three dollars to one dollar. Founded in 1889, the magazine had floundered until the bold move made it incredibly popular. "We can do it," the magazine claimed, "because we deal direct with news dealers and save two profits you pay on other magazines. No middlemen; no monopoly."[8]

Cosmopolitan under Walker had found its success, according to historian David Sumner, in "a niche between the more populist content of *Munsey's* and the more sophisticated approach to celebrity interviews and features taken by *McClure's*." In 1905, William Randolph Hearst bought the magazine from Walker. Under his editor, Ray Long, *Cosmopolitan* began emphasizing fiction from the 1910s through the 1930s. Another of Hearst's magazines, *Good Housekeeping*, followed much the same formula after the magnate purchased it in 1911.[9]

In 1897, Cyrus Curtis, who had already made *Ladies' Home Journal* one of the country's most popular magazines, bought a failing *Saturday Evening Post* and revived it. At the time of Curtis's purchase, the periodical had an average circulation of 2,231 and annual advertising revenue of $6,933. By 1922, its circulation was 2,187,024, and its ad revenue stood at $28,278,755.[10]

Those magazines put an emphasis on fiction, but an emphasis different from that of the genteel literary magazines. As historian Theodore Peterson has noted, "publishers were discovering that the story itself was more important than the literary skill with which it was told." Or, as Frank Munsey explained in 1895: "We want stories. That is what we mean—stories, not dialect sketches, not washed out studies of effete human nature, not weak tales of sickly sentimentality, not 'pretty' writing." What his magazine did want was "fiction in which there is a story, a force, a tale that means something—in short a story. Good writing is as common as clam shells, while good stories are as rare as statesmanship." He argued that fiction "is responsible for enormous circulations, and without fiction the general advertisers would find the magazine proposition a quite different matter and decidedly uninteresting from a business standpoint."[11]

Edward Bok had taken over the *Ladies' Home Journal* in the late nineteenth century and led it to dominance among women's magazines prior to World War I, but Bok retired in 1919. Barton Currie led the magazine through the 1920s, maintaining a strong fiction department, but after Currie left in 1928, the magazine foundered. The Curtis Company, which also owned the *Saturday Evening Post*, transferred in the early 1930s the job of choosing fiction for the *Journal* to the editors of the *Post*. The *Journal* recovered, however, when Bruce and Beatrice Blackmar Gould took over in 1935, improving the magazine's fiction and editorial effort.[12]

Ladies' Home Journal's chief competitor in the women's magazine market was the Crowell Publishing Company's *Woman's Home Com-*

panion. An also-ran through much of the 1920s, by 1932 it had outpaced the *Journal* as the leader in circulation among women's magazines, maintaining that spot through the decade and into 1940 largely, as Mary Ellen Zuckerman has noted, because of "the consistently high quality editorial matter in the journal, particularly the fiction and service departments."[13]

McCall's had been even farther down the list of periodicals, "considered little more than a cheap household journal" before the editorship of Harry Payne Burton beginning in 1922. Burton used name fiction writers like Booth Tarkington, Zane Grey, Kathleen Norris, and others to draw in readers, pushing the magazine's circulation to more than 2.5 million by the end of the decade.[14]

All such magazines built their expansion based on fiction, which became an important part of each in the 1920s and took an even larger role in the 1930s. "I haven't the slightest hesitation in saying that it is next to impossible for any magazine to achieve a circulation of more than half a million without basing it upon good fiction," claimed editor William Frederick Bigelow. *McCall's* did several studies of reader tastes, all of which proved that fiction was the chief pull factor for magazine readers.[15] In 1898, for example, Cyrus Curtis hired *Boston Post* reporter George Horace Lorimer as the literary editor for the *Saturday Evening Post*. Lorimer's *Post* published Stephen Crane, Jack London, F. Scott Fitzgerald, Sinclair Lewis, and William Faulkner and became the unquestioned leader among popular magazines in the first part of the twentieth century.[16]

And such fare unquestionably grew the market for those periodicals. In 1893, for example, Frank Munsey estimated the number of magazine buyers at 250,000. By 1899, he estimated it at 750,000. By 1947, the numbers were quite different. A Magazine Advertising Bureau study that year put the number of magazine reading households at 32,300,000. By 1959, that number had risen to 41,492,000. At the onset of the twentieth century, there was only one magazine with a circulation of a million: *Ladies' Home Journal* reached the mark in 1904. By 1910, so had *McCall's*. By 1920, the *Saturday Evening Post* had achieved a weekly circulation of more than two million. By 1963, at least fifty magazines had reached the million circulation mark.[17]

Table 5.1. Aggregate per-issue circulation of magazines in the United States

Year	Circulation
1900	65,000,000
1923	128,621,000
1929	202,022,000
1935	178,621,000
1939	239,693,000
1947	384,628,000

Source: Theodore Peterson, *Magazines in the Twentieth Century* (Urbana: University of Illinois Press, 1964), 59.

Table 5.2. Growth of magazine circulation

Year	Number of magazines	Average circulation per issue	Annual Sales ($)
1929	365	94,836	1,804,796
1933	365	86,610	1,620,221
1938	492	119,053	2,200,342
1945	472	192,021	2,980,166
1950	567	223,581	3,461,916

Source: Theodore Peterson, *Magazines in the Twentieth Century* (Urbana: University of Illinois Press, 1964), 59.

Table 5.3. Growth of *McCall's* circulation

Year	Circulation
1900	201,200
1910	1,060,300
1920	1,350,100
1930	2,505,100
1940	3,116,700
1950	3,807,100

Source: Theodore Peterson, *Magazines in the Twentieth Century* (Urbana: University of Illinois Press, 1964), 60.

And that growth continued despite the exigencies of the Great Depression. Of the twenty-six leading continually published magazines from 1930 to 1940, twenty-three saw circulation increase.[18]

Table 5.4. Circulation growth of selected periodicals, 1930s

Magazine	1930 circulation	1940 circulation	Percentage change
Cosmopolitan	1,726,623	1,764,974	2.2
Good Housekeeping	1,709,775	2,342,768	37.0
Ladies' Home Journal	2,481,620	3,385,948	36.4
McCall's	2,467,248	3,108,151	26.0
Saturday Evening Post	2,743,199	3,210,940	17.1
Woman's Home Companion	2,501,606	3,370,193	34.7

Source: Republished with permission of Peter Lang Copyright AG, from *The Magazine Century: American Magazines since 1900* by David E. Sumner (2010), 77; permission conveyed through Copyright Clearance Center, Inc.

Much of that growth was built on advertising. As the number of companies wanting their products showcased grew, so too did the periodicals that could showcase them. *Time* magazine's chief economist, Richard G. Gettell, argued in 1951 that from 1935 to 1950 there was a virtual one-to-one ratio of growth in consumer spending and growth in corporate ad spending.[19]

It was also built on the further education of readers. The rise in education and literacy rates facilitated the growth of both magazines and newspapers, the two forms of ephemeral literature that would define the life and career of Hillman. That, in turn, created a synergy between newspapers and fiction magazines, the former seeking to invest venture capital in the emerging market. *Liberty*, for example, was founded in 1924 by the *Chicago Tribune*'s Robert McCormick and the *New York Daily News*'s Joseph M. Patterson. It continually lost money, however, leading the duo to sell to magazine mogul Bernarr Macfadden in 1931. He, too, was unable to make the magazine consistently profitable. *Liberty* changed ownership several times throughout the 1940s until finally closing its doors in 1951.[20]

Macfadden published popular magazines, and he also published pulps. One of those was *Ghost Stories*, founded two years after *Liberty* in 1926. The magazine of supernatural stories was unique to the Macfadden empire but situated itself among other of his pulps like *True Story*. At the same time, while its contents were decidedly the stuff of pulp, *Ghost Stories* was a large-format slick magazine that published authors like Agatha Christie and Upton Sinclair. Hillman published regularly in the magazine in the late 1920s and early 1930s. Though most of his stories appeared in mass national periodicals like the *Saturday Evening Post*, *American Magazine*, and *Liberty*, he also published twenty-one times in *Ghost Stories*, including four stories featuring a psychic investigator named Cranshawe.[21]

Still, such periodicals never achieved the status of their high-circulation counterparts like the *Saturday Evening Post* and others. Lorimer took over the *Saturday Evening Post* in the late nineteenth century and edited it for forty years. Bok did the same for the *Ladies' Home Journal*, staying at his post for thirty years. Editor Ray Long had a similar impact on *Cosmopolitan*, where he was so successful that in the late 1920s he earned an annual salary of one hundred thousand dollars.[22]

They made their respective magazines the most popular in the nation. And despite the American public's rising levels of education as a factor in magazine growth, the Lynds' study of Muncie, Indiana, in 1924 revealed that "the aggregate circulation of the *Post* and the *Journal* was sixty times greater than that of *Harper's* and *Atlantic*." They did so by preaching a decidedly aspirational middle-class ethic, one that, in the words of historian David Minter, "helped to define what being a successful man or woman meant by catering to an audience that increasingly depended on the advice of strangers about everything from morals and mores to hygiene and manners. And in their advertisements they began making wholesale use of the fluid, nonlinear, nonrepresentational techniques that were beginning to dominate fiction."[23]

Whereas smaller-circulation magazines often depended on contributions, those with larger circulations purchased only a slight few freelance contributions. *American Magazine*, one of Hillman's publishers, rejected 98 percent of unsolicited stories. That said, "editors relied largely on professional freelancers with whom they maintained close liaison," as Peterson has explained, which meant that getting a foot in that door increased an author's chances for future sales:[24]

> The freelance writer seems to have been much more myth than reality throughout the entire history of American magazines. It is extremely unlikely that any significant number of authors ever managed to earn a living from magazines unless they held staff positions. The myth of the freelance writer persisted tenaciously; it was encouraged by teachers of writing, by the books on magazine writing which rolled from publishers' presses from the thirties on, by the roseate journals for amateur authors, by the correspondence schools which promised to make anyone a writer in ninety days, and by the editors themselves.[25]

The large magazines did begin paying competitive rates for stories in the early twentieth century. The *Saturday Evening Post*'s Lorimer provided authors with an acceptance decision within one week and paid for stories upon that acceptance. There began as of the 1920s a legitimate competition between magazines for material from authors with name recognition who might sell more copies. In the early 1930s, *Cosmopolitan* paid as much as five thousand dollars for a short story, though the average payment was probably half that sum. It was still a pittance of the magazine's total income. *Collier's* Jerome Ellison estimated in 1946 that only a small portion of the magazine's profits were spent on writers' contributions. "One magazine clears $200,000 an issue and pays $10,000 an issue for material," he claimed. "Another, generally considered fantastically generous, clears $900,000 an issue and pays its contributors $45,000." In 1949, J. K. Lasser estimated that popular magazines spent four cents of every dollar on stories, articles, and pictures.[26]

Jonathan Norton Leonard estimated in 1935 that the magazine industry spent money on contributions to theoretically support a thousand freelance writers at an annual income of three thousand dollars. Since that money was not equally distributed, however, he supposed the industry was only supporting roughly fifty-four. With the glut of would-be authors and the relatively limited page space provided by the magazines, publishers knew they could finesse supply and demand to ensure maximum profit while writers with nothing but the hope of publication had little leverage in negotiations. It was, to be sure, an exclusive club, and freelance fiction writers often held other jobs on newspapers, as academics, or in business.[27]

"Even the successful freelance lived in uncertainty," explained Peterson. "From time to time, he was obsessed by the idea that editors did not appreciate him. He sometimes submitted four article ideas for every one that editors liked. He often earned but $3.50 an hour while writing articles for major magazines, and the money had to support him when editors were not buying his output. He frequently got no more than expense money when commissioned articles did not turn out as editors had expected. He knew that the editors who favored him today might be jobless tomorrow and then he would have to rebuild his contacts in editorial offices."[28]

"Since the decline of the oldtime prospector, few people have worked with less companionship, few have had to rely more on their own resources," explained Morton Sontheimer, former president of the Society of Magazine Writers. "You have to be provident enough, or have good enough credit, to live for months sometimes without income. You have to endure seeing all your capital assets—your ideas and your manuscripts—tied up interminably by indecisive editors. You have to take a philosophical view of payment checks long overdue from rich magazines. You have to preserve your sanity through barren periods when there's no work and through busy periods filled with nothing but cursed revisions. You have to develop a six-inch armor-plate insensibility to what editors may do, or make you yourself do, to those words you all but bled for."[29]

It could be done, however. Authors like Frederick S. Faust published stories throughout the 1920s and 1930s under at least fourteen different pseudonyms, writing roughly two million words per year for pulp magazines and making an annual wage of more than seventy thousand dollars. Such was the rarest feat, but its existence kept the myth of the freelance author alive.[30] Hillman, too, though not as prolific as Faust, enjoyed success in that cutthroat world, but it was not the kind of sustained success that would earn him a place in the canon. For all of his published material, for example, Hillman never appears in any volume of the *Dictionary of Literary Biography*. His aspirational stories of boarding school, Cape Cod, or the publishing industry itself fit the tenor of the growing industry. Despite their ability to maneuver in that labyrinthine system, however, or perhaps because of the system itself, there was a functional ceiling on the ability of authors like Faust or Hillman to gain legitimacy in the field, a different sort of a politics of respectability that denied them a place at the table of more serious authors.[31]

Of course, magazine fiction more broadly experienced its own waves of respectability and popularity. In the 1920s, popular magazines carried a variety of content, but in the 1930s, with the decrease in advertising revenue in the wake of the Depression, fiction became more prominent, as it was the most popular and easiest fare to recruit. As the 1930s became the 1940s, however, fiction became less and less prominent in American magazines, as content shifted during World War II to nonfiction reporting, a trend that would continue after the war's conclusion and into the 1950s and 1960s.[32]

James Playsted Wood described national magazine fiction in 1949 as "'escape' fiction," stories that "take the reader out of the familiar and sometimes drab actualities of his own life into a more romantic and alluring scene where all women are beautiful, all men handsome, and good fortune is assured after exciting interplay of plot and glamorous characters." He worried that "mass magazines ignore much of the better fiction" and that "there is just cause, then, for the unfavorable criticism leveled at the popular magazines for their failure to print more serious fiction." They published instead "light fiction," worried that "the mass public will not accept serious fiction."[33]

Such was the world of Gordon Hillman. The period in which Hillman wrote was the period of modernism in literature, art, and everything else. James Joyce and T. S. Eliot and Pablo Picasso defied the evolutionary flow that had developed since the Renaissance, culminating in the realist and naturalist responses to genteelism in the late nineteenth century. A new emphasis on nonlinear progression and abstraction turned those former ideals on their heads, as modernists, in the explanation of Werner Sollors, "increasingly wished to represent the sense of speed and motion that trains, trolleys, automobiles, and other means of modern transportation made widely available." Hillman was no modernist. Such was not the fare that populated the general-circulation magazines. They were engaged in a moderated version of that late nineteenth century move to realism, and Hillman was part of that effort. Those magazines played to what became known as "middlebrow" culture, and publications like the *Saturday Evening Post* actually used many of their nonfiction pages to rail against modern art as fundamentally un-American. It was a common opinion in society that contemporary artistic and literary trends were either communistic or part of the same trend that brought communism into the country.[34]

The *Post* and other magazines were part of the commercialization of literary production that accompanied the nation's new acquisitive culture after World War I. In the 1920s the *Post*'s pages carried more advertising copy than editorial content. As Werner Sollors has explained, "The development from a literary editor who sought business as a theme to a commercial entrepreneur who paid for content to accompany a journal's advertisements was well underway."[35]

John Dewey made the case that such magazines were made possible by a population "constantly in transit." They were "passengers. Hence the S— E— P— and other journals expressly designed for this intermediate state of existence." Asking, "What becomes of all these periodicals?," Dewey observed that "the man who answered this question would be the final authority on literature in America."[36]

Communist author Mike Gold, writing in 1924, found magazines like the *Post* full of "hired romanticists; hired liars about life; high salaried thimble-riggers, flim-flam men and circus fakers; Rolls Royce captains of fictional industry; sob sisters," a manifestation of mass production and mass culture that was a consequence of the capitalist decadence of the decade.[37]

It was, however, a trend that had been progressing since the Victorian era, as in the 1860s "an unprecedented range of new magazines" featured "fiction with the middle-class family audience in mind." Wilkie Collins referred to that middle-class audience as the "unknown public," rarely taken into account as a readership but actually "the largest audience for periodical literature." That proved to be true throughout

Hillman's career. The literary publications—the *Atlantic*, the *North American Review*, and *Harper's*, among others—managed to move from genteelism to realist and naturalist stories in the first decades of the twentieth century. But for the large-circulation magazines, emphasis on that "unknown public" would always remain dominant, so much so that R. G. Cox looked back at the Victorian period in 1958 and concluded, "From our present vantage point the nineteenth century begins to look like the great age of the periodical."[38]

For Hillman, however, that great age would always be the twentieth. In "Tough Guy," published in *McCall's* in 1935, Hillman tells the story of a fire that destroys a local club and the all-hands-on-deck response of the local newspaper, a tale playing directly to that middle-class family audience while describing the crucial, if stylized, role of periodicals in people's lives. He never wrote a story about the magazine business itself, as the colonial relationship they had with their authors kept them from the kind of close contact necessary to set a proper scene, but "Tough Guy," from 1935, epitomizes the popular magazine style and Hillman's reverence for the periodical press.

TOUGH GUY

Published in *McCall's*, December 1935

"IF DUANE'S drunk again," said Big Ed, "I'll fire him." Big Ed was quite small and slim with bright black eyes, a thin face and an oddly olive skin. He was city editor of the "Courier" and he sat hunched over his desk scowling darkly as he ruffled the still damp pages of the first edition.

"Those day side dunkeys," the Top was saying out of the side of his mouth, "must have had a nice sleep for themselves. There's nothing in the rag but Abyssinia and that won't sell any papers."

The Top screwed himself around in his chair, blew on his glasses and polished them with a rumpled red-bordered handkerchief.

The Top was the news editor and as explosive as a small bomb. He'd once been top sergeant in the artillery and had never gotten over the effects, either physical or mental.

He turned to the men at the copy readers' desk and drawled, "It's going to be a slow night around here, gentlemen, so you might as well stretch out and take a nap for yourselves."

It was seven o'clock, that oddly quiet hour when the day, drained dry of news, had gone slipping into night, whose thunders had not yet begun. It was hot and sticky and Snuffy ran his fingers around the inside of his collar and was worried.

He was worried about Duane. He stood in the center of the long, dim City Room and scowled. Everyone else was in: Daisy, running a comb through her dark hair; Tom Creed, hunched up with his heels on his typewriter; Dan, stiff as a poker and looking a little like a superior sort of clerk; Little Paul in his shirt sleeves, and all the rest. But there wasn't a single sign of Duane.

There was a thin tinkle from above the telephone booths, and the fire gong struck with slow precision. It struck one and four and five and two and no one in the drowsy room, save McAndrew, paid the slightest attention to it.

McAndrew, whose hair was alarmingly pale and whose face almost matched it, scrawled the box number on the edge of a magazine and looked up at his hat. If the gong jangled hysterically into a second alarm, he'd be gone. He was a spark and therefore, according to the staff, quite crazy.

Snuffy sat down on the big bench with the other office boys where they were all reading the comics and chewing gum. It was hot and his clothes stuck to the bench and Duane hadn't come in yet and quite clearly wasn't coming.

Snuffy sat there and tried to imagine the "Courier" without Duane and simply couldn't do it. Duane was the "Courier." If it hadn't been for Duane, Snuffy wouldn't have been here himself.

He had come in a year ago, small and square-jawed and belligerent, and had straightway gotten himself into trouble.

He had gotten into trouble directly he had heard there was such a thing as a head office boy. The head office boy had been a lean and stringy individual with a fine set of freckles and, facetiously, he had sent Snuffy over to the dusty reference room for a half-column cut of the Leviathan.

The librarian had not been pleased. He had lived too long in the atmosphere of yellowed clippings, frayed photographs and long-dead sensation and scandal, to appreciate juvenile jokes.

And the upshot had been that Snuffy, his blue eyes all ablaze, had come storming into the City Room and shouted at his chief tormentor, "You ain't head office boy any more. I am."

The stringy youth, whose name was Al, had been unwise enough to put up his fists, and though a newspaper office was a strange and alien land to Snuffy, he knew what that meant. He had fought his way from one end of B Street to the other, he had fought his way through school, and he hit Al with dearly bought scientific skill.

He was still hitting him and they were rolling over and over on the floor when the managing editor came storming out of his office with a cigar in his mouth, and Big Ed hauled Snuffy abruptly to his feet.

"Stop that," said Big Ed sharply. "He's the head office boy and you'll take his orders and like it."

Snuffy had been so furious he couldn't see. He had yelled, "I won't. I quit! I wouldn't work for you for a million dollars. I'm through!"

He had swung around and gone running down the office, quite small and chunky with his face brick red and his eyes too near tears for comfort.

Someone had caught him by the sleeve and was holding him, someone was saying: "Listen, tough guy, you're going to stay right here and learn something. You're only a little mutt, but we'll make you into a gentleman yet, even if it kills you. You'd better wipe your nose."

Snuffy had looked up and Duane was smiling at him. And he ought to have been mad at Duane, but somehow he wasn't.

He'd pulled out a handkerchief, mopped his face and said, "I ain't a mutt!"

"That's better," Duane had said. "Cool off."

EVEN THEN Snuffy had known there was something special about Duane. It was something that made all the rage go out of him with a rush, that made him feel quite small and empty and unimportant as he scuffed his shoe against the desk.

Duane looked different from anyone Snuffy had ever known. His black hair was brushed straight back on his head, his brown eyes held a hidden hint of merriment, as though everything in the world was really amusing if you only saw it so.

He had slapped Snuffy's shoulder and said, "Go out and get me a bottle of coffee and have it sweet."

And from then on, everything had been all right.

For Snuffy had told Big Ed that he was sorry and he'd stayed, and Al had amazingly disappeared to study for the priesthood, and now Snuffy was head office boy himself.

Big Ed looked up at him now and said, "Fix the weather." He rose, yawned, stretched his arms upward, and went out toward the dark hall.

Snuffy liked writing the weather box for the first page. It was an important thing to do. It made him feel that he was getting on. He sat down in Big Ed's chair and reached for the telephone.

He looked down the long room and, as always, it didn't seem quite real. It didn't seem as if any of these lounging people could ever put out a newspaper; it didn't seem as if any stray current of the world's affairs could filter in through the quiet and set all the typewriters to clacking.

Even Jim, the assistant city editor,

sitting on the other side of the desk and languidly making out photographic assignments, only seemed to be playing some sort of childish game.

Snuffy picked up the phone and the buzzer purred and an orange light flamed up from the desk switchboard and the fire gong began to clang all at once. Imperatively. Importantly.

"Bong—bong—bong," went the gong very fast, and then struck thrice more.

Snuffy was still breathing into the phone and McAndrew had his hat jammed on his head.

"Third alarm," he called.

Jim wearily picked up his own telephone. "Photo Room," he said into it, and sang out to one of the office boys without looking at him, "Get Ed!"

A voice shouted through the phone into Snuffy's ear. "Johnny calling. Tell Ed the Argyle Club just caved in. I'm going over."

Big Ed came running into the room and asked, "What's up?" His eyes were bright with excitement.

Snuffy jumped and said so fast that all the words ran together, "It's the Argyle Club. Caved in. Johnny just called from headquarters. He's on his way over there now—"

A siren screamed through a far-off street, and Big Ed just stood there, tapping the hard surface of the desk with his bony knuckles.

The buzzer whined again and someone screamed into the phone that Snuffy still held, "Cheest! There's hundreds of people under those bricks.

There's hundreds—" The phone went dead.

Big Ed hadn't moved. But his eyes were going over the room so fast that they winked.

"Jerry," he said. "City Hospital. Names and injuries—phone 'em in as soon as you can. Sinbad, Relief Station. Dave, grab a cab to the General Hospital. Get on the phone as soon as you can make it and get the names, and get 'em right."

The fire gong was still tapping out the box number and a clanging bell chipped the dark silence to shreds outside.

Big Ed was still picking the staff over with his eyes. "Paul, Tom, Daisy," he said, "get over to the Argyle Club, Seventh and Main. It's caved in. Phone a flash story. Grab the survivors, Daisy, and see what they have to say. Get going."

THROUGH THE big end windows, Snuffy could see the red revolving target atop a ladder truck. He could only see it for a second and then the whole night broke into shrieking, screaming sound.

On the small desk switchboard every light blazed up, eagerly bright and insistent.

"Snuffy," said Big Ed, "run out to the Photo Room. Tell everybody there to come in, all packed up and ready to go. Everybody!"

The Top swung his feet off his desk. "Boy!" he shouted. "Tell the Composing Room to tear all that junk off the front page. Tell 'em I'm going to replate. Gimme a dummy!"

Snuffy was running down the dark hall, and he could hear Daisy's thin heels clicking a staccato path ahead of him. Paul was struggling into his coat and he said, "It's going to be big."

"Bigger than the time the trolley car went off the bridge," said Tom Creed.

Snuffy jerked at the Photo Room door, and Bruce, the darkest and most dapper photographer, was dancing a hornpipe in his shirt sleeves.

"Ed wants everybody out at the desk," Snuffy gasped. "The Argyle Club's caved in."

"Isn't that simply swell," said Bruce and languidly got into his coat.

Jim, the assistant city editor, bounced into the room like a rubber ball and his red hair was standing on end. "Hey there, you guys," he said, and excitement crackled in his voice. "Get going. The whole town's blown up."

"Let it blow," said Bruce and, in a leisurely way, began sorting flash bulbs into stacks.

Snuffy just stood there and watched. The rest of the camera crew came straggling out of dark rooms and weren't at all excited. They wouldn't have stirred with a single bit of excitement, Snuffy thought, if he'd flung open the door and shouted that the world was coming to an end.

"Keep your shirt on, Jim," said Bruce, and the camera crew were miraculously ready and going out the door. Yet they hadn't seemed to hurry at all. That was the way Bruce managed things.

Snuffy stepped out after them, wondering what they'd do without Duane tonight. Duane was the only one of all the rewrite men who could simply make a typewriter sing. He could sit with his ear to a telephone and take confused notes from some country correspondent and then set them down so sharply in a story that you could see it all just as it had happened. And that was because he saw it that way himself.

T HE DOOR to the feature department was swinging a little open and Snuffy stared in. Someone was stretched out there in the dark on a desk and it was Duane. He was asleep. Sirens screamed unceasingly through the street outside, but he slept on. Snuffy snapped on the light and shook Duane's shoulders and still he didn't stir.

Snuffy shook him again and he didn't move, and Snuffy wondered wearily why Duane did such things. There was no one so calm and cool and perfectly poised as Duane, and yet lately, without a moment's warning, he'd been going on bats.

There must be some reason for it, Snuffy thought, and he went out to the water cooler and clawed out a chunk of ice. He rubbed the ice over Duane's head, and the water went trickling down Duane's neck and over his collar. He slapped Duane's face and slapped it hard. Duane gurgled and sat up, rubbing his head with his hands.

Snuffy scowled at him. "Get up," he said. "Big Ed's goin' to fire you."

"What do I care?" said Duane thickly and slumped back again.

Snuffy put both hands on his shoulders and shook him. "Duane!" he said. "The Argyle Club's just fell in!"

Duane put both feet on the floor and listened to the noise that split the night asunder. Then he said, "Why didn't you say so?"

He knotted his tie and picked up his coat. He started to walk very slowly as if all his mind and all his muscles were concentrating on that. He leaned for a second against the door jamb, and then, as the thin tinkle of a gong came through the corridor, he went into the City Room, sat down at his desk and began fumbling for copy paper.

It was oddly quiet there now. No one seemed to be doing anything save the managing editor, who was standing by the Top and looking over his shoulder.

"Set it all full face, five-column measure," the Top was saying. He turned to Big Ed. "I want about eight paragraphs for this edition."

All the phones began to ring and the buzzer whirred and whirred. Big Ed walked slowly down the room and looked at Duane. He said, "How do you feel?" and Duane nodded.

He said, "Can you write?" and Duane leaned back and said, "Sure."

"Okay," said Big Ed. He sat on the edge of Duane's desk and said quite slowly so Duane would understand, "The Argyle Club, Seventh and Main, collapsed at seven-ten. The West End Improvement Association was having a party there—about two hundred people. They were all in there when the building buckled under them. No estimate on casualties yet. Rescue squad and all the ambulances called. That's all you've got to go on."

He jumped off the desk and though he was quite quiet, Snuffy could see the nerves winking under his eyes.

"Eight paragraphs for this time," he said. "One paragraph at a time and make it fast. Snuffy, rush his copy up!"

For a moment it didn't seem as if Duane could do it. His fingers lay nerveless on the typewriter keys. Then the typewriter stuttered briefly, and soon it began to sing.

Duane tore out the first take and Snuffy snatched it. He read the first sentence as he ran: "Scores of persons were believed trapped as the old Argyle Club collapsed like a house of cards—"

The Top clawed the first take away from Snuffy, ran his eyes over it and tossed it onto the copy desk. "Okay, Ed," he said. "Keep it coming."

He pitched his coat onto the desk and ran toward the Composing Room. Big Ed had a telephone to each ear now and he called out, "Dan! Take Sinbad on twenty-four. First list of injured. Joe! Daisy on twenty-six. Survivor's story."

The managing editor had a phone in his hand too. "Circulation?" he said crisply. "Jack? We'll hit the street in twenty minutes."

The whole room roared with noise: jangling bells, the buzzer, doors that slammed. Duane's typewriter was a low thunder through it all and his face was yellow and drawn.

Big Ed shouted down to him, "Fire Commissioner just got there."

"Got him in the story," Duane said and ripped out the last take.

He sat back, exhausted, and a thin ribbon of cigarette smoke spiraled from his mouth. His hands shook, and he was so limp that every bit of life seemed to have gone out of him.

Big Ed said, "Yes! Yes!" into the phone and then shouted down, "Duane! Take McAndrew on twenty-eight. New lead for the extra."

Snuffy saw Duane stumbling toward the telephone booth, and it hurt to see him so lifeless. They were working him to death and no one, not even Big Ed, cared a bit.

Through the end windows, the little light atop an ambulance shone down the street like a shooting star, and Snuffy knew why none of them, not even Duane, could stop. Trains and trucks and busses were waiting: they were all waiting for the words Duane would put on paper.

Dan came out of a booth and said over his shoulder, "Sixteen at the Relief Station so far."

Duane came back to his desk and his hands were shaking more than ever. He said, "Want to start now?"

"Yes," said Big Ed, and Snuffy hated him. He wouldn't let Duane rest for even a second. He couldn't see that Duane was going to collapse.

Big Ed came down the room and took Snuffy by the shoulder. He pulled a fire badge out of his pocket. "Take this," he said. "Go down to Seventh and Main and get through the lines. See Bruce. He's outside a drugstore. Take him down all this stuff and bring back his plates. Bring 'em back quick."

Someone had made up a big bundle of plates and bulbs and Snuffy stuffed it under his arm. It was an awkward thing to carry and it made him lean a little to one side as he went out into the square.

There were no cabs in sight and the sultry heat beat down on the sidewalk. He tried to run and couldn't, and it was so quiet on the dark street that it didn't seem possible anything could be happening six blocks away.

He moved in a swift shuffle and a round reddish moon had come over the housetops and it was hotter than ever and deathly still. All sense of excitement had left him and he was dog tired. He wished he were in the Peninsula, where a stray soft breeze might be blowing in from the bay, and he thought of Mom, sitting on a bench in Costigan Park, chatting with the neighbors and waiting for the wind to blow the heat away.

Mom would be proud if she could see him now: a person of importance. She had often said she was going to be proud of him yet—even if she had to wear out a strap on him first.

He sniffed and there was the strange smell of dust in the air. He turned a corner and it came drifting, gray and powdery, out of nowhere. For a second all he could see was the dust and all he could hear was a dim roar.

Then he saw it, so suddenly that it made him jump. There, in the sharp flare of floodlights, a gray wall of dust was wreathing over a great mass of crazily slanting bricks, timbers that stuck out at raw fantastic angles, a wall and jagged window-frame seemingly supported by nothing six stories up. A ladder swung up and up and men were like gray moles there in the dust.

Below, there was only a ragged black line where they were driving the crowd back, and the line gaped open and a taxicab came charging out with a policeman on the running board.

The dust settled down again and it gritted on his tongue. He stared as he ran, and it was all unreal, it was all impossible, it was like watching a gray news reel of some dim disaster unroll across a screen.

He looked up at all that was left of the big building and it still wasn't real. It looked like some house of cards that a careless child had kicked aside. Halfway up its sliding mass of ruin a sign still said, "ARGYLE CLUB. DINE AND—" The rest of the sign was gone.

The dust boiled so in the street that he couldn't see very well. He tripped over lines of limp hose and there was a great glare from all the shops on one side of the street. Two firemen went into one of the shops with a stretcher, and all he could see inside were stooped figures in white coats.

A state trooper caught at his shoulder and said, "Y'gotta get outa here, kid!" and he stared upward for a sign that would mean a drugstore.

Someone who must have been Bruce brushed the trooper aside. But Bruce had lost his hat and his face had gone gray with powdered dust.

"Give me those," he said and snatched the bundle from Snuffy. "You certainly took long enough."

He pushed a plate holder into Snuffy's hands. "Second edition stuff," he said. "Rush it back."

Snuffy choked and stumbled across the hose lines into the street again. He pushed through a gap in the ropes and through the crowd back of them. Ahead, the street was dark and empty and the darkness and emptiness were so somehow terrifying that he started to run.

He turned the corner and newsboys were small black dots running through the streets. Their shouts were a constant echo from the dark buildings: *"EXTRA! EXTRA! EXTRA!"*

He was so hot and limp and tired he thought he'd drop. His legs swayed under him as he trotted into the City Room.

Duane was drinking coffee out of a milk bottle and tapping away at the typewriter. The managing editor was shifting a limp cigar from one corner of his mouth to the other and the phones were still ringing.

Jim jumped up and grabbed the plates from him and shouted over his shoulder, "Okay on the second edition stuff." He ran toward the Photo Room and Paul came in the door.

Paul was small and pale and timid and he looked less than ever like a good reporter. He'd lost his hat, he held a package of plates in his shaking hands, and a criss-cross of plaster was on one of his cheeks.

He held out the plates to Big Ed and said, "Harvey's stuff." He sat down on the desk beside Duane and tried to light a cigarette and it fell away on the floor.

Big Ed shouted, "Boy!" and Duane looked up at Paul and said, "What the devil happened to you?"

A boy came running to take the plates and Snuffy hunched down on a desk and drew long breaths and Paul was saying, "Just a cut. I had to crawl in to help get a guy out."

Duane smiled and didn't look so drawn and he said, "Since when have you been a rescue squad?"

Paul tried to keep his hands from shaking. "It wasn't a very big hole to crawl into," he said. "Nobody else was small enough."

He drew his hands across his forehead and left a wet smear of dust and Big Ed said, "How's it feel to be a hero?"

He twisted a cigarette between Paul's lips and lit it and Paul said, "Thanks. Not very good. I'll have the shakes for weeks. That guy was screaming—"

Big Ed slapped him on the shoulder and said, "You'd better be getting back," and Paul said, "Oh, sure," and stumbled out again.

Jim shouted from the desk, "Johnny calling with some new stuff," and Big Ed told Duane, "Bulletin lead all for the second edition. Take it on booth two."

A RED-HEADED girl with her hair and dress all rumpled ran into the room and she was Winnie, the chief telephone operator. She said in one steady scream, "I won't be shouted at! I won't be shouted at if the whole town falls down. We can't handle all those calls. We can't do it." She looked accusingly at Big Ed and said, "Rita just fainted."

At the desk, the buzzer had begun to scream again and Jim tore all the telephone receivers off their hooks and cursed.

Big Ed ran toward the desk and said over his shoulder, "Get in two extra girls, Winnie. And pour some water over Rita."

Jim picked up one of the phones and said, "Hello!" He listened for a second and his back stiffened. He said, "What? You're sure?" He listened again and said, "Can you go over to her house and wait there and call us right away if she comes in?"

He leaned across the desk and said something to Big Ed, and then he turned and called, "Snuffy!"

"Shut up!" said Big Ed sharply.

He turned and waved Snuffy away and said to Jim very fast, "Call up all our staff at the hospitals and tell 'em to check. She may have come in as a casualty. Do it from a booth."

He got up and came down from the desk and told Snuffy, "Go out and wash some of that dust off your face. Take your time." He looked upset and as if he were sorry for something and Snuffy couldn't make out why that was.

He wandered into the wash room and out again and thought how tired he was, and was just turning into the hall when he heard the Top say, "Well, what's all the mystery about?"

The managing editor said, "It's one of the kids. His mother was in there. She went to that Improvement Society party. One of her friends just phoned about it."

Snuffy came slowly out into the hall, wondering which of the office boys it was, and the Top's face went red and he looked like a bantam rooster. He shouted at Snuffy, "Get some proofs! And hustle up!"

HEAT CAME from the Composing Room in sickly waves and the bright lights made it seem even better. Snuffy reached in and tore the proofs from the hook and his hands went wet and cold. He had to hold onto the rack where they stacked the new type and the room went 'round and 'round.

He dropped the proofs and had to stoop to pick them up. Then the hall was a great dark cavern and the stairs were enormous before him. All the old familiar landmarks had somehow changed. They seemed suddenly menacing and grim. Everything was swollen to twice its normal size and something terrible stirred in the back of his brain and wouldn't go away.

He came into the City Room and his feet dragged and were leaden. Big Ed glanced up and by the look on his face, he knew it was true.

He clung to the desk in the midst of a cold silence and said, "Ed, I gotta go home."

For a second, Big Ed didn't answer. Then he said slowly, "You stay right here. Mrs. Corrigan's gone over to your mother's house and she'll phone the minute your mother comes in. If she's hurt, or anything, we'll hear it quicker than anyone else." He said, "I'm sorry, Snuffy. Go and sit down."

Someone was sobbing and that seemed a strange sound to hear in the City Room. Snuffy put one hand to his face and his face was wet. He went blindly past Duane's desk and said, "I gotta go down there."

Duane caught at him so sharply that he ripped his shirt. Duane towered over him and said, "Don't you dare go near that place! D'you hear?"

Mom had always said, ever since he first went to work on the paper, "You do just what Mr. Duane tells you to," and he could see her saying it. He could see her, in her best dress, walking down the street to a dark door under a sign that said, "Argyle Club." And he simply couldn't see any more.

He put his head down on the desk and the bell on Duane's typewriter clinked a little as he finished a line and the second edition story was done.

"They had been dancing in the Argyle Club and the lights had gone out and the music had stopped—all in one split second."

Snuffy said to Duane, "She never had a good time."

That was the terrible thing. Mom had never had a good time. She'd always worked in the little store on the corner of B Street, she'd always been afraid for Snuffy, she'd been afraid he'd go with the gangs. And he nearly had only he couldn't stand the look in Mom's eyes. He couldn't stand thinking of her working all those years, working so he could go through school, sitting and sewing under the lamp through the evenings and smiling at him as he wrestled with his lessons. For she'd never have a good time now.

Duane said very softly, "There's nothing to do but wait. And that's hard. I waited for something once—" His voice trailed off.

Snuffy looked down the dim room and everything was going on just the same. It would go on just the same if he were dead and Duane were dead. It couldn't stop for anything and that was the way life was too. It hurt to think it could be so.

"Listen!" said Duane so sharply that he looked up.

He saw Big Ed lean half across the desk. He heard Big Ed shout into a telephone, "Okay, Dave. Mrs. Robert O'Brien. Check!"

Big Ed came down the room in a rush. He snatched out a dollar bill and said, "Grab a cab to the General Hospital. They've just brought your mother in."

Snuffy's head was spinning. "She isn't—she isn't—"

Big Ed stuffed the dollar into Snuffy's pocket. "Dave couldn't find out how much she was hurt," he said. "Hurry up!"

Duane looked up at Snuffy. "Here's another dollar," he said. "You'll want to take her home in a cab."

Duane smiled and Snuffy suddenly knew that everything would really be all right, because Duane was telling him so. He started for the door and tears were a stinging torment in his eyes.

Some woman was standing by the gate and Snuffy ought to ask her what she wanted, but he couldn't stop to now. She was a big woman, a woman who still had reddish streaks in her gray hair, a woman whose dress was torn and tattered and covered with dust, a woman who had a bandage around one wrist.

"Mom!" said Snuffy.

He felt his legs begin to go under him and suddenly he was in a chair and Mom was sitting beside him and there was a ring of faces all around them.

"Takes after his father," Mom was

saying. "He always got upset easy." She patted Snuffy's head and nobody seemed to think there was anything strange about that.

"He's had a hard night, Mrs. O'Brien," Duane said. "He's a good kid. How'd you hurt your wrist?"

Mom looked up and she was calmer than any of them. "I was right by a window when the lights went out and everything began falling down," she said. "I just stuck my fist through the window and crawled out on a fire escape. I dunno just how long I was there, but all of a sudden I saw old Ladder Seven from D Street comin' round the corner. So I yelled down, 'Here I am!' and they swung up the big stick and Clem McCafferty come up for me."

She smoothed down the rags of her dress and said, "I only cut my wrist a little, but the boys shoved me into an ambulance before I could say anything."

SHE SAT there quite calmly, and though her dress was torn and her face was streaked with dust, she was somehow more important than anyone in the room.

She got up and said, "Well, I guess you've all got some work to do. I'd better be going home."

Duane rose and bowed just as if she'd been a great lady and she told Snuffy, "You stop getting excited over nothing and do what Mr. Duane tells you to."

She went out as unconcerned as if she'd been sitting on a bench in Costigan Park all evening, and Duane grinned at Snuffy and said, "Isn't she swell!"

Just the way he said it made Snuffy feel all right again and he listened to Jim, shouting over the phone to a country correspondent. "So you thought we'd like a story about the chief of police's dog being run over," he said. "Well, let me tell you—"

Big Ed said, "Keep your hair on. The Top wants a freak for page six and the dog'll do."

He grinned and called down the room, "Duane, take a good big story for a change. All about a policeman's dog in Pembroke."

It was some time later when Snuffy sat with Duane in a little restaurant where white tables glared. The five star edition had gone in and Snuffy was so sleepy he couldn't keep his eyes open.

Duane looked down at him and grinned and said, "Take your spoon out of your coffee cup and maybe we'll make you into a gentleman yet."

6. HOLLYWOOD

In 1938, RKO Pictures purchased the rights to Hillman's story "The Great Man Votes." It was a minor coup for Hillman, whose profile only benefited from the exposure that came from Hollywood. The studio's original plan was to use the story as a vehicle for character actor Victor Moore, but instead it gave the lead role to John Barrymore. Bob Sisk produced the film, and John Twist wrote the screenplay. Shooting began on October 10, and the movie appeared in January 1939.

The movie, like Hillman's story, followed the life of Gregory Vance, a "shiftless, drink-loving, Harvard graduate, night watchman," according to the Production Code's analysis, played by Barrymore. The story takes place during the Coolidge administration in 1923 and serves as a takedown of city machine politics. Vance's alcoholism leads his two children, whose mother had died years prior, to take care of themselves to a large degree, but when they get into a fight with the son of the local political boss, "Iron Hat" McCarty, played by Donald MacBride, attempting to defend their father against schoolyard taunts, McCarty responds by having Vance fired from his job as a night watchman. Vance's children, however, stay involved, and when McCarty discovers that he needs Vance's vote to maintain his hold on ward supremacy, they convince him to appoint their father commissioner of education in return for his vote. Meanwhile, the uppity parents of Vance's deceased wife are scheming to have the children taken from him but are thwarted when he takes the commisionership. The story's ultimate denouement is that Vance does not vote for the ward boss, despite the quid pro quo. It was a story that typified Hillman's work, combining an aspirational narrative with a depiction of the liminal space between failure and legitimacy.[1]

"Though it has little social significance and less than no grasp on reality," began the *New York Times*' review, *The Great Man Votes* was "a picture with its heart in the right place." The reviewer applauded Barrymore, and fellow stars Peter Holden and Virginia Weidler, but they were working on a film with "a certain unevenness of structure." And that unevenness ultimately made for a disappointing picture. "Its amateurish approach and the fact that its secondary characters exist merely as comical, priggish, or sentimental set-ups to be bowled over by the protagonistic Vance family do not impair the story's freshness," the reviewer complained, "yet the story itself would have been more amusing for sounder characterizations and a few facts of life to base them upon."[2]

The creation of pre–World War II films moved with relative alacrity. Hillman's original story was published in *American Magazine* in 1931. After RKO purchased the rights and produced a screenplay in 1938, the studio submitted its script for *The Great Man Votes* based on Hillman's story to the Production Code Administration in September 1938, almost seven years after its original publication late in 1931. After three rounds of minor script changes to meet the Code's draconian standards, the production was given the go-ahead to film in October, it did so in November, and got the Production Code Administration's final approval in December, releasing the film in early January 1939.[3]

It was a movie, despite the negativity of the *New York Times*, almost universally loved, as much as any movie can be. Outlets as disparate as the *New Yorker* and the Daughters of the American Revolution both approved. For the former, *The Great Man Votes* was a comedy "to tide you over a bad afternoon hour." For the latter, it was the "unusually interesting story of how the love and admiration of children" can rehabilitate a wayward parent. Even *Time* found value in the picture, despite its claim that director Garson Kanin's "specialty is making silk purses out of sows' ears."[4]

The trade papers were more effusive. The *Hollywood Reporter* saw the film's screenplay based on Hillman's story as "one of the best screen documents that has been turned out in a long time. Granted it was an excellent premise to begin with, Twist has transferred it into a picture the screen can be proud of because of its finesse and the meatiness of its lines and characterizations." *Film Daily* and *Motion Picture Daily* showed a similar enthusiasm. Meanwhile, *Motion Picture Herald* and *Variety* both saw the class aspects of the film. It was "as suitable for the greatest city as the smallest town, and its natural audience is composed of all those Americans who vote or ever intend to," according to the *Herald*, while *Variety* assumed that it would "be hailed by class audiences as a fine example of the film art, yet carrying sock appeal for mass patronage." Its warm reception even led RKO to discuss a sequel to the film titled "The Great Man in Politics," though the project never came to fruition.[5]

It was the kind of praise that Hillman's fiction had never really produced, a distillation not only of his own literary aspirations but of the embellished legacy of his mother's acting career. A Hillman, or at least a film derived from the work of a Hillman, was, however briefly, the talk of the Hollywood trade papers. Darryl Zanuck of Twentieth Century-Fox wanted to take advantage of the seeming success of RKO and in September 1938 bought the rights to Hillman's story "Here I Am a Stranger," originally published in *McCall's*. Or, soon to be published. It was a mark of Hillman's newfound success that Zanuck bought a story in September that wouldn't actually appear until the October issue of *McCall's*. "The Great Man Votes" had originally appeared seven years prior to its big-screen debut. Its success, however, meant that Hillman's next story would be purchased even prior to publication. Hillman was using agent Gerald Drayson Adams, who would go on to become a screenwriter in his own right in the next decade. According to the *Hollywood Reporter*, Zanuck and Adams worked a deal to put Hillman under a term contract with Fox, with his first assignment adapting the story into a screenplay. There is not, however, any corroboration of that report, and whatever deal the two made may have fallen through. Though Hillman loved to claim in autobiographical statements that he spent time working in Hollywood, veteran Fox screenwriters Milton Sperling and Sam Hellman adapted his story into a screenplay.[6]

It was a common event. The popularity of middlebrow fiction magazines provided ripe fodder for filmed content. The stories in magazines like *McCall's*, the *Saturday Evening Post, American Magazine*, or *Liberty* told concise stories with quickly resolved character arcs that had already proven successful enough to keep such magazines popular in the "golden age of American reading." Unlike novels, which were also often adapted, there was little content to cut for length. The stories were readymade screen treatments, and many short story writers, like Hillman, found occasional income from adaptations of their work. Some, unlike Hillman, were able to parlay such adaptations into studio work as writers for the movies, which provided a more consistent paycheck than submitting stories to magazines and hoping they would sell in time and volume to make ends meet. Hillman's was, again, a common case.[7]

In February 1939, Zanuck began choosing personnel for the film, pegging Gregory Ratoff to direct, and Warner Baxter, Richard Greene, and Nancy Kelly to star, though only some of that personnel would make the final cut. In April, Twentieth Century-Fox announced its program schedule of fifty-two films for the 1939–40 season. Zanuck planned to personally supervise the production of twenty-four of the films, five of which would have two-million-dollar budgets. *The Rains Came, Stanley and Livingston,* and *Drums along the Mohawk* headed the list, along with an adaptation of a Rida Johnson Young play and a biographical drama about Brigham Young. Somewhere further down the list, however, was *Here I Am a Stranger*, the second film to be made based on a Gordon Malherbe Hillman story. Sperling and Hellman adapted the story and, despite early reports, Roy Del Ruth directed it.[8]

Here I Am a Stranger, which appeared later in 1939, was more complex and less funny than *The Great Man Votes*, combining the three core stories that dominated HIllman's writing: that of the newspaperman, the boarding school, and the challenges of family. When his wife leaves newspaper writer and chronic drunk Robert "Duke" Allen, she takes their young child, marries into money, and raises him in a life of privilege while Duke suffers through alcoholism and failure. When that child, David, enters college, his experiences lead him to reconnect with his father, which helps Duke return to his career. When one of David's college acquaintances—the brother of his girlfriend, the son of his adopted father's boss—kills a woman in a drunk driving accident and one of David's friends is arrested for the crime, David first promises to protect his acquaintance, pressured by his family to maintain the esteemed reputation of the upper class. David's conscience, however, will not allow him to let his innocent friend sit in jail for a crime he did not commit, and he tells his reporter father the story, forcing a confession from the killer. It was a screed against the caprice of the rich and another in a long line of Hillman's celebrations of newspaper journalism as a stabilizing force and vessel of salvation.[9]

While the Production Code Administration had fewer problems with *Here I Am a Stranger*'s script, the production was not without its problems. The film's star, Richard Greene, who played David, shattered his leg in a freak accident only six days after production began. He was fixing the bumper of his car on a neighborhood street on an incline. Another motorist had parked on the street but had failed to use his parking brake. The unmanned car rolled down the hill and crushed Greene's leg, leaving him unable to perform for eight weeks (and briefly worried doctors that they would have to amputate). Twentieth Century-Fox's Zanuck had hired several freelance actors for the movie and did not want to lose them because of the accident. So actors like Richard Dix, Roland Young, Gladys George, and Russell Gleason received a long-term paid vacation, as Zanuck felt the broader expense was worth keeping the actors in the movie and away from rival studios.[10]

Frank S. Nugent, writing for the *New York Times*, bemoaned this second attempt, as well. "Its performances are generally sound," he noted, referencing star Richard Greene and costars Gladys George, Richard Dix, and Roland Young. "There are a few sequences that couldn't be bettered." But that only made the confusing plot and disappointing ending all the more frustrating: "With it all, we still haven't the faintest notion of the author's intent, unless it be to demonstrate that a boy's best friend is his mother—or sometimes his father—or maybe neither." It was a telling quote, cutting at the heart of the film, the story, and its original author. The Boston press, however, was far more pleased, reveling that a movie "written by a Boston man, Gordon Malherbe Hillman, is the leading attraction at the Paramount and Fenway Theatres."[11]

The trade sheets were complimentary if less enthusiastic about the second Hillman film adaption, describing the movie as a father-son genre picture with just the right dose of moralism. "Thus, while it scarcely assumes impressive importance," described the *Hollywood Reporter* in a representative analysis, "it will prove a gratifying top-of-the-bill fixture and can be counted on to bring in satisfying grosses." The *Reporter* liked the cast and several of its poignant episodes, but the screenplay sought to do too much, attempting "to elaborate a simple story with too many characters, purposes and cross-purposes. Likewise, it is overcrowded with noble purpose and deeds, which result in some confusion as to who actually is the hero of the piece, and give it a pretty thickly applied saccharine over-toning." Such was the tenor of much of the film media's response.[12] *Here I Am a Stranger* was good. It was not great. It would be the last full-length Hollywood feature based on a Hillman story.

It was a demonstration of how fleeting relationships with the film industry could be. When the second adaptation wasn't as well received as the first, Hillman's relationship with Hollywood abruptly ended. Still, the fulfilment of aspiration was not solely measured by movies. Gordon's success of the late 1930s continued into the next decade. The year after Hillman's *Here I Am a Stranger* premiered, in April 1940, he published his only novel, *Fortune's Cup*, with Thomas Y. Crowell Company. Crowell wasn't the largest publisher in the country, but it was a good one. Founded in the 1830s, Crowell had produced popular reprints of Milton, Tennyson, and Longfellow. Its most popular original work was the mystery writing of Frank Heller, whose Philip Collin novels became a minor sensation in the 1920s. And Hillman's novel, to a much lesser degree, was a minor sensation in 1941. First, Crowell wasn't a vanity press. Second, the *New York Times* was far kinder to Gordon's novel than they were to the film adaptations of his stories. "There is a credible maxim to the effect that hard writing makes easy reading," wrote Margaret Wallace. "If so, an extraordinary amount of application and self-discipline must have gone into the construction of 'Fortune's Cup.' It can be absorbed by a process more like breathing than reading." Wallace praised the story of the hardworking, overqualified newspaper critic and his manic, underqualified son. It was "an understanding study of the barriers which separate, always and stubbornly, one generation from the next." Even those less awed by the debut still seemed satisfied. The *New Orleans Times-Picayune* described *Fortune's Cup* as a "fast-moving" book, "a readable, workmanlike novel."¹³

It told the story of Larry and Stan Evans. Larry was dramatic editor for Hillman's fictional *Courier*, who toiled at the job for years against his better judgement in order to fund his son Stan's education, only to find that Stan had been expelled from college. Stan's college experience was spent making friends, falling in love, and socializing. Thus a dejected and floundering Larry brings dejected and floundering Stan home and gets him a job at the *Courier*. Stan finds his new job tedious in the extreme and waits daily to light off to the Green Dragon cafe to be with his friends. His newfound hard-drinking lifestyle only exacerbates the burden on his father, who had already been beset by so many burdens, but eventually his father, his friends, and, ultimately, the *Courier* teach him the value and dignity of hard work and give him over to the effort of a legitimate newspaperman. It is the story of a kid who thinks he is extraordinary only to discover that he is not, and the story of a father who thinks he is ordinary only to discover that he is much more to so many. Like so many of Hillman's newspaper stories, it revolves around the inherent virtues of the newspaper business and its ability to provide an education that formal training never could. That Larry is a dramatic editor, like the book's author, only adds to the broader self-justifying autobiographical nature of the plot.¹⁴

Not only was *Fortune's Cup* a chance for Hillman to continue his newspaper stories in longform, but it was his chance to join the likes of Streeter, Poole, and MacGrath by becoming a novelist. It was his chance to write the great newspaper novel in the tradition of Evelyn Waugh's *Scoop*. While the paper, as in Hillman's stories, is both a setting and a character in *Fortune's Cup*, the story more broadly is concerned with Sam's coming-of-age. In that sense, it also incorporates the elements of his boarding school stories, wherein young men seek to find themselves as they experience a world larger than they knew before. As such it also follows the tradition of Alec Waugh's *The Loom of Youth*.

Along with the Waugh nexus in which the novel falls, the book also does for Sam what Ernest Poole's *His Family* does for the three daughters of Roger Gale, finding themselves in a larger world in relation to their concerned father. That novel, written by one of the authors who served as an early example of Hillman's career, would be the first to win the Pulitzer Prize for Fiction. Those same dynamics are also present in Edward Streeter's *Father of the Bride*, which plays for laughs the fraught relationship between parent and newly adult child navigating the larger world, as Stanley Banks attempts to organize a wedding for his daughter. Hillman, then, is playing on both his two most common writing tropes, the newspaper story and the coming-of-age story, and modeling the work of two of his most public predecessors.[15]

The success of the book was reassuring for Hillman, but it would not pay the bills. Whether Hillman actually moved to Southern California and returned to Boston, as he sometimes claimed, or whether he never actually left, which seems far more likely, by the end of the 1930s, he began working for the *Boston Record* and would stay with the publication until his death. The *Record* was as central to Hillman's late biography as the *Transcript* was to his early work. The *Record* was originally founded in 1884 as a supplemental paper to the *Boston Daily Advertiser*. When William Randolph Hearst bought the *Advertiser* in 1914, the *Record*, too, became a Hearst publication. It would remain as such until it merged with another Hearst paper, the *Boston American*, in 1961.[16]

By the late 1940s, however, Hillman's success outside of his newspaper reporting had slowed. His paper, the *Record*, reported that at the end of the decade, the author had "been in ill health" and "has done little writing."[17] Less writing, of course, meant less money coming into the family coffers, meager as they might have been. For the bulk of that decade, for example, Gordon and Carolyn lived at the Hotel Vendome but had been forced to leave because of financial difficulties. The Vendome was built in 1871 and expanded a decade later, a massive, luxurious edifice in Boston's Back Bay. The hotel was just north of Copley Square, where the pair would move after their eviction. The Vendome would later earn infamy for a 1972 fire that destroyed the building, killed nine firefighters, and wounded eight others. It was the worst firefighting disaster in Boston's history, destroying what had become, by the late 1940s, a living space that was well beyond the Hillman family's means.[18] The disaster for Hillman a quarter century before 1972 was far less dire, as the struggling author and his mother were forced to leave the Vendome, but that act, too, would ultimately produce a casualty.

THE TROUBLE IN ROOM 519

By that time, memories of Hillman's successful film debut seemed a million miles away. The story that follows is the one upon which that film was based, "The Great Man Votes," from 1931.

THE GREAT MAN VOTES

Published in *American Magazine*, November 1931

It was seven o'clock on a gray New York November morning, and steamer whistles wailed dismally from the water front.

Mr. Gregory Vance sat gingerly upon a broken-down red sofa. A slate-covered Latin book was in his hand.

"Sheer stupidity!" Mr. Vance was saying. "Won't you ever get it into your heads that Julius Caesar was the first war correspondent in history? Just imagine the bald-headed old bird sitting down in a damp tent with six secretaries and dictating the details of a battle he'd been in!"

Donald in the big, rickety chair, with Joan perched on one of its arms, attempted to visualize that dull fellow, Gaius Julius Caesar, dictating to six irritable centurions that mass of material about battles and bridges which was destined to harass the schoolboys of several centuries.

In the cold, gray light of early morning, and with no breakfast inside him, Donald found this very hard to do. They could not be blamed if they saw Gaius Julius in terms of their father, nor if the impression persisted that about the noble Roman lurked a faint aroma slightly suggestive of stale whisky, that his hair was always uncombed, and that he lolled on crimson sofas after a bout of night-watching a hole in the ground that would shortly be a skyscraper.

"Damp!" sighed Mr. Vance. "It's damp as the devil through all France and Belgium. Caesar probably had the rheumatism. If he didn't, I have. Ugh!"

He looked longingly at the dingy brown cupboard in the corner.

But Mr. Vance was a man of honor. He did no more than look. He did not even move toward the cupboard. He did not even consider opening it. He did not want his children to see the tall bottle that it contained; he did not want them to suspect that he had the lamentable habit of drinking rather more than was good for him.

And not for worlds would they have admitted that they did know. The cupboard and its contents had been there ever since they could remember, but it was a polite fiction to ignore both.

Mr. Vance ceased looking at the cupboard and ruffled the leaves of the Latin book again.

"I guess that's a long enough lesson for today," Joan said severely. "You look tired. You'd better be going to bed."

"Tyrant!" said Mr. Vance, but he stumbled heavily into the bedroom, all the same.

A few seconds later, a heavy creaking of springs testified to the fact that Mr. Vance had retired for the day.

His son and daughter found him asleep when they tiptoed into the room. As Mr. Vance had thrown his bedclothes into utter disarray, they straightened them without waking him and then set about getting their breakfast on the gas stove.

"It's too bad," mused Donald, "that Pop has to get so tired."

"Eat your cereal," his sister advised him, and then said suddenly, "You know, if Pop put his mind to it, he could be a great man!"

Donald considered this as they gathered their books and made ready to set out for school.

"How could Pop be a great man?" he asked.

"I don't know," his sister told him loyally, "but I sort of guess he could."

She continued to consider this question as they went down their ramshackle front steps into the very center of New York.

Ever since they could remember, they had lived there, while Mr. Vance lost one job after another, and now it was the only dwelling house in the district.

That Gargantuan giant, New York, had swallowed up all the other houses, and where they had stood, huge buildings were now mountainous against the sky. Only the Vances' house was left, and that was long, low, rickety, and wooden. It looked like a house in a sleepy Southern town, and its next-door neighbor was thirty-six stories high.

"I wisht we lived in the country!" said Joan, as Broadway traffic blared and jangled before them.

Police whistles shrilled, trolley bells rang, and the elevated roared, as Donald asked, "What's the country like, Jo?"

"I dunno 'cept from pictures," his sister told him. "It's all green trees and grass, I guess, an' horses an' cows." A motorcar bumped another in the middle of the street, and Donald said longingly, "If we lived in the country, then I could have me a black-and-white rabbit."

IT WAS a long way to their public school, past ill-smelling fur stores and warehouses. Traffic-heavy streets slowed their progress, and, even though it was November, heat had begun to beat up from the pavements.

They always approached the school warily, for they were used to taunts and even physical onslaught from their fellows, but now all the children were

THE TROUBLE IN ROOM 519

grouped about Master Egbert Holtzenhoffer, who was dancing up and down with excitement.

"His poppa fell off'n a ferryboat! His poppa fell off'n a ferryboat!" proclaimed Margie Gillings in rapt awe. "Egg's poppa fell into the drink, he did!"

"An' his pitcher's printed in all the papers!" seconded Davy Linehan, a large, lumpy boy whose father was the most important man in the ward. "My old man'll make a kick about them ferryboats, I guess."

The young and pale Master Holtzenhoffer was in the seventh heaven of joy. Heretofore he had been more or less of a football for kicking purposes, but now, in the twinkling of an eye, he had become a second assistant hero at least, and was making the most of it.

"They brought Pop home in an amb'lance," he was shouting, "an' Dugan, the cop, comes upstairs first. An' then comes the stretcher with Pop layin' back an' takin' it easy an'—"

"You needn't," said Joan disgustedly, "be so stuck up about it. After all, you didn't fall off'n a ferryboat your own self!"

Margie Gillings glared at her. "His pop's pitcher's in the papers!" she declared. "On the front page. Your pop's pitcher ain't never been in the papers."

It was quite true. Mr. Vance's countenance had never adorned the public press, and even at school his progeny were regarded as pariahs. The student body demanded one exacting form of social status, and that was distinction in the conduct of the male parent. Not the iron-bound distinction of Park Avenue, but the loose and lively standards of the West Side.

True, the father of the freckled Rafferty twins was only a longshoreman, which was not remarkable, but he beat up his boss and lost his job on Saturday nights, and that was admirable. Mike Massucio's fond parent was connected with the bottling trade and reputed, in his son's proud words, to be able "to put a fella on the spot, and then the fella gets rubbed out; see?"

Of course, there was Davy Linehan, uncrowned king of the school because Peter Aloysius Linehan, his father, was the district leader; and Margie Gillings' parent was hailed as "Hot Shot," wore violent plaid suits, and had originally come from Chicago. Not to speak of Mr. McGann, Senior, who had driven the topmost silver rivet into the tallest building in New York, nor Mr. Sapirowitz, who was a sand hog and built tunnels under the river.

"Wot's your pop do?" was the stock question addressed to new scholars, and woe betide those pupils whose parents did not measure up to the standard. That was where Joan and Donald were unfortunate. Everyone knew that Mr. Vance was merely a night watchman for a big building that was at present only a hole in the ground.

Both Joan and Donald adored their parent; they admired his manners and his conversation and could see few flaws in his conduct. But they had to admit that he was a parent of whom they could not be publicly proud, and they understood the fine distinction between Mr. Massucio, who dispensed bottled goods and was famous, and Mr. Vance, who drank them and was not.

THE SCHOOL gong rang with a brazen roar, and Master Holtzenhoffer stopped midway in the recital of his parent's saga. It was too bad, he thought, that school bells had to ring, for, in all probability, his father would not fall off any more ferryboats and his span of fame in school would not last until the next sensation came along.

The class straggled reluctantly into Latin recitation. Miss Maxfield was waiting for them. Miss Maxfield was always cool and calm, and since she was still young and pretty, little humorous quirks came and went at the corners of her eyes. She was amused at the idea of Mr. Holtzenhoffer's being the current hero, for she knew that he very unsuccessfully ran a small grocery shop and that his wife henpecked him.

"Teacher! Teacher!" piped Margie Gillings. "Egg's pop fell off'n a ferry boat, he did, an'—"

"And the police fished him out and his picture is in all the papers," said Miss Maxfield calmly. "Isn't that perfectly splendid! I suppose, Davy Linehan, that ferryboats wouldn't suggest to you what Caesar did when he went to Britain?"

Davy got himself to his feet slowly, for he had been playing handball against the front wall of his house when he should have been studying and he suspected Miss Maxfield was aware of that fact.

"He went to Englum for tin," he muttered. "He went for tin—tin—tin—"

"Yes, tin," said Miss Maxfield. "One of the baser metals, I believe. Does anyone else in the class know what Caesar did when he crossed the Channel?"

Donald's hand went up. "Please, teacher," he said, "he built himself a big wall all over Britain to keep out the Picts and the Scots, and there was a big town all back of the wall with hoss racing and cock fights goin' on all the time. It was open all night like Broadway, an'—"

Miss Maxfield sat up in surprise. "That's perfectly true," she said, "though it's not in the book. Where did you learn all that?"

"My father told me," murmured Donald with an apprehensive glance about the classroom.

Miss Maxfield sat and wondered about Mr. Vance. She had heard that he was a lamentable outcast, and she knew that he sat outside a shanty in most deplorable clothing and smoked an equally deplorable pipe. On the other hand, he seemed to have all the knowledge that properly belonged to a public-school teacher, and his children would certainly head the class that year.

"Very good, Donald," she said. "Go on and translate!"

Donald translated the remarks of that bald-headed old war correspondent, Gaius Julius Caesar, very well indeed, despite the fact that he could quite clearly see Davy Linehan shaking a doubled fist at him, and he knew that there would be retribution later on.

T**HERE WAS.** He and his sister were slipping inconspicuously down the street after school when Davy caught up with them, his lumpy face lumpier than ever and his red hair standing on end.

"Your pop thinks he's smart, don't he?" he began.

"Is smart!" retorted Joan, who was the bolder of the two.

"Yeah?" remarked Davy, shifting his schoolbooks in preparation for seizing Joan's dark froth of bobbed hair. "He'd better keep his fingers outa this school, he had. An' you better quit makin' a fool outa me in Latin, d'you hear, young kid?"

Donald's lazy drawl was precisely that of the elder Mr. Vance as he said, almost in an undertone, "Who could?"

Master Linehan's blue eyes blazed with outrage. "Look here, Pretty Face," he growled, "you think you're pretty smart, don't you? An' your pop thinks he's pretty smart. Well, he ain't!" He pushed his face forward with the jaw outstretched in an attitude reminiscent of the finer days of Mr. Jack Dempsey. "Your pop," he shouted, " is just a bum! An ol' bum!"

Joan's books went flying across the street as she threw back her head to shout, "*R-rinehart!*"

"*Rine-har-rt!*" roared Donald, and his fist smote Master Linehan amidships.

Master Linehan did not know that the shout was the traditional rallying cry of Harvard Yard; he did not know much of anything save that he was enwrapt in what seemed to be a double-barreled tornado. Someone seemed to be biting one of his wrists, so he flung out the other fist and also kicked. This was regrettable, for his leg was jerked out from under him and he hit the pavement with a thud. It was the more of a thud since two small demons had fallen on top of him.

A block away, Miss Maxfield, who came from Cambridge, jumped as she heard the rallying cry of the battles of Harvard Square: "*Rinehart! Rinehart!*" She turned the corner swiftly, half expecting to see the Harvard Club in the midst of a riot.

Instead, she saw an inverted pyramid, the base of which was the fast-weakening Master Linehan, and the apex, polite and ladylike Joan Vance, who was hammering away like a heavyweight champion in the last round.

"Children!" she cried. "Children!"

Two-thirds of the pyramid's most acute angle arose and ran. Its base, which had once been Master Linehan, staggered weakly upright and sobbed, "Wait till my pop gets yuh! Wait till my pop gets yuh!"

"Children!" shouted Miss Maxfield again. "Children!"

But all she saw was the battered blond head and the equally battered dark one as they turned the corner of Broadway.

Not till they had covered two blocks did the junior Vances stop to take account of damage. Donald's nose was swollen and his stockings were torn. Joan's skirts were in a like condition and a black ring was widening about one eye.

"S-say," panted Donald, "you g-got a s-swell shanty, sister!"

Joan stopped and looked in a plate-glass window. As she looked, she considered the situation.

"Donny," she said, "we c-can't go back home. We've lost all our books and Old Man Linehan will be over to tell Pop about us, and what'll Pop do then?"

"Spank us," said Donald suddenly, "and then he'll get terrible upset about spankin' us an' wish he hadn't."

"We're too old to be spanked," sniffed Joan.

They both gazed about in apprehension. It was likely that Master Linehan would rally his gang and pursue them. They trembled. One trembles easily before the terrors of the world at the age of twelve.

"Oh, gee!" sighed Donald brokenly. "Ol' Man Linehan's just mean enough to get Pop's job taken away from him, he is."

Joan came to the great decision first. "Donny," she proclaimed, as Broadway crowds drifted by them in a humid tide, "we've gotta run away! We've gotta!"

"Run where?" asked Donald cautiously.

"To the country," called his sister, who had already started up Broadway.

Now, Donald did not know that "the country" lies far beyond Yonkers and Hastings and Scarsdale and Tuckahoe, but he did have his doubts.

A sudden, shrieking roar split asunder all the other noises like a scarlet arrow of sound, and his nose elevated itself in the air.

"Fire emjims!" he howled. "Fire emjims!"

A policeman leaped into the street, his whistle shrilling. The tide of traffic split with a wide river of warm asphalt between. A crimson car went by like a streak, its driver shirt-sleeved and helmeted, the big bell banging.

"Deppity chief!" howled Donald. "Two bagger! Two bagger! Lookit 'em come!"

Traffic lights began to blink red as if they had gone mad, the big scarlet rescue truck went by with a roar. Behind it, as far as the eye could see, all was scarlet and gold and brass, shrieking sirens and pounding bells.

They had been running for blocks now and it was rather unfortunate for their ambition to see the fire that at that moment Joan spotted a green delivery truck shouldering its way into the Broadway traffic.

With a single whirl she deposited herself in the rear of this vehicle among bottles and milk cans, while the unfortunate Donald, being of a slower mold of mind, had to run after the truck till his legs threatened to collapse. Finally his sister hauled him aboard, and they both settled back to observe the scenery.

It was a warm day and the Broadwayites were mopping their brows and buying orange drinks. The roar of the fire engines had died away to a dull drone in the distance, and there was no smoke to be seen.

Columbus Circle flashed past them, and they united in making faces at the discoverer of America, who had caused them so much trouble in school. At Seventy-seventh Street, they sat up and took notice, for this was the end of the civilized world. They had penetrated this far on a school pilgrimage to the Museum of Natural History. Beyond, as far as they knew, lay utter darkness.

"We ought," said Donald," to be comin' to the country pretty soon!"

"It doesn't look like it," his sister told him.

It did not. The red street cars still jangled beside them, the Broadwayites still mopped their brows, slate-colored apartment houses stood up like cliffs.

"I guess there ain't no country left," Donald sighed. "We must be most in Connecticut now."

"You can't," his sister told him, "believe the maps you see in school. They don't mean anythin'."

"We come miles an' miles an' it's still New York!" Donald complained as ranks of apartment houses still rose before them.

"It's probably all New York till you get to Nevada or some such place," his sister said, "an' then it's desert without camuels."

"Nor fire emjims!" Donald suddenly remembered. "We've lost the fire emjims. They'd never come this far."

THE TRUCK suddenly stopped before a drug store, and the driver let out a hot howl as he saw his two passengers among the milk cans. He had no chance to do more, for they passed rapidly across Broadway, making faces at him.

They were already nearly at the river when Donald clutched his sister's arm. "Golly!" he cried. "Trees!"

There were several tired-looking dust-covered trees ahead, and, beyond, it seemed that a sea of yellowish green leaped at them. There were no "Keep off the Grass" signs; there were no prowling policemen. Beneath them a cliff dropped sheer away to the broiling blue of the river; still farther away, Jersey rose green and fair from the purpling cliffs of the Palisades.

"Gee," Donald gasped, "I guess it's real country over there!"

His sister shook her head. "We haven't got a dime for the ferry fare," she said. "Come on up here!"

There was no traffic on the street, there were no blinking red and green lights nor orange drink stands nor fire escapes loaded with mattresses. There were only a few houses, and these were set sparsely, with houses at all, save one immense mansion that sat on its terraces behind huge iron gates and sleepily surveyed a string of barges going up the river.

"The guy that lives there," said Donald learnedly, "must be the ward boss."

But the spirit of adventure spurred them on even past this inviting and enchanted land. It was so quiet now that they were almost afraid to talk, and the roar of the city was only a dull monotone in the distance.

There was another vacant lot before them, a clump of trees, a scraggly hedge, and then, rising out of a yard rank with tall, yellowish grass, a real round-towered castle such as may be seen in storybooks. It was not a castle in good repair—its windows glowered glasslessly—but there were some late apples left hanging on a tree by its side.

Swinging half open between the hedges was a wooden gate. Joan's feet hurt her and she wanted to sit down. She also wanted an apple. She went in the gate.

"You'll get arrested for trespassin'!" warned Donald.

"Scared cat!" said his sister.

On the whole, Donald was more afraid of his sister's wrath than of policemen. He followed her.

Half an hour later, they were sitting on the castle steps when a dark shadow fell upon them. Strangely, Joan was not at all surprised. It had been such a magical day that whatever happened next would mean still more magic. She was sure of it. Donald was merely frightened, and he trembled.

"What on earth are you doing here?" asked the stern-faced man with the neat little gray mustache that merrily belied all the sternness.

"Eatin' appuls!" said Joan easily. She knew, though she could not have told how she knew it, that the stern man with the gray eyes was going to play some tremendous part in their lives. So she smiled.

"So that's what you're doing!" said the stern-faced man, and his mustache twitched as if he were smiling, too. "And how on earth did you get that black eye?"

"It's a peach, isn't it?" said the placid Joan. "Davy Linehan did it. We beat him up."

"You mean to say that a boy hit you?" asked the stern-faced man, and sat down on the steps beside them.

"Sure, mister!" said Joan, startled by his innocence of the ways of the world. "Is this your castle, mister?"

"A castle?" said the stern-faced man, and then looked up at the windowless round turret. "Oh, yes, of course, it does look like a castle. It was a boys' school before I bought it."

"It's a swell castle, mister," said Donald timidly.

The stern-faced man really did smile this time. "I'm glad you like it," he said. "I'm glad you like the apples, too. Tell me all about the big fight."

135

THE TROUBLE IN ROOM 519

Joan flipped her apple core away, and he gazed at her night-black hair that curled in two crescents on each side, her eyes that for some reason reminded him of someone.

"Well," she said briskly. "There was nothin' to it. We just yelled 'Rinehart!' and jumped the big slob."

"'Rinehart'?" asked the stern-faced man. "Why did you yell that?"

"Donny and me," Joan told him, "always say that when we're goin' to jump someone. It comes from Harvard, and that's a college and my father went there. This guy called my father a big bum, so of course we had to jump him."

"Of course," the stern-faced man agreed. "And who, precisely, is your father?"

"Mister Gregory Vance," said Donald. "He's a grand father."

"Suppose," the stern-faced man said, "if you don't mind, you tell me a little something about yourselves."

Somehow, Joan had expected this question. "Sure, we don't mind," she said. "We're trespassin' on your property, anyhow."

So she told him of how Mr. Vance spent his nights guarding a hole in the ground, of how tired he got, of the early morning coaching he gave his children in their lessons, of his rheumatism and the cure for it that lived in the cupboard, of the perils of public school and the imminent danger of the arrival of Peter Aloysius Linehan on vengeance bent.

To her great surprise, she found that the stern-faced man violently disapproved of all these commonplace happenings of a happy, normal life in New York.

"Terrible!" he said. "Frightful for two children!"

"Oh, no!" Joan assured him sagely. "That ain't nothin'!"

But the stern-faced man didn't believe that at all. "I'm going to put you into a taxicab and send you home," he said. "And you tell your father he's not to punish you, and that if he does, Mr. Reginald Welch will personally and delightedly skin him when he sees him tomorrow. You tell him to stay in for Mr. Welch, and that Mr. Welch is going to give Donny a rabbit and a whole countryside full of cows."

"But we been to the country!" said the appalled Donald. "This is it, and there ain't no rabbits."

Joan was far more matter-of-fact. "Thanks," she said, "but we don't need a taxi, Mr. Welch. Just lend us a dime and we'll take the subway."

"Hereafter," said the stern-faced man, "you're always going to ride in taxicabs. I've been neglecting my duty toward you."

"But," said Donald dizzily as they slid downtown in a blue-and-scarlet taxi, "he ain't got no duty toward us. What's he mean, Jo?"

Joan did not answer. She knew that something tremendous was going to happen to them, she knew that Mr.

Vance's star was going to be exalted beyond all other stars, but she did not wish to even guess about such great happiness before it came. She knew surely and certainly that, somehow, she and Donald were at the gates of utter Paradise.

SHE REMAINED sure of this even when they were home in their dingy apartment once more and the doorbell rang and a sudden thumping came up the stairs.

The door opened, and before them stood that apostle of vengeance, the Honorable Peter Aloysius Linehan, complete with silk hat and blackthorn stick.

She looked uneasily at the blackthorn stick as Peter Aloysius boomed, "Where's yer pop?"

Donald was frightened to death. He knew very well why Peter Aloysius had come, but something made him stride protectingly between his sister and the blackthorn stick. If Peter Aloysius touched her, he suddenly knew, he would bite him.

"He's out," said Donald, and his voice trembled.

Peter Aloysius sat down without being bidden. He did not look at all vengeful but only rather old and hot.

"Would yuh get me a drink of water, please," he said, "and would yuh tell yer pop that I'm hopin' he votes the straight ticket tomorrow, and there'll be a machine waitin' below to take him to the polls when he pleases."

"A nautomobile?" asked the startled Donald, as Joan ran to get the glass of water. "A real nautomobile?"

"A real automobile," sighed Peter Aloysius, mopping his face with a bright red bandanna. "Sure, nothing's too good for yer pop, kid." He surveyed Joan as she brought him the water. "Who hung the shanty on yuh, sis?" he asked.

Joan crossed her legs to hide her ripped stockings. "It ain't nothin', Mr. Linehan," she said.

"Davy done it," said Peter Aloysius. "Davy done it, and I'll tan him proper."

He rose and looked at Joan appealingly. "Could yuh," he said hesitantly, "could yuh get yer pop to the polls in proper shape? They're gettin' pertic'ler—"

Joan could not see why Peter Aloysius should be so delicate about the habits of Mr. Vance. After all, they were public property.

"Sure, Mr. Linehan," she said. "Pop'll be sober."

THE GRIM, gray east was just turning to pale rose when Mr. Vance ceased his labors and stumbled homeward. Mr. Vance thought the rose light rather fine and he strove to recollect a line of Swinburne to commemorate it. Then he remembered that it was only the soiled New York sky, that the east really held nothing but First Avenue and its gas tanks, and that he was no longer a blithe young fellow with a great and glittering future, but only Old Vance, the night watchman.

Such moments were always being spoiled by unpleasant recollections, and the remedy was always contained in the tall bottle in the cupboard. He was just about to open the cupboard when his daughter came into the room, arrayed in a pair of her parent's cast-off pajamas.

She regarded her father and said, "It's locked. I locked it up. Mr. Linehan says you're to be in proper shape when you vote."

Mr. Vance flung himself on the red sofa, and one end of it promptly collapsed. He swore softly and said, "Since when has old Plug Hat Linehan been interesting himself in my affairs?"

"It's 'lection day," his daughter told him, "and there's no school, and Mr. Linehan's very nice when you know him and you're to vote the straight ticket. He said so."

Mr. Vance shifted to the other end of the sofa. "Little did I know," he said, "that I had fathered a female politician."

"I think," his daughter advised him, "that you'd better be getting yourself shaved."

"Why?" inquired Mr. Vance. "Am I a myrmidon of the city government? How in the devil did you get a black eye?"

"Pasting Davy Linehan," said Joan shortly. "He said you was nothing but an ol' bum. Donny and I pasted him plenty. Yessir, and Mr. Reginald Welch is comin' to see you, too. He sent Donny and I home in a taxi."

"Sent Donny and *me* home," corrected her parent.

Donald emerged, sleepy but fully dressed, from the rear room. "He's gonna gimme a rabbit," he announced. "He's a good guy!"

Mr. Vance did not seem to have heard about the rabbit. He sat twisting and untwisting his fingers, thinking of an even grayer dawn than this when gay laughter had been stilled and all the light had gone from everything. It had been eleven years since Joan the First had died.

And now Joan the Second poked her face about the bedroom door to ask, "You aren't going to get—get tight, are you?"

"No, indeed," said Mr. Vance with a tremendous effort at cheerfulness. "I'm going to press my pantaloons so I may appear in the proper aspect of a gentleman at the polls.

"Would you two most complete devils," he called, "mind taking my shoes down to the Greek philosopher's to be shined?"

Joan and Donald knew there was a can of shoe polish on the closet shelf, but they forebore to mention it. If Mr. Vance was going to honor the State of New York by voting, it was no more than right that he should have his shoes shined in style.

As they went out, Mr. Vance dully stirred himself to action. He wondered what Joan the First would think if she could see him now—young Vance turned into Old Vance. It had been a long path down which he had slowly slipped, and he had slipped, because he did not care—he did not care about anything save Joan the First, and she had gone to a green land where whistles never blew and no grim gas tanks rose to bar the dawn.

Mr. Vance put the iron on the stove. He put up the ironing board. Dimly, even as he thought of Joan the First, he had the sense of great things stirring, great things impending. It may have been because Joan the First had that gift of foresight.

"I've got," murmured Mr. Vance, "to straighten up. I can't let the kids down."

He spat upon the iron, he laid his trousers on the board.

THERE WAS A clatter of steps on the stairs, the outer door flew open, and a brisk, red-headed young man with incredibly blue eyes flew in.

"Hullo, Mr. Vance!" he hailed. "I'm from the *Record*. How do you feel?"

Mr. Vance turned with as much dignity as a trouserless man can. "Since when," he inquired, "has the *Record* been interested in my health?"

"Today only!" said the red-headed young man. "The camera's coming up in a cab. What d'you have for breakfast, Mr. Vance?"

"I haven't," said Mr. Vance, "had my breakfast. Am I supposed to have committed a murder, or what brings this attention from the press?"

"The fact is," said the red-headed young gentleman, "that you're a great man!"

"Of course," said Mr. Vance. "But what led the newspapers to suspect my undoubted prominence?"

"Say!" the red-headed individual told him. "You're the only registered voter in this precinct. The city of New York is keeping a special polling place open for you from eight A.M. to six P.M. It's keeping two registrars in the booth and two cops outside, and there'll be a couple of watchers from both parties on hand—and all for you!"

The overwhelmed Mr. Vance stared. "Is that all straight about my being the only voter?" he asked.

"Say!" remarked the red-headed one. "Would I, Alec McAllister, lose my beauty sleep if you weren't going to be a front page story with half-column cuts?"

"Whew!" whistled the amazed Mr. Vance. There was a series of horrendous shrieks from beneath his window, and he went to look out. Below was a handsome car. In it was Mr. Hot Shot Gillings attired in his loudest checked suit. He had his finger on the horn.

"That must be," said Mr. Vance dreamily, "my official chariot."

Mr. McAllister had also advanced to the window. "Let it wait," he counseled. "The cameras aren't here yet."

MR. GILLINGS tired of blowing the horn; a hurdy-gurdy came from nowhere and began to wheeze out *The Sidewalks of New York*. Around it gathered a circle of ragged children.

"Poor kids!" sighed Mr. McAllister. "Poor New York kids!"

"*Boys and girls together, Me and Mamie O'Rourke,*" wheezed the hurdy-gurdy, and all the children began to dance.

"They aren't," said Mr. Vance reprovingly, "any poorer than other kids. New York's good for 'em. It toughens 'em. It teaches 'em self-reliance. It's the most liberal education in the world."

Mr. McAllister shook his head as the hurdy-gurdy whined. "That's the saddest tune in the world," he said, "and they're the saddest kids in the world. Of course, New York toughens 'em. It toughens 'em too much."

He pointed down the street with a lean forefinger. "Look!" he said. "Here's a child bringing home her old man's boots. And I'll bet her old man gave her that black eye!"

Mr. Vance hastily looked. It was Joan the Second.

"Young man," he choked, "I've got to be getting ready!"

Joan and Donald, bearing Mr. Vance's boots, had halted wide-eyed on the steps of their home. They were staring at Mr. Hot Shot Gillings and the motorcar and at a cameraman who was untangling his tripod from a taxi.

They were also being stared at by a solid line of the younger citizenry, and a shrill voice piped up: "That's them! That's Joan Vance. I know her! I do! See if I don't! Hi, Joan! Hi, Joan! Has your pop had his pitcher taken yet?"

It was all too miraculous to believe, especially as the cameraman insisted on going upstairs with them and their door opened on a vista occupied by a red-headed young man energetically scribbling notes on three pages of tattered copy paper.

"Gosh!" Donald's voice rose in the air. "They's a nautomobile outside, an' reporters an'—"

"Certainly! Certainly!" said Mr. Vance and bent toward them both. It was occurring to him that it was not quite decent for his daughter to have a black eye, so he said very softly, "Now, listen carefully! Do you like living in New York?"

Joan looked up sharply, but Donald said, "Druther live in the country. 'Druther have a black-an'-white rabbit!"

Mr. Vance gazed upon that great philosopher of the press, Mr. Alexander McAllister. "Alec," he inquired, "how many children have you?"

"None!" said Mr. McAllister.

There was a tap on the door, and Margie Gillings made her appearance as timidly as if she were intruding upon royalty. "My pop," she whispered, "wants to know when Mister Vance'll be starting for the polls."

Joan looked down on her as if from immeasurable heights. "You tell your pop," she said majestically, "that my pop'll be down when he gets good and ready!"

She peered out the window, and most of the pupils of her public school gazed up at her with that awe and admiration so eminently fitted to the great daughter of a great man.

A great man? Why, Mr. Vance was gaining greatness every instant! There were so many reporters now that they had overflowed into the hall as he put on his hat and the parade began. Traffic stopped as it came down to the street, cameras clicked, heads came out of windows, the sidewalks were quite black with people.

The pupils of the public school had come for blocks to see such a sight. They stood dumb and mute before such parental prominence, and Joan surveyed them with a cold eye, surveyed the degraded Davy Linehan, the pop-eyed Master Holtzenhoffer, the groveling Miss Gillings. Her pop was the greatest pop in her school; he was probably the greatest pop in the world, for what was the world if it wasn't New York?

"In here, little lady," said Mr. Hot Shot Gillings, and he held the door open for her as if he had been a chauffeur.

"Golly!" breathed Donald as they set off down the street with the press crammed into a snarl of taxis behind them, "this's better'n twenty millium black rabbits!"

IT GREW better still on Broadway, for Canavan, the cop on the corner, held up his hand in utter disregard of all green lights, and traffic growled to a stop to let the Great Man through.

It growled to such an abrupt stop that Mr. Reginald Welch was hurled forward in his limousine. Mr. Welch's mental processes were very much mixed at the moment. He was reproaching himself for neglecting his brother-in-law and he felt badly about having abandoned his brother-in-law's children.

He had decided that he would take them all, even Mr. Vance, to his country place in Connecticut, where there were cows and even rabbits. It was quite lonely at the country place and he would relish the society of the children. He would also, though he hated to admit it, enjoy the society of his renegade brother-in-law.

At the same time, he recalled that Mr. Vance had been publicly proclaimed "an old bum," and as he had a neat little lecture to read to him, he secretly hoped that his brother-in-law would be very sodden and down on his luck, indeed. It would make things easier.

He was in a hurry to get this part of the program over with, and so he leaned forward and addressed his chauffeur. "Jennings," he ordered, "ask the officer what's holding us up."

Officer Canavan put his elbows on the window ledge of the car. "Sure," he said. "It's Mr. Gregory Vance. He's on his way to vote!"

7. THE COPLEY

"Hillman had been one of the most successful magazine writers in this country a decade ago," explained the *Boston Post*, but those days had long gone. "In the past few years however he had been plagued by ill health and seemed to have lost the golden touch for writing that had brought him success as an author." After the eviction from the Vendome, however, things seemed briefly to improve. Hillman sold a story to *Good Housekeeping*, which allowed him to rent rooms for himself and his mother at the nearby Copley Plaza Hotel.[1]

The Copley was designed by Henry Janeway Hardenbergh. It opened in 1912 to immediately become one of Boston's most important luxury haunts. Hardenbergh had already, in 1907, built the Plaza Hotel in Manhattan, and did his best to transfer that sense of opulence to his Boston project. The Copley's Oval Room had an angel painting on the ceiling by John Singer Sargent, and the restaurant and lounge areas became one of the most trendy visiting places for the city's elite. Still, the hotel wasn't a stranger to controversy at the time of the Hillmans' arrival. On November 20, 1921, Frederick Kerry, a prominent Boston businessman and grandfather of the former senator and one-time presidential candidate John Kerry, killed himself with a gunshot to the head in a first-floor bathroom of the Copley. Kerry's finances had faltered, and his resulting suicide scandalized the lunch crowd who heard the shot from the dining area.[2] For the most part, however, the Copley had existed in a state of quiet luxury through the first half of the twentieth century.

Hillman and his mother, a now seventy-four-year-old semi-invalid, moved into a suite encompassing rooms 518 and 519 at the Copley in either January or February 1950. The weekly rate was an exorbitant $110, but such was the price for a luxury that Hillman's mother had come to expect, a lifestyle fitting a famous actress, poet, and Wellesley professor, one that Gordon continued to try to provide for her despite his dwindling finances. By early May, he hadn't been able to pay the rent in several weeks, and the Copley, like the Vendome before it, evicted the pair. They were required to leave by Monday, May 8.

Hillman searched desperately for the money, asking to borrow funds from several acquaintances, but no one was willing or able to help. Until the morning of Sunday, May 7, when he found someone who was able to float him a loan. But when the would-be Samaritan became ill, they were never able to meet. The Hillmans would have to leave the Copley, after all.

It was a difficult blow, and only exacerbated the writer's depression. He was broke. He had been drinking heavily lately, and he was drinking throughout that lonely Sunday. He "was on the verge of delirium tremens." Then there was the additional stress of hiding his financial problems from his mother, blinded by her own largesse and unaware that they were scheduled to move again the next morning.

The *Boston Globe*'s fiction magazine that morning featured a story by James B. Hendryx reminiscent of so many of Hillman's stories over the years. "Black John Smith was dimly conscious of a vast discomfort," the story began. "His head ached, there was a terrible throbbing at his temples, and a continuous thumping against his back. He opened his eyes which smarted so that he closed them again. His chest was heaving and as he coughed and retched a deluge of water cascaded from between his parted lips. The monotonous thumping continued, and again he opened his eyes and blinked in the dim half light that surrounded him. Gradually his brain cleared and his vision penetrated the gloom."[3] It was an ominously fitting opening to an ominous day, a feeling Hillman knew well.

At 4:15 that evening, after his last attempt to borrow had failed, Hillman called room service and ordered dinner to Room 519. He ordered two bowls of cream of tomato soup, two martinis, and a piece of pie, and it was delivered by a Copley waiter named Albert Gaudette. Mother and son ate dinner. They drank their cocktails. The hotel fetched the trays an hour after they were delivered. Hillman then sat down in his room with a crossword puzzle while his mother retired to her room to read the newspaper, perhaps the James Hendryx story so reminiscent of her son's writing, written by another in a long line of marginal fiction writers, paid on the promise of acceptance by an outlet willing to publish. She sat quietly at the foot of her bed in a red armchair.

"Suddenly, everything went black." Gordon began thinking about his dire straits, the trouble he was going through, all for her, and how much easier survival would be without having to care for this elderly woman who could no longer care for herself. She was the problem. She was the anchor pulling him down slowly into the Boston harbor. "I got an empty cocktail bottle, filled it with water, and put a cork stopper in it. Then I carried it into my mother's room. She was sitting in a chair at the foot of her bed, reading. I walked behind her and struck her four or five times on the head with the bottle. She made no outcry, just fell in a heap on the floor. I guess I killed her with the first blow." He stood for several minutes staring at her body. "Then I went back to my own room and called the police."

It was just after seven o'clock when Hillman dialed police headquarters. "I've got some trouble in my room," he told them. When detectives arrived, Hillman was resolute. "You are the police. Good. I have just murdered my mother."[4] The police initially sent just one car to the hotel, assuming the call was a hoax. They soon, however, discovered otherwise. Moving into his mother's room, police found Carolyn Hillman lying at the foot of her bed. She was facedown. The back of her head was a porous mash. Her blood spattered the walls.

The scene was one that the self-aggrandizing, grandiose younger Carolyn would have abhorred, but the *Boston Globe* would have provided her slight recompense. Carolyn was "a woman of small stature whose features still bore the traces of the beauty that had won her fame on the stage half a century ago."[5] Still, it was no difficult task for Dr. Theodore G. Echdoy of Brookline to pronounce Carolyn Hillman dead. Medical examiner Timothy Leary also viewed the body before it was carefully removed from Room 519 and taken to the ominous, four-story city morgue, known to locals as the Southern Mortuary.

The Southern Mortuary first appeared in the 1930s, an imposing structure. The foundation for the building was laid in 1929, soon after the discovery of the tomb of King Tutenkamen, and the design of the building evinced an Egyptian-revival theme. The tunnels beneath its Albany Street location were passageways for dead bodies pushed by orderlies. They led directly into the morgue's storage facility, where bodies were stacked in drawers four high around the room. Those who entered from the street, rather than from underground, were able to avoid the stifling formaldehyde smell but could not miss the sphinxes, ancient symbols of death, that guarded the main stairway that led into one of the storage rooms. The lobby was built by the Works Progress Administration and featured an hourglass sculpted in the archway of the main entrance to remind visitors of the temporal nature of life. Though its upper floors housed the Mallory Institute of Pathology, an important research facility, the Southern Mortuary evinced in its living visitors far more dread than optimism.[6]

Leary had been the Suffolk County medical examiner for forty years. He was eighty years old. Ten years prior, it appeared that the county was going to force him to retire, but he was able to stay on for another decade. Leary's career was distinguished. He had been a professor of pathology at his alma mater, Tufts College, from 1898 to 1929. In 1908, he was appointed associate medical examiner of Suffolk County, then two years later took over the head post. He had, in his long career, investigated more than 44,300 deaths. By 1950, however, he was eighty years old and tired. On May 16, the day of Hillman's arraignment, Leary told reporters that he would announce his retirement the following day at a meeting of the Medical Legal Society.[7]

"This is a sad case," Leary told reporters. "It is simply a case of where a man will probably spend the rest of his days in a State institution at the expense of the taxpayers." He listed the official cause of death as fractures of the upper and lower maxillary bones and of the nasal and frontal bones, as well as exsanguination, shock, and "homicidal blows of a bottle." Carolyn was buried in Boston's exclusive Forest Hills Cemetery in Jamaica Plain. The venue, founded in 1848, matched Carolyn's sense of her own place in the social order. It was the home of governors and judges and admirals; of Francis Cabot Lowell and William Lloyd Garrison; of e.e. cummings, Eugene O'Neill, and Anne Sexton. Thus Carolyn found herself in death next to those she so longed to accompany in life.[8]

Soon after the body was removed, Police Commissioner Thomas F. Sullivan and Superintendent Edward W. Fallon joined lead detective Captain Francis G. Wilson at the Copley. Hillman sat in his armchair smoking a cigarette. He told them his gruesome story carefully and with detail, like an author. "I've written plenty of murder stories," he told them, "but I never thought I'd be mixed up in a real one."

Hillman's "murder stories" veered wildly from the pseudo-biographical plots of his stories of prep school or the Cape or the newspaper business. There was no trouble paying the bills, no family strife, no real-world desperation. The stories instead featured an occult detective, a psychic investigator named Cranshawe who solved supernatural crimes. Cranshawe was stylish but cynical, living in a large New York mansion with his Japanese valet before jetting off across the country and across Europe to solve mysterious paranormal crimes. The stories were, in other words, a far cry from Room 519, as Hillman sat there under the watch of police, afraid and alone. There was no mansion, no Japanese valet, and the ghosts, this time, had won.[9]

Hillman's Cranshawe investigated his crimes in stories like "Death and Sunrise," "The Headless Shadow," "The Thing That Limped," and "Stolen by Spirits," all of them published in *Ghost Stories* magazine. Published first in 1926, *Ghost Stories* was one of the first competitors to *Weird Tales* magazine, debuting three years prior as the original American effort at occult and fantasy stories. Both were continuations of the pulp magazine tradition of sensational literature that began in the United States in the 1880s and only grew through the Gilded Age and early twentieth century, playing to a decidedly different audience than did *Liberty*, *McCall's*, and *American Magazine*. That audience tended to be "lowbrow," as opposed to Rubin's "middlebrow" culture. It was an audience that was less educated, less compensated, who had been defining themselves against middle- and upper-class cultural forms since the antebellum period, in which culture in working-class neighborhoods separated themselves by manliness and physical prowess as a sign of strength. Blood sports became popular. Theater riots helped create space for melodrama. As the century progressed, that emphasis on blood sports and melodrama combined with new publishing mechanisms in the postbellum era to create the pulp phenomenon.[10]

As historian Lee Server has explained, in the early 1900s, pulp magazines began specializing in specific sensational genres like crime, adventure, romance, and westerns. It was that inclination to specialization that made space for authors like Rex Beach, another of Hillman's models and contemporaries. Beach's western adventure stories of Alaska and other northern climes found a home in the pulps, which led to the success of his novels. Hillman never penned western stories, having none of Beach's experience as a prospector, but his incorporeal mysteries depended on the same pulp tradition.[11]

Francis G. Wilson, lead detective in the case and the Cranshawe to Hillman's spectral crime, was himself an object of attention from the local media. Wilson was the first African American to make captain in the Boston Police Department. When he arrived at the Copley to apprehend the haggard Hillman, Wilson was knee-deep in an investigation of the January 17 Brink's Robbery, a heist of Boston's Brink's Building that bagged almost three million dollars and was, up to that point, the largest robbery in American history.[12]

Wilson arrested the lone surviving Hillman, described by one officer as "calmly irrational," and led him out of the Copley. The following morning, May 8, Hillman appeared before Judge Frank W. Tomasello, dazed and seemingly unaware of his surroundings. He didn't react when Tomasello read the complaint that the author "did assault and beat" his mother by "striking her with a bottle and such assault and battery did kill and murder." He didn't react when he was charged with murder.

But his lawyer did. Joseph M. McDonough requested bail and a continuance. He wasn't able to get bail, but the arraignment was held over until May 16, when Hillman would again be scheduled to appear in Boston Municipal Court. Until then, Tomasello remanded Hillman to Charles Street Jail, the famous nineteenth-century prison built on the Auburn Plan that had housed Sacco and Vanzetti, German World

War II POWs, and other infamous criminals.[13] On May 16, Hillman again appeared before Tomasello, who ordered that the defendant again be held without bail for the grand jury after Hillman waived examination on his murder charge.[14]

Prior to his judgeship, Tomasello served as an assistant U.S. attorney in Boston. It was there, in the U.S. attorney's office, where he made his early reputation, prosecuting high-profile cases. He first came to the public's attention in 1936, when he helped prosecute *United States v. Chelsea Trust Co.*, a case involving a World War I veteran who, estranged from his family, lived the last decade of his life in the National Home for Disabled Volunteer Soldiers in Hampton, Virginia. He willed everything to the home, which led to a lawsuit by the estranged family. Tomasello and his fellow attorneys successfully got the government its proper inheritance. Less than a month later, he defended the government again in *Nugent v. Murphy*, a habeas corpus case where the defendant claimed he was not the suspect the police thought he was and thus should not be extradited from Massachusetts to Maine. Again Tomasello was successful. In 1938, he appeared again in the Massachusetts district court, this time for a case less lurid but more politically charged. *Clyde-Mallory Lines v. Cardillo* involved a shipping company trying to avoid paying workers' compensation to an injured employee, even though the United States Employees' Compensation Commission had ordered the payment under the Longshoremen's and Harbor Workers' Compensation Act.[15]

Tomasello was a successful attorney, but he was also a community leader. He was active in the Knights of Columbus, and his family was involved in many Catholic charities, including the Home for Italian Children. Several Tomasello family members had served on the Home's board of directors. In 1942, Tomasello, already president of the Italian American Charitable Society, began a two-year term as a state officer for the Knights. A devoted member of the Democratic Party, he also served as a Massachusetts delegate to the 1944 Democratic National Convention, where he would help nominate Franklin Roosevelt to his fourth presidential term. That kind of devotion to both Catholicism and Massachusetts Democratic politics put Tomasello in some heady circles, and his acquaintances included, among others, John F. Kennedy. He had, by that point, made the move from the U.S. attorney's office to the Boston municipal bench, where he would stay for most of the next decade.[16]

As Tomasello was representing Massachusetts at the 1944 Democratic National Convention, attorney Joseph M. McDonough was serving as Boston campaign manager for the successful gubernatorial run of Maurice Joseph Tobin. The ambitious young lawyer then ran his own less successful campaign against Francis E. Kelly in 1948 to become the Massachusetts attorney general. His loss was a disappointment, to be sure, but McDonough was primarily a defense attorney—always a hard sell to an electorate choosing the state's chief prosecutor. And so he continued his practice, where, in 1950, he met Gordon Hillman.[17]

Hillman petitioned after his arrest "that he is without funds to properly prepare his defense," and thus the municipal court appointed McDonough as his public defender. McDonough was a good lawyer. Hillman was ordered to undergo a mental evaluation after his arrest, but on McDonough's advice refused to answer questions. "He was friendly, apologized profusely for not answering questions," the psychiatric report explained, "stating that his lawyer forbid him to do so. He stated he felt better than he did when he first came into the Charles Street Jail and everybody is treating him well. The guards report there has been no abnormal behavior."[18]

There were sixteen different witnesses called for his indictment hearing in Superior Court, with the result that he was indicted on a second-degree murder charge, but the court allowed him to plead guilty to manslaughter. In the larger iteration of the story, Hillman claimed that he was struck by an automobile in Copley Square earlier in the day, which had contributed to his disorientation. He had cared for his mother, he claimed, since his father's death when he was fourteen years old, "giving her everything she asked for so long as he could afford it," explained the *Boston Post*. Police Captains Francis G. Wilson and Leo Masuret testified about the debts, the eviction. Suffolk Superior Court Chief Justice John P. Higgins sentenced Hillman to three to five years in prison.[19]

Hillman's crime was not necessarily the anomaly that it might have seemed. His story was grotesque, tragic, but it was in so many ways representative of both the state of marginal fiction writers in America and the kinds of crimes prosecuted in Boston.

Later that month in Bridgeville, Delaware, novelist Ursula Parrott was jailed along with her poodle for failure to pay her hotel bill. Former Boston newspaperman Myles Connolly was in Hollywood selling scripts after the success of his novel *The Bump on Brannigan's Head*. In June, another Boston man was charged for second-degree murder and committed to Bridgewater State Hospital for observation by Suffolk Superior Court. James J. McCarthy was on trial in Middlesex for bludgeoning his mother-in-law to death with a quart beer bottle.[20]

Parrott's life typifies the liminal world these fiction writers occupied. A Boston native who wrote and published romance stories, she came to prominence in 1929 with her debut novel, *Ex-Wife*, which was made into a movie, *The Divorcee*, starring Norma Shearer, who won an Academy Award for her effort. It was a success that led to several more novels and film adaptations in the 1930s, but that success was, like Hillman's, ephemeral. Not only was she in similar financial straits to Hillman in 1950, but eight years prior, in 1942, she was indicted on federal charges after visiting an army private in a Miami Beach stockade, having sex with him, then using her car to crash through the gate to help him escape. The private was Michael Neely Bryan, former guitarist for Benny Goodman, and the case drew national headlines because of the prominence of both. Ultimately, Parrott admitted responsibility, claimed she just wanted to take Bryan to dinner and planned on returning him, and was acquitted by a jury.[21]

If Parrott's story had many of the elements of Hillman's, Connolly's had everything Hillman always wanted. Another Bostonian fiction writer and novelist, Connolly was able to make the successful transition from having his stories adapted for movies to writing and producing movies himself. He became a friend and confidant of Frank Capra and had a long Hollywood career.[22]

Even James Hendryx, whose story appeared in the *Globe*'s fiction magazine on the morning of Hillman's murder, fit in many ways the Hillman profile. He was a novelist of western fiction who worked for much of his life as a journalist to supplement his income. Originally from Minnesota, Hendryx wrote stories that took place in the northern climes of Canada, Alaska, and Montana, and they were more violent than the work of Hillman. But Hendryx was another marginal fiction writer who worked as a journalist to make ends meet. He never found the kind of Hollywood success that Connolly achieved, but he also never ran afoul of the law like Parrott or Hillman.[23]

Of the eight deaths classed as homicides in Boston that year, Hillman's was the only one to see a courtroom by the end of November. Two of the assailants committed suicide after their crimes, one died of natural causes. One of the assailants was committed to a mental hospital. One homicide had yet to be solved, and two others were awaiting trial. It was a situation that boded well for the two pending defendants. Hillman was allowed to plea down to manslaughter. Of the six cases that began as manslaughter charges, two were allowed to plea down to assault and battery. The city's homicide unit had investigated 284 cases of violent deaths in 1950. "Presiding justices of the courts," admitted the 1950 annual police report, "deemed it unnecessary to conduct inquests in two hundred and seventy-seven."[24] If there was ever a time and place to murder one's mother with minimal consequence, it was Boston in 1950.

The story that follows is one of Hillman's Cranshawe detective stories, representing a decidedly different theme for a decidedly different audience. "Panic in Wild Harbor" was originally published in *Ghost Stories* magazine in September 1929.

PANIC IN WILD HARBOR

Published in *Ghost Stories*, September 1929

IN ALL my friend Cranshawe's portfolio of psychic experiences, there is none more ghastly or unearthly than the weird affair at Wild Harbor. Cranshawe, being a trained psychic investigator and perhaps one of the best-known in America, catalogues it simply as "phenomena in a New England coast town." But Cranshawe is always conservative.

It all began when a telegram was laid on our table.

Cranshawe read it, signaled to his Japanese valet and tossed the wire over to me. It read:

> *Engage you immediately to probe ghastly mystery. Come at once.*

It was signed by the town officials of Wild Harbor.

"I know the place," said I, but Cranshawe had already called to the valet.

"Pack the bags and get two seats on the Boston train," he snapped.

"This may be a most remarkable case," he turned to me. "I've heard something, I believe, about his place. A bell rings at uncanny intervals."

"Rot," said I. "You can't expect to find ghosts in a summer resort nowadays. Wild Harbor's full of artists and barelegged girls in the season. The only thing that's ghastly about the town is the smell of fish."

Cranshawe was already sorting out his equipment: his note-books, his camera, the telescope he always took with him, and a dozen other odds and ends.

"You're always so skeptical," he said. 'That's why I'm taking you with me. If what I fear is true, horror stalks in that town, and a good, sane, sensible scoffer is exactly what I need as a witness. Come along."

I must confess that, as we began our adventure, I shivered a little at the memory of my other experiences with Cranshawe. But the sight of Wild Harbor reassured me. It was such a sleepy little fishing town, and more sleepy now than it would be later, for the summer season had not yet begun. Ordinary, box-like New England houses were everywhere. The inhabitants were peaceably going about their business, while a quarter of the town's police force was down at the station, picking his teeth and watching the train come in.

"Well, here we are," said I, "and not a ghost in sight."

A short man in a faded blue suit came running up to meet us, and if ever a man was agitated, he was. His very eyes held a hint of dark terror, and his voice shook when he spoke.

"Mr. Cranshawe?" he said "Thank God you've come. These things can't go on—they mustn't! It's too ghastly—"

"I have brought a friend to help me," said Cranshawe, and the three of us climbed into one of the town taxicabs and went rattling over the cobblestone streets.

"The whole town's terrified," the little man was saying, "and if the tourists get wind of it, our summer season's ruined. We count on you, Mr. Cranshawe; we count on you!"

It was quite idiotic. Here was the little man babbling away as though we were living in the Dark Ages; yet through the cab window I could see the fish nets drying, and the red front of a five-and-ten-cent store, and could hear the newsboys crying the Boston papers.

I couldn't catch much more of the conversation, for the little man was leaning toward Cranshawe and whispering in his ear. But I could tell from the way his hand shook that he was frightened out of his wits.

We stopped in front of a big white house, with a green lawn in the rear sloping gently to the harbor. The house stood by itself, away from all others, and at the far corner of its ground rose the red chimney of a paint factory.

"You'll come in?" said Cranshawe to the little man.

"*Me?*" he shuddered. "I can't. I don't dare. That bell and the face and . . . Goodbye!" With that he slammed the door in our faces.

The cab was gone in a cloud of dust, and Cranshawe and I stood in front of the white picket fence looking up at the old house.

"What's he afraid of?" I asked testily, for I was tired from the long train ride.

"Horrors," said Cranshawe. "Horrors that he does not understand. One of them's the bell above you."

I looked up and, there, just below the flat widow's-walk that adorns the top of all sea captains' houses, hung a bell—an old, worn ship's bell, gone green in places from rust and damp. No rope led to it.

"Every Friday at midnight, it tolls ten times," said Cranshawe. Then he led the way to the front door of the house, opened it, and we stepped inside.

A very ordinary house it was, too. Old haircloth chairs and sofas, a ship's lantern in the hall, rugs and bric-a-brac picked up from the four corners of the earth, lithographs of sailing vessels on the wall. In short, the house of a sea captain.

Then I thought of something.

"How can the bell ring?" I asked. "It has no rope."

"It tolls," insisted Cranshawe calmly. "It tolls ten times."

"But why ten?"

Cranshawe lifted one of the lithographs from the wall.

"Ten men," he said, "went down on the schooner, *Golden Wind,* at twelve o'clock on a Friday night two years ago. What's that?"

It was a long, drawn-out hello, and as we stepped outside on the porch, a stout, red-faced seafaring man was waving to us from beyond the fence.

"Mr. Cranshawe!" he called. "It's Cap'n Starbuck."

"Come in!" Cranshawe called back, but the Captain shrugged his shoulders.

"Not I!" he said. "Will you come out here, sir?"

Cranshawe and I walked over to the gate. I could not help marveling how men could entertain such supernatural fears when the sun shone down and all the day was fair. Now, I marvel how they could have lived at all, side by side with that house of evil.

"I haven't been in that house," said the Captain shakily, "since what happened a year ago today. Nothing on earth would ever get me in there again. Clear out, sir! Clear out quick! I warn you!"

"Now my advice to you, Cap'n," said Cranshawe, quite seriously, "is to clear out yourself. Go far away, go to California, and straighten out your nerves. And go at once . . ." he paused, looked still more serious. "At once—before it's too late."

The Captain's hands shook.

"I been ready to go," he muttered, "and now I got my affairs in shape, I will. But I'm bound to sail to the banks tomorrow in the *Hallowe'en*. The moment I get back, I'll start for California, and thank you kindly, sir."

He turned quickly and shambled off down the road. Cranshawe raised his voice in a last warning. "Don't go near the sea, Captain! Don't go near the sea!"

Stark fear glinted in the old seaman's eyes, but he shouted angrily: "By God! Alive or dead, I'm not afraid of *him!*"

When we went back into the house, the swift twilight was already falling.

"What the devil did he mean!" I said.

Cranshawe calmly lit his pipe. But his eyes were not calm; they darted about as if he were expecting something weird—something uncanny and horrible.

"Two years ago," he droned, "the *Golden Wind* was racing the *Hallowe'en* up the coast, racing to be in first with the catch of fish. Cap'n Starbuck drove his ship headlong into a fog; a fisherman's horn sounded dead ahead. Cap'n Starbuck was at the wheel. He took a chance and kept to his course. There was a crash, and that's all he knows—except that the *Golden Wind* went down with nine men and its Portuguese skipper."

"Ten men in all," said I, shuddering. "And the bell tolls ten!"

Cranshawe knocked out his pipe.

"Precisely," he said. "Cap'n Starbuck came back here to this house. A year ago he was found unconscious, with his hand upon the knob of this very front door. He has never stirred a foot onto his own land or into his own house since. Now, if the summer colony gets wind of this, they'll stop coming to Wild Harbor, so the city fathers called on me. Let's have a sandwich."

The sandwich and the cup of coffee which Cranshawe had provided made me see again how foolish the whole business was. An old sea dog falls unconscious in his house, the wind makes a bell toll—and there you have a pretty tale of terror. Besides, I reasoned, all seafaring folks are superstitious.

By half-past ten, I was yawning my head off. By eleven, I said to Cranshawe, "I'm not going to wait for your old bell. I'm going to bed."

"Righto," Cranshawe said, with a yawn. "The front room's made up."

The lights were on in the hall; they were on in the cheery little bedroom, and, after a last look out at the harbor, I undressed and slipped placidly between the covers. Then I switched the lights off and waited for that phantom bell.

I watched the hands on my radium-faced watch racing toward midnight. They came together on the hour, and I strained my ears.

The bell did not toll on the hour, nor at the quarter nor at the half, so

I shrugged my shoulders and turned over to sleep.

At last, I chuckled, Cranshawe had come on a wild goose chase!

It must have been a foghorn that wakened me—for its eerie wail was still ringing in my ears when I sat bolt upright in bed.

The horn sounded suddenly again, on a keen, high note of terror, and I stepped to the window from which the sound seemed to come.

As far as I could see stretched a white sheet of fog, and through it twinkled the red and green riding lights of a schooner. The horn had stopped; there was no sound; but out of the fog loomed the broken bow of a ship, heading into shore. That ship was ghastly white, and she seemed to move in her own circle of light, a dull, greenish, corpse-colored glow. In she came and in, till it seemed she must touch the sea wall. Her foremast was a tangled wreck, her bulwarks broken down and slimy with weed.

The fog clung close about her; yet that ghastly green glow illumined the long, rutted, weed-hung decks, the splintered wheel-house, the ribbon of sail stringing from the broken mast. By the mast, and seemingly supported by a spar, a tall shadow was twisted.

A sudden shift in the light revealed it plainly as that greenish flicker played about the bows. Sailors call that light "corpse-fire," and in a flash I knew why. The tall shadow was not a shadow at all—it was a sailor, his arms outflung as if to clench some unknown thing, and his face was not the face of any living man!

As I shuddered and gripped the window curtains, I saw plainer still— the splinter of the spar had pierced clean through that silent shadow!

For a moment I fancied I knew, recognized, remembered the man who bore that ooze-green face, the man cut clean through by that splintered spar. Then horror upon horror loomed from the wreathing fog.

A ship's lantern made a spark of white upon the lawn—a loathsome, deadly white; but outside of that one spark, the lantern threw no light at all. There was no glow around it; the fog was no brighter there, and stare though I might, I could see nothing behind or beside that lantern. Waist-high it was, as though a man were carrying it. It even swung with the motion of a man's arm, but there was no man there.

Straight it came, as if bearing down upon me. Then, with a start, I realized it was rising to the height of a man's shoulder, then above his head—a shuddering, eerie dead-white spark in a sea of fog, a silent signal of horror.

Behind it lay the silent ship, the figure was inert upon the transfixing spar—and terror held me fast. Move my legs I could not; my head seemed riveted to one position on my shoulders. But even so, my fear-crazed brain registered the approach of something sinister.

Something, I knew, was creeping out of that fog, creeping down upon me like the hunter of a wild animal. And I was the animal, caught in a mesh of cold fear, my legs paralyzed, my arms like water, my eyes staring straight into the white welter.

In a panic I stretched a clammy hand out to the revolver under my pillow. A jerk and it was mine, though I could scarcely hold it.

Then the lantern glowed level with my eyes, glowed with its dead light that illumined nothing. It moved as if a man were carrying it across the veranda roof, but no man was there. And all the time I had the feeling of some Terror coming from the fog...

The lantern's light was so bright it hurt my eyes; yet it lit nothing in the night outside nor in the room. I raised my revolver and then I saw—

First a hand, misshapen, twisted like a claw; and though that hand held no lantern, held nothing at all, the light was still there. The hand moved blindly toward the window pane. It had no thumb, and the nails were like long talons.

As I stared, a scream—a hideous, racking scream—came through the fog. It came from that sepulchral ship, from that ghastly shape impaled upon the splintered spar. It was the scream of a man in utmost agony—of a man on the point of death—and the claw crept close to the catch on the window.

My icy finger slid on the trigger and my revolver, slid slowly as death, and I could see the hammer rise as that "corpse light" shone full upon me and I was face to face with the Horror of all Horrors.

There was a Thing behind the lantern—huge, transparent, so that I could see the death ship through it—a Thing in the semblance of a man.

Long earrings such as Portuguese seamen wear glittered dully, the hair above them was matted with salt and seaweed, and—it is nearly beyond me to tell it, even now—that Thing had no face!

More because my finger twitched than because I willed it, the revolver went off with a deafening roar. The window crashed. My wrist was caught as if by claws, the revolver clattered to the floor, and I could see nothing—nothing that can be mentioned even now—save two long earrings.

I must have screamed. I must have struggled, for my arm was slashed as if by sharp claws—and suddenly I was at the door, with the soft patter of footfalls behind me! Not the footfalls of a living man—rather those of an animal, and I wrenched at the knob and stumbled down the stairs, scream upon scream tearing from my throat.

Above my cries, drowning them out, arose the deafening tolling of a bell. Slow strokes and sure—like the toll of a dead man's doom. *One—two—three—*

I caught feebly at the stairhead, and screamed again, while those footfalls patterned soft behind me, closer—closer—

"Four—five—six," the bell was still tolling.

A cold shiver seized me. *Eight—nine—ten—*

Though the clamor still went on, I could not cry out again.

The bell tolled thirteen, and stopped dead!

Then I lost track of everything.

I awakened in the warm sunshine of the library, with Cranshawe bending over me, a whisky glass in his hand.

"The bell!" I whispered, for my voice seemed gone. "The bell tolled thirteen!"

"Thirteen!" said Cranshawe, and his face went even paler. "I didn't count. I heard you calling and rushed out. Lucky I caught you as you fell."

"I didn't fall," I said weakly. "There was some Thing—"

But Cranshawe was not even listening.

"Thirteen?" he mused. *"Thirteen!* And there's a fishing schooner just come up the bay with her flag at half-mast. Old man, I'm afraid we're in for more terrors."

"There aren't any more," I whispered. "There can't be." And, still shivering all over, I told him the horrors of that awful night.

He was just helping me to rise, when a shout came from the outer door, and the little man we had met at the station came in, creeping fearfully, as if in abject terror.

"Mr. Cranshawe!" he cried. "Oh, my God, it's horrible! The *Hallowe'en* was sunk last night and every man aboard save one."

Cranshawe looked stunned. "I told Starbuck to stay away from the sea," he said, as if to himself.

"The *Hallowe'en*," said the little man, peering about him in fear, "sailed on the evening tide. The *Mary B.* picked up one man. He says—he says that off the Graves Shoal, they ran into a fog, and out of it loomed a ship—all white—and the white ship ran them down! Its foremast was a wreck—What say, sir?"

"Nothing," I shook my head. "Go on."

"And as they struck, Cap'n Starbuck was up for'ward, and one of the white ship's spars pierced him through and through. All that the man the *Mary B.* picked up can remember is the Cap'n screaming, and one more thing—"

"What's that?" asked Crenshawe.

"He says that the white ship—the one that struck them—was the *Golden Wind*—the ship that Cap'n Starbuck sent to the bottom two long years ago last night!"

The little man was ashen pale; his hands were quivering, and he flinched as Cranshawe suddenly spoke.

"How many were lost aboard the *Hallowe'en?*"

I could have told him, even before the little man spoke.

"Thirteen!"

Cranshawe snapped his notebook shut.

"We'd better help my friend out of here," he said. "He's had—a bad fall!"

The little man lifted me on one side, and Cranshawe on the other. I was hardly able to walk.

"What are them?" said the little man, and drew back swiftly.

I looked down. My pyjama sleeve was crushed back, and on my forearm there were four red marks, like the gashes left by four sharp talons. My wrist was so stiff I could not move it.

"I tripped in the night," I said weakly. "The fog was so thick I couldn't see—"

The little man took hold of my arm again, but he was shaking all over.

"There wasn't any fog in Wild Harbor last night," he said.

Cranshawe snapped at him.

"Don't mind about that," he said. "Take him across the street and get him a cup of coffee. I'll bring down his clothes. I'm going upstairs, anyway, to have a look around."

I was propped up in an easy chair in a pretty little cottage across the street. Out on the porch, the housewife and the little man were still rattling on about the horrible wreck of the *Hallowe'en*, when Cranshawe came in and shut the door on them.

"Old man," he said solemnly, "I found everything as you said. The window is smashed, there are pools of sea water on the floor, the whole place smells of dank weed and ocean bottoms—and I found your revolver with one chamber empty. Only it's not a revolver any more. Some terrific force has twisted it into scrap iron."

I shuddered.

Just then a boy came shouting down the street. I could not help hearing what he cried from door to door:

"There's a wreck come ashore at the Graves with a dead man on it."

"Was it the *Hallowe'en?*" I could hear a woman ask, but the boy's voice blurred so I could not hear it any more.

The little man came hastily into the room, his face a mask of utter horror, and I asked weakly, "Is it the Hallowe'en?"

"It isn't the *Hallowe'en!*" cried the little man in near hysteria. "It's the *Golden Wind*, up from the sea bottom after two years—and aboard her, hung on a spar is . . ."

I waved him to silence. I knew who hung on that spar. I remembered at last the dead face on the dank deck of the dead ship. And I wanted to know no more.

"Mr. Morse," said Cranshawe, "that ends the tolling of the bell and the apparitions of the face—that is not a face—in the fog. Nothing more will disturb you or your summer visitors. The dead man's vengeance is complete."

I rose weakly. The talon marks were still scarlet on my arm, and I put on my coat gingerly.

"But what's the explanation of this whole terrible business?" quavered the little man as we walked out into the sunshine.

"You must make your own," Cranshawe told him. "One man's guess is as good as another's."

8. BEACON HILL

The literature on matricide is limited at best, but research indicates that single-victim, single-offender incidents are most common, as is the fact that most matricide victims are white and that adult sons are usually the killers, the vast majority of them deemed to have some form of mental illness. Most such assailants have an intense, overly close relationship with their mothers. There have been, of course, female, child, and minority offenders, and some of them have been involved in multiple-victim incidents. But Hillman's act does fit the pattern of American matricide. The analysis of such patterns, however, did not appear in any systematic way until after the younger Hillman's death.[1]

An understanding of matricide was developing at the time of the Copley Plaza attack. Freud had described the act as the "primal crime of society as well as the individual," making the case that most people experienced matricidal impulses, which served as the primary source of guilt in human society. At the time of Hillman's crime, research in England and Columbia had depicted case studies of adult male matricidists. Several others in the United States and England had evaluated juvenile offenders. Further studies followed in the 1950s and 1960s, all creating the broad portrait that became the standard assumption of parricide research and one that very much fit the profile of Gordon Hillman.[2]

After his particular matricide was complete, and after his surprisingly short sentence for the crime, Hillman had no choice but to continue to work. In 1954, the CBS series *Four Star Playhouse* purchased

Hillman's story "The Wild Bunch" for a half-hour episode. The story, which had originally been published ten years prior for a 1945 edition of *Liberty* magazine, concerned a quiet, orderly bachelor who marries a beautiful wealthy widow and moves into her large estate with her three unruly children. The period of adjustment for all of them ultimately leads, in typical Hillman fashion, to an understanding and ultimate acceptance. It was another common theme of Hillman's stories. The only child who lived alone with his mother after the death of his father often wrote of full families and the politics such families created, though the situational problems those families faced always culminated in a satisfactory ending. "The night wind came soft and sweet and it smelled of warm earth and growing things," Hillman wrote in one such tale. "The stars were brilliant and close. Kenny sank onto the grass and pulled Joe down beside her. People said you could never go back into that enchanted country of childhood, but Kenny could take you back. It was all gone, all the tautness in his head, for he was a boy again; almost a boy again." Hillman's family stories also fell in line with tales of his progenitors, like Poole's *His Family* and Streeter's *Father of the Bride*. "The Wild Bunch" was in line with the themes and tropes of the genre.[3]

Four Star Playhouse, running from 1952 to 1956, worked on the premise that each week a half-hour teleplay would feature one of four stars, David Nivin, Charles Boyer, Dick Powell, and Ida Lupino. Appearing on February 17, 1955—the twenty-first episode of the series's third season—the Playhouse's "The Wild Bunch" episode starred Charles Boyer and featured Natalie Wood as one of Boyer's precocious new stepdaughters. Frederick Brady adapted Hillman's story for William A. Seiter to direct. The production was a minor coup for Hillman, who had been through so much controversy.[4] Hillman's fiction publications had stopped after the murder. Though no one knew it at the time, the *Four Star Playhouse* episode was the last gasp of Hillman's fledgling fiction career.

Gordon also continued to work in the Boston media and hooked on, after the murder fiasco had run its course, with his old employer the *Boston Record*. The manslaughter conviction, treated by many as a bout of temporary insanity that killed someone soon to die anyway, was surprisingly quickly forgotten by those in a newspaper business that often covered criminal activity and had perhaps been hardened to its dictates. No record exists of concerns expressed by Hillman's co-workers about working with someone who had committed murder in the recent past, no evidence of a scarlet letter attached to his name as he resumed work. Quite the opposite. Hillman's crime was never mentioned publicly again in the Boston media that had been his home since his teenage years. Without the demands of freelance fiction writing and the burden of the aging invalid Carolyn, Hillman actually thrived in his new life, bucking the trends of historical assumptions and statistical norms. It was there at the *Record*, for example, that he and a team of reporters won the Boston Press Club's Amasa Howe award for its coverage of a mysterious plane crash. On October 4, 1960, an Eastern Airlines plane with seventy-one people aboard left Logan Airport, only to crash minutes later into the murky Boston harbor. Sixty people died in the disaster, but much of the coverage focused on the Air Force's Office of Special Investigation and the FBI searching for a "secret document" aboard the plane that was never recovered. The other journalistic emphasis focused on the fact that the crash was caused by a bird being sucked into the jet engine and causing it to fail. This was different territory for Hillman, who had largely concerned himself with cultural topics and reviews in his earlier work. But this new effort would serve him well, as the Boston Press Club award demonstrated.[5]

The *Sunday Advertiser* was associated with the *Record*, as the whims of the incestuous world of the Boston print media and a shrinking market left continuing conglomeration. In 1965, Hillman and another journalist, Tom Berube, teamed for the *Advertiser* to document yet another plane crash—this one causing injuries to Massachusetts senator Edward Kennedy, the thirty-two-year-old brother of the former president. While campaigning for reelection to the Senate seven months after his brother's assassination, Kennedy's small twin-engine plane crashed while en route to the state's Democratic convention. It was June 19, 1964. The senator had planned to leave earlier, but it was a monumental day in Washington that wouldn't let him leave until later than scheduled—the Civil Rights Act of 1964 passed the Senate. And so with the late start and bad weather at Barnes Memorial Airport in Westfield, Massachusetts, the pilot attempted a landing sometime after 11:00 p.m. Kennedy's legislative aide, Edward Moss, would die from his injuries, as would the pilot. The senator escaped with three broken vertebrae, two broken ribs, and a collapsed lung. He ran his reelection campaign from a hospital bed, where he would spend the next five months. Hillman's coverage, with Berube, of Kennedy's slow but steady recovery earned the team another prize for news writing by the United Press International Newspaper Editors of Massachusetts in 1965.[6]

As veteran Boston journalist Bruce McCabe remembered in the 1970s, Hillman was "a superb rewriteman who used to ward off the tedium of listing the names of people who had passed the bar examinations by including the name and address of his pet parakeet."[7]

It was a period of recovery for Hillman, and that recovery was more than professional. It was during this period that Hillman married Barbara Tibbets. Known to her friends as Tibby, the new Hillman, seventeen years Gordon's junior, was born on October 6, 1917, to parents G. Wallace and Maude Tibbetts. The Tibbetts were an upper-class family, G. Wallace serving as director of the Massachusetts Division of Employment Security and Maude a graduate of Syracuse and the Leland Powers School, a teacher at Leland Powers, and "a direct descendant of Israel Bissell, Revolutionary War dispatch rider who carried the news of Concord and Lexington to Philadelphia in 1776." Their children thus grew up with that legacy and those expectations, an upbringing that Gordon surely found familiar.[8] Tibby was a twin, and, as her niece Diane Kessler noted, the twin sisters "were exactly alike, except they went in two totally different directions." While her sister was a typically conservative suburbanite, Tibby was a bohemian, and those differences often kept them estranged for extended periods of time. Still, that isn't to say that Tibby wasn't responsible. She wrote for the society pages in the Boston press, where she met the older copy editor who would eventually become her husband. Tibby satisfied the vanity that Gordon and his mother had always fostered. She was a younger woman with social connections that led her to friendships with all of the city's social and cultural elite.[9]

Together the newlyweds moved to 79 Mt. Vernon Street in the artsy Beacon Hill neighborhood of Boston. There they lived on the top floor of a five-story brownstone, with a window looking down on Mt. Vernon Street. It was an apartment with two large rooms and a galley kitchen, which the couple cordoned off with a bookcase.[10]

"Gordon was very kind to Barbara and put up with her," said Kessler. "No, he accepted her and adored her." There was plenty to accept. Tibby first convinced her husband to acquire a pet monkey, which they named Gregory. But then she wanted a bird, the parakeet described by McCabe. She first kept the bird at her parents' house, hoping to ease Gordon into the idea of owning two different exotic animals in a two-room apartment. She named it Malherbe, after her husband's middle and family name. In the end, though, Gordon happily accepted the new pet. "They were perfect together."[11]

Along with that love and companionship, Tibby served a compensatory function for Gordon. She was outgoing and extroverted while her husband was quiet and introverted. She was a burst of youthful vitality for a man tortured by his past, who spent much of his free time smoking in an armchair. Still, whatever Gordon's demons, he did have the same dry, clever sense of humor that appeared in his fiction. He always, for example, left a pint of liquor on the iron fence post separating the brownstone from the street, "just in case," he said, "someone needed a nip."[12]

In the spring of 1968, lung cancer forced Hillman's retirement from Boston journalism. He was sixty-seven years old, and he spent the last months of his life in the quiet Mt. Vernon Street apartment with his fifty-year-old wife, their monkey, and their bird. As spring became summer, and summer became fall, Gordon's illness took a turn for the worse. He died quietly, on Friday, October 4, 1968, at Massachusetts General Hospital. His body was taken to Harvard Medical School, donated to better medical education in his adopted hometown. His funeral would be conducted at the J. S. Waterman & Sons Funeral Home on Commonwealth Avenue in Kenmore Square, followed by a public memorial service at Arlington Street Church. Waterman & Sons was an institution in Boston, originally founded in 1832, but it paled in comparison to the legacy of Arlington Street

Church. Founded in 1729 as a Presbyterian congregation, the church went Unitarian in 1803, when William Ellery Channing took over its ministry. It was from the Arlington Street pulpit that Channing declared religion "a social principle," and as the church developed through the centuries, it continued to live up to that Unitarian vision.

In 1959, Jack Mendelsohn became the church's minister, and he kept Arlington Street in the news during the tumultuous 1960s. In 1965, James Reeb, a Unitarian minister and a member of the Arlington Street congregation, was killed in Selma, Alabama. After participating in Martin Luther King's aborted attempt at a Selma-to-Montgomery March on the morning of March 9, Reeb and several other ministers ate dinner at an integrated restaurant. All were beaten for their effort, and Reeb would die from brain injuries two days later. In 1967, the church held a draft card "Turn-in and Burn-in" service to protest U.S. involvement in Vietnam. Earlier in 1968, prior to Hillman's death, Arlington offered sanctuary to two Vietnam War draft resisters.

It was, in other words, a perfectly fitting place to hold a memorial service for Gordon Malherbe Hillman. It had a venerable legacy in the city stretching back to the colonial period, a legacy of seriousness and erudition in the pursuit of some version of truth. At the same time, it embraced the bohemian progressivism of the age. It was Gordon, and it was Tibby. And it was attended by the full panoply of Boston's print media literati. No one at the memorial service mentioned Carolyn. No one mentioned the trouble in Room 519. Gordon was dead, but he was finally free.[13]

Hillman's story is representative of many in the era. In dealing with aspirational themes within his stories, and by providing class-aspirational narratives that ignored the real-life suffering happening during the Great Depression, the author was playing to the tropes that drove popular fiction magazines of the era. He was, like so many other authors, almost famous, having brushes with real success before disappearing into relative obscurity. His was the fate of most authors who existed outside of the canon, outside of the literary elite. The difficult financial straits in which many such authors found themselves at various points in their careers usually did not create the kinds of psychoses that would lead to matricide, but that never diminished the reality of economic trouble.

Hillman's story vacillated between that of exemplars like Ursula Parrott, on one hand, and Myles Connolly, on the other, as he experienced equal measures of success and desperation throughout his life. His writing career was an effort to navigate the terrain laid by Ernest Poole, Harold MacGrath, and George Barr McCutcheon, to find the success of contemporaries like Edward Streeter, Booth Tarkington, and Katherine Ann Porter. In the end, Hillman never found that kind of success, but neither did most American journalists and authors of short fiction in the first half of the twentieth century. The story of Hillman is the story of most American writers. Most didn't have a pet monkey. Most didn't commit matricide. But the path from privilege to journalism to fiction to a glass ceiling on the level of individual success described a far more common career arc for American writers than did the Pulitzers of Poole or Tarkington. Thus it is that in an enigmatic life awash in contradiction, surviving in an industry that itself seemed counterintuitive in its standards and practices, the author's biography provides the contradictory truism that undergirds this account: Gordon Malherbe Hillman was a murderer, and Gordon Malherbe Hillman was a representative example of early twentieth-century American fiction writers.

He both bought and sold the myth of privileged exceptionalism. It was a myth that sustained him when times were flush but destroyed him when it went away. Or, perhaps, he was able to see himself in the contentment of his fiction until fiction dissipated and left the reality of debt and despair that never broke his characters like it broke himself. It is not difficult to imagine him diving headlong into his later reporting on plane crashes, seeing in the wreckage a metaphor for the idealized American dream that he had portrayed for so long before it ultimately failed him. He had watched his own version of that privileged position crash against the rocks, thudding with the reverberating sound of a heavy carafe in the Copley Plaza Hotel.

The final included story in his biography is the one adapted for CBS's *Four Star Playhouse* after Hillman's time in prison, "The Wild Bunch," originally published in 1945.

THE WILD BUNCH

Published in *Liberty*, October 1945

"They'll just love you, Georgie," said Lenora and shamelessly held her husband's hand.

Mr. Daniels flushed, for he was still a little surprised that he was actually married to such a beauty. He sat back in the taxi and took comfort in Leonora's flood of copper-colored hair, in her red, red cheeks, in her dark eyes that were enormous. For the fact was that he was a trifle frightened.

When you are a neat, quiet bachelor, growing a little precise, it is exciting enough to have married a dashing red-headed widow without having wed yourself to her family and her enormous country house besides.

Mr. Daniels had done just that and was desperately trying to recall what his new family were like. There were three children, two girls and a boy, and since they had been away at school during the sudden storm of his courtship of Leonora, he had seen them only once, at the wedding.

And then he and Leonora had gone dashing away on their honeymoon, leaving them with an angular governess named Miss Hyde.

"They'll simply adore you, Georgie," said Leonora, and he heartily hoped they would.

They would certainly find him somewhat different from their deceased father, Major Alee Drew, who seemed to have been a gentleman rider in steeplechases, a tennis champion, and a notable hand with small boats.

Mr. Daniels, who was quite tired, sunned himself in the radiance of his wife, who never seemed to tire at all, and allowed himself to think of her house, which would now be his. He had never seen it, since, when he had met, wooed, and married Leonora, she had been living in a friend's apartment in New York.

His wife thrust her head out the taxi window. "Here's Connemara! Here it is. Welcome home, Georgie!"

With superb indifference to what the taxi driver might think, she gave him a soft warm kiss.

Mr. Daniels tried to see what his estate was like and couldn't because his wife was in the way. He had an impression of a long driveway through a tangled wilderness, and then the taxi stopped by the front steps.

There was the house and it was enormous: a huge dark red pile, whose upper tiers broke out into an astounding rash of turrets and towers and gables. He had very little time to look at it because Leonora was leaping from the taxi and tugging him by the hand.

Mr. Daniels was now about to meet his new family in a hurry.

The first was a huge yellow object, identifiable as a boxer dog, which glared at him and growled.

And those persons, those quite large and alarming persons who were so thoroughly hugging and kissing Leonora were undoubtedly his new children. They were making a great deal of noise.

Mr. Daniels, lost and alone, looked upward. On the steps he beheld an enormous colored woman, billowing in an apron, and a lean, tall, doleful colored man—dressed all in black—who sorrowfully descended to collect the bags.

His lips moved as he did, and Mr. Daniels had the astounding idea he was saying, "Sodom and Gomorrah."

Whether this were true or not, he didn't know, for Leonora suddenly snatched him into his family circle.

"David! Carlotta! Louise! Here's your father. Come kiss Georgie!"

Mr. Daniels, now infinitely alarmed, saw a small boy with straw-colored hair, clad in a filthy pair of shorts, who seemed to be followed about by a large gray-and-black-striped cat. He beheld a dark leggy girl in riding breeches, and another—a blonde one—in as little of a sun suit as he had ever seen.

They all stared at him and scowled.

Mr. Daniels did wish his wife wouldn't be so overpowering, and he hastily said, "Of course they don't want to be kissed. Why should they?"

Luckily Leonora was now off on a new tack. "Where's Miss Hyde?"

David calmly rubbed a sneaker-clad foot against his other leg. "Oh, old Iron Face? She went off in a huff two weeks ago. She slapped Carlotta, so Carlotta tripped her up and sat on her."

The enormous colored woman slowly came down the steps. "Miz Daniels, they'm a telegram for you."

Leonora ripped it open. "Oh, my Lord! Aunt Kate's sick down in Virginia and she wants me to come at once."

The boxer dog began to bark violently, the children's voices rose, and on a strident tide of sound Mr. Daniels found himself being hauled, pushed, or somehow propelled into the house.

He had the impression it was vast, disorderly, and dusty, and then Leonora was addressing him: "I know it's dreadful, Georgie, but I've just got to go. And it'll be such a nice chance for you to get acquainted with the children."

Mr. Daniels, beyond words, managed a feeble nod. He had, after all, known that Leonora was an unusual woman when he married her.

She hurled her hat onto the sofa and started issuing orders. "Carlotta, call the air-lines office and get me something on a southbound plane. I want my light brown suitcase. Where's my case, Louise?"

"I guess it's in Little Hell," said the blonde girl in the sun suit.

Leonora pounced down the hall, she wrenched open a closet door, and torrents of things began to fall out. Mr. Daniels, fascinated, beheld fishing rods, riding boots, a pair of white jodhpurs, two umbrellas, and a wooden decoy duck.

Leonora and Louise plunged bodily in and began throwing out even more alarming articles.

Carlotta's heels came clattering down the hall. "Seat on the six-o'clock plane, Leo. You'll have to snap into it."

THREE QUARTERS of an hour later, Mr. Daniels came to the uncomfortable realization that he was in a strange house, surrounded by the most frightening set of children he had ever met.

The lean colored man, more doleful than ever, was picking up his bags, and Mr. Daniels dutifully followed.

"Miz Daniels's a mighty sudden lady," said the lean colored man in tones of utter despair.

Mr. Daniels nodded and wished he could have married Leonora without wedding her family as well.

They came into an enormous cavern of a bedroom and the lean colored man said, "Sodom and Gomorrah" quite clearly.

"Huh?" said Mr. Daniels in some surprise.

The lean servitor began opening bags. "These chilluns. They way they acts. An' me an elder in mah church. They calls me Uncle Sim, and why I stays heah I don' know."

He slid silently away and Mr. Daniels met his bedroom face to face. There were crossed rapiers over the mantel; a fox's mask glared at him from a corner; a huge silver cup seemed to have been won by the late Major Drew at polo. The major had all too evidently been the hell of a fellow.

With such a dashing, sporting father, it was unlikely that his progeny would care much for Mr. Daniels as a substitute, even if he was vice-president of a large publishing house. For Mr. Daniels was somewhat afraid of horses, his tennis was extremely bad, and his only desire in regard to small boats was to get out of them as quickly as possible.

He went over to the large dusty mirror to see if he could find any redeeming qualities in himself. What he saw was a rather short, apple-cheeked, dark-haired gentleman who looked like a small cherub and was undoubtedly unsuited to deal with rough, vigorous children.

The large colored woman came around the door. "Ah'm Aunt Cassie an' dinna's ready when you are." She gave him a compassionate look. "Now, suh, don' you worry about anything."

Mr. Daniels began to worry a good deal.

Aunt Cassie went away and Mr. Daniels began to dress himself beautifully to meet his family.

He descended half an hour later to find they hadn't bothered to wait for him. There they sat about the major's really fine mahogany dining table dressed precisely as Mr. Daniels had seen them earlier.

That would be Carlotta, the darkly handsome olive-skinned girl, though it was rather reprehensible that she still wore her breeches and boots and seemed to be carving patterns on the floor with her spurs.

This would be Louise, a beauty, blonde, as pink and white as a milkmaid, displaying a great deal of skin in her rose-colored halter and shorts. And that would be David, as good-looking and dirty as ever.

"Good evening, Carlotta. Good evening, Louise. Good evening, David," said Mr. Daniels rapidly.

His family snarled, 'Good evening, George," and went on eating.

Mr. Daniels moved gingerly around the large boxer dog, which bared its teeth. On his other side he observed the striped cat.

"Shut up, Alcibiades," said Carlotta and slapped the dog.

Mr. Daniels helped himself to excellent fried chicken, and so missed the start of the savage argument between his female children.

"After all," he heard Carlotta observe, "you might do something besides mush with every boy in town."

"Just because no boy'd ever want to mush with you!" said Louise. "And let me tell you, sister dear—"

Mr. Daniels plunged manfully into the fray. "If I were a young man, I'm sure I'd like nothing better than to ah—mush with anyone as handsome as Miss Carlotta."

There was a dead and depressing silence and all his family stared at him. He had been told he had uncommon charm with women; it had been said he was simply wonderful with children. Mr. Daniels realized woefully that this wasn't so.

After dinner they retired to the living room, and Mr. Daniels stared at antlered heads while his new offspring stared at him with a cold, hard, utter dislike.

Mr. Daniels wilted, and the tiger cat suddenly leaped, purring, into his lap.

"Well, will you look at Peter!" David cried. "Gosh, Peter *never* sits on anyone's lap."

"Cats haven't any sense," said Carlotta pleasantly.

Mr. Daniels went to bed with the uncomfortable feeling that all his children hated him and that his only ally was a large cat.

NEXT MORNING was Sunday, gloomy and gray, and Mr. Daniels' spirits took a sharp drop when he entered the dining room.

Several Sunday papers were strewn about the floor. And on the floor reclined or sat his family with plates and coffee cups beside them.

Mr. Daniels sat down primly in his proper place at table and started to sort his horrid children out.

Carlotta had on a soiled blue shirt and overalls and a slight scent of stable surrounded her. Mr. Daniels decided she must be about seventeen.

Louise, who was eighteen at least, had encased her really remarkable figure in dark dungarees rolled up to the knees. She was drinking her coffee and reading the comics at the same time. David was still in his shorts and still quite dirty.

"Do you always breakfast on the floor?" inquired Mr. Daniels with as much brightness as he could muster.

"When we want to," said Louise shortly and began to talk to Carlotta.

Mr. Daniels, snubbed, had a strong desire to spank his whole family and was sorry his daughters seemed a little too large for it.

So he stared around the dusty room instead and perceived that the late major's furniture and his silver and glass showed discrimination and taste. The only trouble was that no one seemed to look after them and even the brasses had gone green.

He felt a paw soft against his leg, and it was his friend the cat.

That dreary dismal afternoon he was extremely glad he had an important manuscript to read, for the very house seemed to resent him, his children most certainly did, and he could quite easily imagine he heard the late major's ghost chuckling to itself as it surveyed its unhappy successor.

The manuscript was quite absorbing and he was much annoyed to glance up and see David standing before him.

David's face had a different look: an alarmed look. "I can't find Peter," he said. "You haven't seen him, have you, *Georgie?*"

Mr. Daniels did not like to be called Georgie by dirty and disagreeable small boys. "No." He went back to his manuscript. When he looked up again, David was still there.

David said, "Something's happened to him."

Mr. Daniels had the swift sense that his stepson was asking for help. He put the manuscript down. "Oh, he's just gone about his own business. Cats do, you know."

David looked despairing, as if he'd known this new father of his wouldn't be any good. "But, Georgie, he isn't that kind of cat. He always follows me around. And he didn't come home to lunch. He didn't come home at all."

It was one of Mr. Daniels' weaknesses that he never could stand seeing anyone in trouble. He jumped up and rain was streaming against the window. "All right, David, we'll go look for him. Get a flashlight, will you?"

Half an hour later he was very wet and it was growing dark. But David—a quite different sort of David, was holding him tightly by the hand.

"I g-guess," David was saying, "we'll have to give up."

Mr. Daniel had to keep on because someone was depending on him. "Oh, no we won't, Davy."

He thought he heard a soft sound

and he turned the flashlight to where the driveway met the main road. The big striped cat was dragging itself along with one leg limp behind it.

MR. DANIELS was quite tired that night after he had got the vet and the vet had set Peter's leg and had gone away again.

The big cat lay on a soft blanket in a basket and it licked Mr. Daniels' hand as he set it down in David's room.

David, very small in white pajamas, looked down on it.

"Will Peter be all right, Georgie? Will he really be all right?"

"Oh, yes, he'll be quite all right," said Mr. Daniels.

He was conscious of a small bony arm about his waist and of a very shy voice too.

"Good night, Georgie."

Mr. Daniels hadn't known it would be so pleasant to have a son.

The next day was different, quite different. For David was most appreciative, and even the girls seemed to have softened toward him a trifle.

After breakfast they all abruptly vanished, so Mr. Daniels decided to do two things: read the Greek Anthology to rest his nerves, and explore his new and alarming house.

He put the small book in his pocket and went gingerly up the stairs. The more vast and dusty bedrooms he saw, the more he became convinced that nobody had ever bothered to clean up anything, dust anything, or even pick up anything.

Mr. Daniels sighed at such wild disorder and climbed a winding flight of stairs to a turret room. On a window seat Carlotta was hunched up, writing in a leather-bound book.

She saw him and slapped the book shut. "Don't you dare look!"

Mr. Daniels sat down in a shabby chair.

"I won't."

Carlotta swung her boots down to the floor and her eyes were defiant.

"It's poetry. I write poetry. Now start laughing."

He'd have to go very softly, Mr. Daniels thought, for Carlotta wasn't what she seemed.

"I don't see anything to laugh about," he said mildly. "Do you know this one of Callimachus'?"

He drew the book from his pocket and began to read:

They told me, Heraclitus, they told
    me you were dead,
They brought me bitter news to hear
    and bitter tears to shed.
I wept as I remembered how often
    you and I
Had tired the sun with talking and
    sent him down the sky.

And now that thou are lying, my dear
    old Carian guest,
A handful of gray ashes, long, long
    ago at rest,

Still are thy pleasant voices, thy
nightingales awake;
For Death, he taketh all away, but
them he cannot take.

The defiance drained from Carlotta's eyes. "It makes me want to cry."

"Quite all right," Mr. Daniels told her. "I always cry when I hear anyone sing Loch Lomond."

"So do I—buckets."

They sat smiling at each other as if they'd found they were friends.

Her voice was much softer when she spoke again. "Georgie, would you do something for me?"

"Surely, unless it's something terrible."

Carlotta looked quite troubled. "I don't know whether it is or not. I'm supposed to stay at Miss Hammond's school to be finished, and I don't want to. I'd like to go up to a little college in Vermont instead—where I'll learn something."

Mr. Daniels pulled out his pipe and lit it, for he suddenly felt quite comfortable with this dark daughter of his.

"About poetry?"

"Poetry and a lot of other things. I'd major in English Lit, I think. You see, Georgie, at old Hammond's I'm just the girl who's good at games. Nobody dreams I'd ever want to learn anything, nobody ever will."

Yes, Mr. Daniels considered, they'd think you were a girl without an idea in her head. I did, myself. But he only said, "What does Leonora say?"

Carlotta put her chin in her hands. "Leo's a dear, but she always thinks everything's lovely just the way it is, and she can never see anything right under her own nose. She was sent to Hammond's, herself, and she loved it, so—"

"So you wish I'd talk to her?"

Carlotta nodded. "There's no reason why you should, for I've not been very nice to you."

Mr. Daniels puffed away on his pipe and admired his new daughter. "You couldn't be expected to cheer at having a strange father flung at you."

Carlotta gave him a shy smile. "You see right inside people, don't you, Georgie? Alec never did, though he was a swell father. Alec just decided we'd be a ridin', huntin', shootin' family, and he never bothered to find out whether that was what we really wanted or not. And Leo can't see us because we're too close to her. So, because we're not quite happy, we're an awful set of little savages."

Mr. Daniels put the book back in his pocket. "Not so awful," he said.

LUNCHEON WOULD have been a very pleasant meal if it hadn't been for Louise.

Louise said grandly, "Shan't be home to dinner. I'm going to the Deans' party."

Carlotta raised her dark head. "I don't think you'd better, Lou."

Louise became angry at once. "Oh, you don't! And why shouldn't I, sister dear?"

"Because," Carlotta said flatly, "They're too old for you and too tough."

Mr. Daniels remembered he had heard Leonora speak of the Deans with disapproval. So he hesitantly intervened. "I shouldn't go if I were you, Louise. After all, you are pretty young and—"

"I'm sick of being told I'm young!" Louise said and flung herself out of the room.

Mr. Daniels was much disturbed. He was even more disturbed late that afternoon when he came around the corner of the terrace to see Louise being driven rapidly away in a car that was crammed with people. They did not look like nice people to Mr. Daniels and they did look tough.

He wondered what he might have done about it and could think of nothing short of having locked Louise in her room. He wondered just what a stepfather's status was in regard to a violent rebellious daughter, and was sure he didn't know.

He still didn't know after dinner that evening when he sat in the disordered living room and watched the sudden rain stream down the long leaded windows.

He was all alone with a book on his lap, and then wasn't, for the big boxer dog had come into the room.

The dog was quite close to Mr. Daniels now. It sat down and put an apologetic paw on his knee.

"Alcibiades," said Mr. Daniels sternly, "you need a bath."

The door opened and Louise came in. Her hair was plastered to her head, her long dress was one wet ruin, her slippers were a mass of mud.

"I didn't like the party," she said.

Mr. Daniels rose in determination. He seized his erring daughter by the arm. "You come straight out to the kitchen and I'll make you a hot drink."

He had never seen a more agitated young woman nor a meeker one. She collapsed into a chair at the kitchen table. "They all got beastly drunk, Georgie."

Mr. Daniels said he wasn't surprised.

"So," Louise told him dimly, "nobody'd bring me home, so I just climbed out a window and walked and walked—"

Mr. Daniels set a cup of cocoa before her and told her to drink it down.

Louise did, and then sat looking at him. "Aren't you going to start yelling at me, Georgie?"

"Why should I?"

Louise's eyes narrowed. "Saving it to tell Leo, I suppose?"

Mr. Daniels shook his head. "Let's just forget it, shall we? You've had a tough enough time."

Louise suddenly seemed defenseless.

"Georgie," she said, and it was an appeal, "I wouldn't make such a fool of myself if I had something to do."

Mr. Daniels pulled out his pipe. "What do you want to do, Louise?"

She said softly, "I'd like to try to learn to be an actress."

Mr. Daniels' pipe began to puff. Louise's face and figure might not be her fortune, but they'd certainly help. Moreover, she sounded dead serious, as if it were something she'd thought about for a long time.

"I know a man who runs a summer theater. He might take you on as an apprentice. But you'd have to work like the devil."

Louise said surprisingly, "I don't mind work, and I might be rotten, but I'd like to try."

They were all right—really all right, these children of his, if you could only get through the hard tough core they'd built around themselves, Mr. Daniels thought.

"All right, Louise. Now get off those wet clothes and take a hot bath and go to bed. Hustle up!"

Louise rose wearily. "You know, Georgie, in the end we'll always do just what you want us to—all of us."

"Will you?" said Mr. Daniels, highly surprised. "Why?"

"Because you're very patient and keep calm and never yell."

She stopped by the door. "I suppose I ought to tell you that Carlotta's heading for trouble."

"How?"

"She's never had any boy friends, Georgie, and now she's fallen hard for Johnny Miles, whose family have just moved in down the road. He's very correct and proper and we're not. So she's going to get hurt." She kicked off her sodden slippers. "Carlotta's quite sensitive."

Mr. Daniels was still rolling that around in his mind next morning when he arrived on the terrace in time to see Carlotta waving good-by to a sandy-haired young man.

He was wondering if it were the correct Mr. Miles when Carlotta, breeched and booted, charged up the steps.

"Georgie," she cried, "Johnny says our place looks like a pigpen! Does it?"

Mr. Daniels perceived that a crucial moment had arrived. "Pretty much."

Carlotta flung herself desperately down in a deck chair. "Oh, dear. I do like Johnny and he'll never stand for us. Why, Georgie, his family dress for dinner every single night, even if they're all alone."

Mr. Daniels said he'd heard of its being done.

Carlotta turned to him. "Georgie, what shall I do? Uncle Sim's not here because his church's holding a revival, and Aunt Cassie'll quit if we ask her to clean up."

Mr. Daniels calmly took off his coat. "Well, we two seem to be reasonably able-bodied. Shall we unpig the place?"

Carlotta gave him a joyous grin. "Let's. Where'll we start?"

Mr. Daniels grimly led the way down the hall. "The worst spot of all."

Carlotta quailed. "Not Little Hell?"

"Why not?" said Mr. Daniels dryly. He opened the door and things began falling out.

An hour later Louise came upon them.

"Whatever are you up to?" she shrilled.

Mr. Daniels held the decoy duck in one hand and a pair of mold-greened field boots in the other. "We are cleaning the Augean stables so Carlotta can have a boy friend. Want to help?"

Louise started rolling up her sleeves. "I don't, but I will. Only, hold on a sec. I am the bearer of ill tidings."

Carlotta raised herself from hands and knees. "What new woe now, fair sister?"

"Aunt Cassie's sister's having a baby, so Aunt Cassie's lit out for days and days. Whatever are we going to do?"

Mr. Daniels stroked the decoy duck. "Oh, that's all right," he said. "I can cook."

Louise flung her arms about him. "Why, Georgie, you're wonderful!"

D<small>EEP PEACE</small> dwelt in the big house that Saturday night. Mr. Daniels, in his best dinner jacket, surveyed the scene. The major's mahogany gleamed, the glass glistened, the brasses shone. The living room was clean and neat and full of flowers.

Roses lay in a bowl on the dinner table; tall candles were lit. It was unlikely that even so correct a young man as Johnny Miles could find any fault when he shortly came to dine.

Alcibiades, actually clean, sat at Mr. Daniels' side and lovingly licked his hand.

Carlotta was dark and lovely in a dress of deep yellow; Louise was blonde and delightful in foamy green. Even David, scrubbed to a high polish, had been forced into a dark blue suit.

Mr. Daniels surveyed all his handiwork and found it good.

"Georgie," Carlotta said softly, "I can't believe it's really us."

There was a tremendous racket outside. A taxi stopped; a rich voice could be heard commanding something.

The door crashed open and there was Leonora, tawny, copper-haired, more breath-takingly beautiful than ever.

She stood there for a second, taking them all in, apparently taking everything in.

She flung open her arms in a sweeping gesture. "Isn't it nice!" she cried ecstatically. "Nothing's changed at all!"

NOTES

INTRODUCTION

1. Arthur B. Maurice, "A New Golden Age in American Reading," *The World's Work* 39 (March 1920): 488, 507. The Hawthorne quote was originally in a letter the author wrote to publisher William Davis Ticknor (quoted in Nina Baym, "Again and Again, the Scribbling Women," in *Hawthorne and Women: Engendering and Expanding the Hawthorne Tradition*, ed. John L. Idol Jr. and Melinda M. Ponder [Boston: University of Massachusetts Press, 1999], 21).

2. Maurice, "A New Golden Age in American Reading," 489–506. Commentary on Maurice's thesis appeared in "The New Golden Age of American Reading," *Wisconsin Library Bulletin* 16 (April 1920): 43; and Agnes Repplier, "In Case We Read: Thoughts about Books for the Vacation," *Weekly Review* 4 (25 June 1921): 602.

3. For more on Beach, see Lee Server, "Beach, Rex," in *Encyclopedia of Pulp Fiction Writers* (New York: Facts on File, 2002), 24–25.

4. For more on McCutcheon, see George Barr McCutcheon Papers, Harry Ransom Humanities Research Center, University of Texas at Austin.

5. For more on MacGrath, see Harold MacGrath Collection, Special Collections Research Center, Syracuse University, Syracuse, New York.

6. For more on Streeter, see Edward Streeter Papers, 1909–1976, MSS 39, Fales Library and Special Collections, New York University.

7. For more on Poole, see Truman Frederick Keefer, *Ernest Poole* (New York: Twayne, 1966).

8. Katherine Anne Porter, "Go Little Book . . . ," in *The Collected Stories of Katherine Anne Porter* (New York: Harcourt, Brace, 1965), v–vi.

9. Katherine Anne Porter, *Pale Horse, Pale Rider*, in *The Collected Stories of Katherine Anne Porter* (New York: Harcourt, Brace, 1965), 269–317.

10. Theodore Peterson, *Magazines in the Twentieth Century* (Urbana: University of Illinois Press, 1964), 48.

11. Peterson, *Magazines in the Twentieth Century*, 50.

12. Peterson, *Magazines in the Twentieth Century*, 445–46. See also Joseph T. Klapper, "The Mass Media and the Engineering of Consent," *American Scholar* 17 (Autumn 1948): 419–29; and Patricke Johns-Heine and Hans Gerth, "Values in Mass Periodical Fiction, 1921–1940," *Public Opinion Quarterly* 13 (Spring 1949): 105–13.

13. Peterson, *Magazines in the Twentieth Century*, 446–48.

14. Margaret Widdemer, "Message and Middlebrow," *Saturday Review*, 18 February 1933, 433–34; Joan Shelley Rubin, *The Making of Middlebrow Culture* (Chapel Hill: University of North Carolina Press, 1992), xi–xv, 30–33.

15. Richard Ohmann, *Selling Culture: Magazines, Markets, and Class at the Turn of the Century* (New York: Verso, 1996), 24–26, 295.

16. Gordon Malherbe Hillman, "Guns at Shiloh," *Liberty* 15 (4 June 1938): 20.

17. Gordon Malherbe Hillman, "The Sound of Trumpets," *Liberty* 18 (9 August 1941): 25.

CHAPTER ONE

1. New Hampshire, however, did not issue a birth certificate for Piper. Carolyn Piper, Certification of Vital Record, State of New Hampshire, Department of State, Division of Vital Records Administration, Concord; Thirteenth Census of the United States, 1910, Population Schedule, Brookline, MA (NARA microfilm publication T624), Roll 608, sheet no. 18A, Records of the Bureau of the Census, Record Group 29; "Carolyn Hillman," Certified Copy of Record of Death in Office of the City Registrar, Registry Division, City of Boston, 15 May 1950.

2. Federal Writers' Project of the Works Progress Administration, *New Hampshire: A Guide to the Granite State* (Boston: Houghton Mifflin, 1938), 46–47, 536–37; Wilfrid H. Paradis, *Upon This Granite: Catholicism in New Hampshire, 1647–1997* (Portsmouth, NH: Peter E. Randall, 1998), 111–12. For more on the history of New Hampshire, particularly in the post–Civil War period, see Harold Fisher Wilson, *The Hill Country of Northern New England: Its Social and Economic History, 1790–1930* (New York: Columbia University Press, 1936); Andrew Leonard Slap, "Transforming Politics: The Liberal Republican Movement and the End of Civil War–Era Political Culture" (PhD diss., Pennsylvania State University, 2002); and Elizabeth Forbes Morison and Elting E. Morison, *New Hampshire: A Bicentennial History* (New York: Norton, 1976).

3. *Boston Post*, 8 May 1950, 6; Tenth Census of the United States, 1980, Population Schedule, New York, NY (NARA microfilm publication T9), Roll 896, sheet no. 8, Records of the Bureau of the Census, Record Group 29; and Marriages Registered in the City of Boston for 1899, p. 34, Massachusetts Vital Records, 1840–1911, New England Historic Genealogical Society, Boston.

4. Though she lived with her father, she was always listed separately in the city directory as a boarder in his house. Though she disappears from the record between 1895 and 1899, there is no mention of her as an actress, much less a successful actress, in any of the Boston or New York papers during that lapse, under her own name or any

variation thereof. *The Concord Directory, 1891* (Boston: Littlefield Directory Publishing Co., 1891), 238; *The Concord Directory, 1893* (Boston: Littlefield Directory Publishing Co., 1893), 266; *The Concord Directory, 1895-6* (Boston: Littlefield Directory Publishing Co., 1895), 226; Marriages Registered in the City of Boston for 1899, p. 34, Massachusetts Vital Records, 1840-1911, New England Historic Genealogical Society, Boston, MA; and Edwin M. Bacon, *The Book of Boston: Fifty Years' Recollections of the New England Metropolis* (Boston: Book of Boston Company, 1916), 493.

5. *The Evanston Directory, 1901* (Evanston, IL: Evanston Press, 1901), 195; *The Lakeside Annual Directory of the City of Chicago, 1902* (Chicago: Chicago Directory Co., 1902), 937, 2627; *The Lakeside Annual Directory of the City of Chicago, 1903* (Chicago: Chicago Directory Co., 1903), 982, 2745; *The Evanston Directory, 1905* (Evanston, IL: Evanston Press, 1905), 205; *The Lakeside Annual Directory of the City of Chicago, 1906* (Chicago: Chicago Directory Co., 1906), 1059; *The Lakeside Annual Directory of the City of Chicago, 1907* (Chicago: Chicago Directory Co., 1907), 1075; *The Lakeside Annual Directory of the City of Chicago, 1908* (Chicago: Chicago Directory Co., 1908), 1112; "Gordon Hillman," Massachusetts, Social Security Death Index, Master File, 024-12-1783.

6. See Donald L. Miller, *City of the Century: The Epic of Chicago and the Making of America* (New York: Simon and Schuster, 1996), 89-171, 224-353, 378-84, 488-515; Upton Sinclair, *The Jungle* (New York: Doubleday, 1906); and James Barrett, *Work and Community in the Jungle: Chicago's Packinghouse Workers, 1894-1922* (Urbana: University of Illinois Press, 1987).

7. See Leon Fink, *Workingmen's Democracy: The Knights of Labor and American Politics* (Urbana: University of Illinois Press, 1983); Sidney H. Kessler, "The Organization of Negroes in the Knights of Labor," *Journal of Negro History*, July 1937, 248-76; and Susan Levine, "Labor's True Woman: Domesticity and Equal Rights in the Knights of Labor," *Journal of American History* 70 (September 1983): 323-39.

8. See Carl Smith, *Urban Disorder and the Shape of Belief: The Great Chicago Fire, the Haymarket Bomb, and the Model Town of Pullman* (Chicago: University of Chicago Press, 1995); Paul Avrich, *The Haymarket Tragedy* (Princeton, NJ: Princeton University Press, 1986); Risa Lieberwitz, "The Use of Criminal Conspiracy Prosecutions to Restrict Freedom of Speech: The Haymarket Trial," in *In the Shadow of the Statue of Liberty: Immigrants, Workers, and Citizens in the American Republic, 1880-1920*, ed. Marianne Debouzy (Urbana: University of Illinois Press, 1992), 275-91; and James Green, *Death in the Haymarket: A Story of Chicago, the First Labor Movement and the Bombing That Divided Gilded Age America* (New York: Anchor, 2006).

9. Studs Terkel, *Division Street, America* (New York: Pantheon, 1967), 379.

10. See J. Seymour Currey, "Chicago's North Shore," *Transactions of the Illinois State Historical Society for the Year 1908* (Springfield: Illinois State Journal Co., 1909), 101-14.

11. See Ross Miller, *American Apocalypse: The Great Fire and the Myth of Chicago* (Chicago: University of Chicago Press, 1990); Erik Larson, *Devil in the White City:*

Murder, Magic, and Madness at the Fair That Changed America (New York: Crown, 2003); and Gail Bederman, *Manliness and Civilization: A Cultural History of Gender and Race in the United States, 1880–1917* (Chicago: University of Chicago Press, 1995), 31–41.

12. William Lant Carpenter, *A Treatise on the Manufacture of Soap and Candles, Lubricants and Glycerin*, 2nd ed., ed. Henry Leask (London: Spon and Chamberlain, 1895); "The History of Soap," https://blog.udemy.com/history-of-soap/, accessed 8 September 2016. See also F. W. Gibbs, "The History of the Manufacture of Soap," *Annals of Science* 4 (April 1939): 169–90; and, for the long history of soap production through history, focusing particularly on Britain, see R. Lucock Wilson, *Soap through the Ages* (London: Unilever Educational Booklets, 1959).

13. *Chicago Tribune*, 15 December 1901, 1.

14. *Chicago Tribune*, 26 October 1896, 12; 24 February 1897, 12; 24 February 1901, 12; 28 September 1901, 7.

15. *Chicago Tribune*, 23 September 1900, 1; 15 December 1901, 1.

16. *Chicago Tribune*, 11 April 1900, 9. Later, in 1908, Fairbank would be involved in another scandal in the city, when an investigation into fraudulent water tax meters discovered that six of the seven meters at Fairbank's principal Chicago factory were faulty, costing the city roughly six thousand dollars per year in water tax revenue. The following year, a lawsuit charged that the estate of the late Nathaniel Fairbank had been involved in tax evasion since 1903, saving more than five hundred thousand dollars owed to the government (*Chicago Tribune*, 27 March 1908, 5; 4 May 1909, 3).

17. The group had to make such claims because of a secret meeting held in Chicago in 1899 between various soap companies that sought to create a price-fixing trust. Fairbank was part of that meeting, as well. "The soapmakers have had trouble lately over price cutting and the increase in the size of cakes by ambitious manufacturers," the *Tribune* reported, and thus began the process of collusion that so many other industries were starting in the late Gilded Age (*Chicago Tribune*, 8 March 1899, 4; 11 April 1901, 5).

18. *Boston Daily Record*, 8 May 1950, 3. For more on Malherbe, see Gilles Henry, *Francois de Malherbe: Gentilhomme et poète, 1555–1628* (Paris: Cheminements, 2005); and David Lee Rubin, *Higher, Hidden Order: Design and Meaning in the Odes of Malherbe* (Chapel Hill: University of North Carolina Press, 1972). For more on Guyon, see Patricia A Ward, *Experimental Theology in America: Madame Guyon, Fénelon, and Their Readers* (Waco, TX: Baylor University Press, 2009); and Nancy C. James, *The Pure Love of Madame Guyon: The Great Conflict in King Louis XIV's Court* (Lanham, MD: University Press of America, 2007).

19. Gordon Malherbe Hillman, "Woman Power," *Woman's Home Companion* 69 (January 1942): 16–17, 75–78.

20. Gordon Malherbe Hillman, "For Your Own Good, Dear," *Woman's Home Companion* 71 (December 1944): 32, 68–70; Gordon Malherbe Hillman, "Miss Baby Intervenes," *American Magazine* 137 (March 1944): 34–36, 135–38; Gordon Malherbe

Hillman, "This Is Fair Warning," *American Magazine* 134 (December 1942): 38–41, 117–19; Gordon Malherbe Hillman, "Visitors from Vermont," *Liberty* 19 (28 November 1942): 27–33; Gordon Malherbe Hillman, "A New Love for Freddy," *American Magazine* 137 (January 1944): 90–91, 134–36.

CHAPTER TWO

1. *The Lakeside Annual Directory of the City of Chicago, 1909* (Chicago: Chicago Directory Co., 1909), 1109, 3135; *The Lakeside Annual Directory of the City of Chicago, 1910* (Chicago: Chicago Directory Co., 1910), 604; *Bumstead's Evanston City and North Shore Directory, 1909-1910*, vol. 1 (Chicago: Bumstead & Co., 1909), 307; Thirteenth Census of the United States, 1910, Population Schedule, Brookline, MA (NARA microfilm publication T624), Roll 608, sheet no. 18A, Records of the Bureau of the Census, Record Group 29; *Boston Globe*, Morning Edition, 8 May 1950, 1, 15; 5 October 1968, 20; *Boston Globe*, Evening Edition, 8 May 1950, 1, 11; *1917 Brookline Directory* (Boston: Greenough, 1917), 300; *1918 Brookline Directory* (Boston: Greenough, 1918), 279.

2. See Van Wyck Brooks, *The Flowering of New England* (Boston: Dutton, 1936); Mark R. Schneider, *Boston Confronts Jim Crow, 1890-1920* (Boston: Northeastern University Press, 1997); Ellery Sedgewick, *A History of the "Atlantic Monthly," 1857-1909: Yankee Humanism at High Tide and Ebb* (Amherst: University of Massachusetts Press, 1994); Susan Goodman, *Republic of Words: The "Atlantic Monthly" and Its Writers, 1857-1925* (Hanover, NH: University Press of New England, 2011); and Sam Bass Warner, *Streetcar Suburbs: The Process of Growth in Boston, 1870-1900*, 2nd ed. (Cambridge, MA: Harvard University Press, 1978).

3. See Neil Miller, *Banned in Boston: The Watch and Ward Society's Crusade against Books, Burlesque, and the Social Evil* (Boston: Beacon, 2010); Paul S. Boyer, "Boston Book Censorship in the Twenties," *American Quarterly* 15 (Spring 1963): 3–24; Moshik Temkin, *The Sacco-Vanzetti Affair: America on Trial* (New Haven, CT: Yale University Press, 2009); and David Felix, *Protest: Sacco-Vanzetti and the Intellectuals* (Bloomington: Indiana University Press, 1965).

4. *Private Independent Schools*, 43rd ed. (Wallingford, CT: Bunting and Lyon, 1990), xv–xvii.

5. Richard T. Flood, *The Story of Noble and Greenough School, 1866-1966* (Dedham, MA: Noble and Greenough School, 1966), 38, 74; *The Handbook of Private Schools*, 83rd ed. (Boston: Porter Sargent, 2002), 203, 1196.

6. Flood, *The Story of Noble and Greenough School*, 48–51.

7. Noble died on 7 June 1919. Flood, *The Story of Noble and Greenough School*, 40, 45–46, 52; Gordon Malherbe Hillman, "Turn the Hour," *Good Housekeeping* (October 1937): 76–79, 191–99.

8. *The Handbook of Private Schools*, 1196; Flood, *The Story of Noble and Greenough School*, 37, 52–55.

9. Flood, *The Story of Noble and Greenough School*, 56–57.

10. Meanwhile, at Nobles, the opening of the school in 1918 was delayed for a month because of the influenza epidemic (World War I Selective Service System, Gordon Hillman, Registration Card, Serial No. 3467, Order no. A748, National Archives and Records Administration, M1509, roll 1685167, Draft Board 4, Middlesex County, Massachusetts; Flood, *The Story of Noble and Greenough School*, 60).

11. "History of the Class of 1917," *Noble and Greenough 1917 Class Book*, 15–16, Nobles Archives, Noble & Greenough School, Dedham, MA; Flood, *The Story of Noble and Greenough School*, 57.

12. *Noble & Greenough School, 1913-1914, Catalog* (Boston, MA), 22–23; "New Boys—1911," *The Nobleman* 1 (October 1911): 9; and "History of the Class of 1917," *Noble and Greenough 1917 Class Book*, 15–16, Nobles Archives, Noble & Greenough School, Dedham, MA; Ernest Poole, *The Harbor* (New York: Macmillan, 1915), 59; Truman Frederick Keefer, *Ernest Poole* (New Haven, CT: College and University Press, 1966), 45–46.

13. *Boston Post*, 17 October 1950, 3; *1915 Brookline Directory* (Boston: Greenough, 1915), 293; *1916 Brookline Directory* (Boston: Greenough, 1916), 278.

14. William Stanley Braithwaite, ed., *Anthology of Magazine Verse for 1918* (Boston: Small, Maynard, 1918), 266.

15. Gordon Malherbe Hillman, "But Never to Take Your Place," *McCall's*, May 1937, 18; Gordon Malherbe Hillman, "Kid Brother," *American Magazine* 118 (July 1934): 58.

16. Gordon Malherbe Hillman, "Day to Remember," *McCall's*, June 1940, 20.

17. Hillman, "Kid Brother," 60.

18. Gordon Malherbe Hillman, "Schoolboy's Return," *Liberty* 17 (5 October 1940): 36–42.

19. Gordon Malherbe Hillman, "Turn the Hour," *Good Housekeeping*, October 1937, 76.

20. Hillman, "Kid Brother," 67, 118.

21. Gordon Malherbe Hillman, "Gentleman's Estate," *American Magazine* 123 (January 1937): 129.

22. Gordon Malherbe Hillman, "Wind in the Valley," *Liberty* 21 (3 June 1944): 16, 67.

23. Gordon Malherbe Hillman, "Nine Lives to Love," *McCall's* 64 (January 1937): 18.

24. Gordon Malherbe Hillman, "It's All Over Now," *McCall's*, March 1940, 28; Gordon Malherbe Hillman, "Day to Remember," *McCall's*, June 1940, 20.

25. Hillman, "But Never to Take Your Place," 18, 118–21.

26. Gordon Malherbe Hillman, "The Sound of Trumpets," *Liberty* 18 (9 August 1941): 23.

27. Hillman, "The Sound of Trumpets," 22–25, 59–60; Gordon Malherbe Hillman, "Square Peg," *American Magazine* 122 (July 1936): 50–53, 142–44.

28. Gordon Malherbe Hillman, "From Now On," *American Magazine* 120 (July 1935): 18–21, 86, 88, 90.

29. James T. Farrell, *Young Lonigan* (New York: Vanguard, 1923); James T. Farrell, *The Young Manhood of Studs Lonigan* (New York: Vanguard, 1934); James T. Farrell, *Judgment Day* (New York: Vanguard, 1935); Robert Elliott Burns, *I Am a Fugitive from*

a Georgia Chain Gang! (New York: Vanguard, 1932); John Steinbeck, *The Grapes of Wrath* (New York: Viking, 1939).

30. Dale Carnegie, *How to Win Friends and Influence People* (New York: Simon and Schuster, 1936); Zora Neale Hurston, *Their Eyes Were Watching God* (New York: Lippincott, 1937); Stella Gibbons, *Cold Comfort Farm* (New York: Longman, 1932); F. Scott Fitzgerald, *Tender Is the Night* (New York: Scribner's, 1934).

31. Thomas Hughes, *Tom Brown's Schooldays* (London: Macmillan, 1857); Alec Waugh, *The Loom of Youth* (1917; London: Methuen, 1984); John Knowles, *A Separate Peace* (London: Secker and Warburg, 1959).

CHAPTER THREE

1. Richard T. Flood, *The Story of Noble and Greenough School, 1866–1966* (Dedham, MA: Noble and Greenough School, 1966), 57–58.

2. Manny E. Paraschos, "Boston," in *Encyclopedia of Journalism*, vol. 1, *A–C*, ed. Christopher H. Sterling (Los Angeles: Sage, 2009), 176–77; Joseph Edgar Chamberlin, *The Boston Transcript: A History of Its First Hundred Years* (Freeport, NY: Books for Libraries Press, 1930), 7.

3. Eliot's "Boston Evening *Transcript*" was originally published in his collection *Prufrock and Other Observations*, much more well known for its eponymous "The Love Song of J. Alfred Prufrock" (see *Prufrock and Other Observations* [New York: Knopf, 1920]).

4. Paraschos, "Boston," 177.

5. Richard Ohman, *Selling Culture: Magazines, Markets, and Class at the Turn of the Century* (New York: Verso, 1996), 19, 21.

6. Chamberlin, *The Boston Transcript*, 203–13.

7. Chamberlin, *The Boston Transcript*, 220–24.

8. Chamberlin, *The Boston Transcript*, 225–28.

9. Frank Norris, *McTeague: A Story of San Francisco* (New York: Doubleday and McClure, 1899); Theodore Dreiser, *An American Tragedy* (New York: Boni and Liveright, 1925). For more on Norris, see Joseph R. McElrath Jr. and Jesse S. Crisler, *Frank Norris: A Life* (Urbana: University of Illinois Press, 2006). For more on Dreiser, see Jerome Loving, *The Last Titan: A Life of Theodore Dreiser* (Berkeley: University of California Press, 2005).

10. Evelyn Waugh, *Scoop* (London: Chapman and Hall, 1938); George Gissing, *New Grub Street* (Troy, NY: C. A. Brewster, 1904); Sherwood Anderson, *Winesburg, Ohio* (New York: Huebsch, 1919); Ben Hecht and Charles MacArthur, *The Front Page* (New York: Times Square Theatre, 1928). One other example of high-profile fiction writing with newspapers as a setting is Mark Twain, *Editorial Wild Oats* (New York: Harper and Brothers, 1905).

11. Fictionalized accounts of newspaper reporting were common, but so too were newspaper authors who used fictionalized personas to get across a particular message

or protect an identity. It was an act that began in the colonial era with authors like Benjamin Franklin and continued well into the twentieth century. Edward Streeter, one of the comparative authors for this study, himself used what has become known as "the newsprint mask" for a series of letters from a persona who was a World War I soldier named "Bill" writing home to his beloved Mable. For more on the phenomenon, see Welford Dunaway Taylor, ed., *The Newsprint Mask: The Tradition of the Fictional Journalist in America* (Ames: Iowa State University Press, 1991), 3–31, 224–29.

12. Gordon Malherbe Hillman, "Tough Guy," *McCall's*, December 1935, 9.

13. Gordon Malherbe Hillman, "No Place for a Nice Girl," *American Magazine* 132 (December 1941): 10.

14. Gordon Malherbe Hillman, "Copy Girl," *American Magazine*, January 1952, 124.

15. Gordon Malherbe Hillman, "The Unhappy Union Boss," *Liberty* 23 (1 June 1946): 27; Gordon Malherbe Hillman, "Lead All—Baby," *Liberty* 24 (7 June 1947): 21.

16. Hillman, "Tough Guy," 9–10, 25–26.

17. Hillman, "Lead All—Baby," 21, 71–74; quotes from 21.

18. Gordon Malherbe Hillman, "Hats Off to O'Hara," *Liberty* 21 (18 November 1944): 30–31, 79–82; quote from 30; Gordon Malherbe Hillman, "Inside Story," *Woman's Home Companion* (April 1950): 22–23, 114–15, 118–20; quote from 120.

19. Gordon Malherbe Hillman, "A Chair for the Captain," *Good Housekeeping*, December 1938, 34–35, 196–201; quote from 200–201.

20. Hillman, "The Unhappy Union Boss," 26–27, 57–60; quote from 60.

21. Gordon Malherbe Hillman, "A Happy Man," *Liberty* 23 (7 September 1946): 31, 72–76; quotes from 73, 75, 76.

22. The *Transcript* would ultimately succumb to the Depression, ceasing publication in 1941 ("Boston Transcript Folds after 111 Years of Genteel Journalism," *Life*, 12 May 1941, 34–35).

23. Braithwaite's devotion to the cause of Black literature would ultimately take him to Atlanta University in 1935, where he would serve as professor of creative literature for the next decade. In 1918 he was awarded the NAACP's Arthur B. Spingarn Award for Outstanding Achievement in Literature. He moved to Harlem in 1941, where he would live until his death in 1962 (*Encyclopedia of the Harlem Renaissance*, vol. 1: *A–J*, ed. Cary D. Wintz and Paul Finkelman [New York: Routledge, 2004], s.v. "Braithwaite, William Stanley," 175–77; *Encyclopedia of the Harlem Renaissance*, vol. 1: *A–J*, ed. Cary D. Wintz and Paul Finkelman [New York: Routledge, 2004], s.v. "Cornhill," 252–53; Margaret Haley Carpenter, foreword to *Anthology of Magazine Verse for 1958 and Anthology of Poems from the Seventeen Previously Published Braithwaite Anthologies*, ed. William Stanley Braithwaite and Carpenter [New York: Schulte, 1950], xxviii; W. E. B. Du Bois, "Book Reviews," *Crisis* 31 [February 1926]: 193).

24. Carpenter, foreword, xxx–xxxii.

25. William Stanley Braithwaite, introduction to *Anthology of Magazine Verse for 1958 and Anthology of Poems from the Seventeen Previously Published Braithwaite Anthologies*, ed. Braithwaite and Margaret Haley Carpenter (New York: Schulte, 1950), xxxix–xli.

26. Braithwaite, introduction, xlii–1.

27. William Stanley Braithwaite, ed., *Anthology of Magazine Verse for 1918* (Boston: Small, Maynard, 1918), 266.

28. Braithwaite, ed., *Anthology of Magazine Verse for 1918*, 136–37.

29. William Stanley Braithwaite, ed., *Anthology of Magazine Verse for 1919* (Boston: Small, Maynard, 1919), 66; Gordon Malherbe Hillman, "The Tankers," in *Contemporary Verse Anthology: Favorite Poems Selected from the Magazine, 1919-1920* (New York: Dutton, 1920), 143.

CHAPTER FOUR

1. Carolyn Hillman and Gordon Hillman, *Rhymes Grave and Gay* (Boston: Cornhill, 1919); *Boston Globe*, 5 July 1919, 13.

2. Hillman and Hillman, *Rhymes Grave and Gay*, 32–33.

3. Gordon Malherbe Hillman, "Tides of Memory," *American Magazine* 122 (October 1936): 30.

4. Hillman, "Tides of Memory," 30–32, 135–39.

5. Gordon Malherbe Hillman, "As Long As You Want Me," *American Magazine* 134 (August 1942): 39, 41, 93.

6. Gordon Malherbe Hillman, "Infatuation," *Liberty* 24 (19 July 1947): 43, 82–85.

7. Gordon Malherbe Hillman, "My Fair Lady," *American Magazine* (October 1943): 25, 92.

8. Gordon Malherbe Hillman, "Storm Song," *Liberty*, 23 January 1937, 26–30.

9. Richard Ohmann, *Selling Culture: Magazines, Markets, and Class at the Turn of the Century* (New York: Verso, 1996), 309.

10. *Boston Globe*, 14 July 1935, A30.

11. Gordon Malherbe Hillman, "For Your Own Good, Dear," *Woman's Home Companion* 71 (December 1944): 32, 68–70; Gordon Malherbe Hillman, "This Is Fair Warning," *American Magazine* 134 (December 1942): 38–41, 117–19; Gordon Malherbe Hillman, "Miss Baby Intervenes," *American Magazine* 137 (March 1944): 34–36, 135–38; Gordon Malherbe Hillman, "Broadway Doll," *Collier's*, 4 September 1948, 18–19, 56–58; Gordon Malherbe Hillman, "Woman Power," *Woman's Home Companion* 69 (January 1942): 16–17, 75–78.

12. Gordon Malherbe Hillman, "Visitors from Vermont," *Liberty* 19 (28 November 1942): 27–33; Gordon Malherbe Hillman, "Roman Holiday," *American Magazine* 133 (March 1942): 44–45, 93–98; Gordon Malherbe Hillman, "A New Love for Freddy," *American Magazine* 137 (January 1944): 90–91, 134–36.

13. Rollins would soon move to New York, in 1926, where he again moved in literary circles and opened his own theater school. "Hillman, Gordon Malherbe, 1900–, 2 letters to W. S. Braithwaite; 1920 and [n.d.]," bMS Am 1444 (514a), William Stanley Braithwaite Collection, Houghton Library, Harvard University, Cambridge, MA; Marian Janssen, *Not at All What One Is Used To: The Life and Times of Isabella Gardner*

(Columbia: University of Missouri Press, 2010), 34; *Wellesley College News*, 10 November 1921, 3; "Our Interesting Past," Boston Hotel Buckminster, http://bostonhotelbuckminster.com/aboutus.html, accessed 26 January 2012.

14. "Hillman, Carolyn, 2 T.I.s to W. S. Braithwaite; 29 Mar [19—] 1922," bMS Am 1444 (513), William Stanley Braithwaite Collection, Houghton Library, Harvard University, Cambridge, MA; "Harriet Monroe, 1860–1936," Poetry Foundation, http://www.poetryfoundation.org/bio/harriet-monroe, accessed 26 January 2012; William Stanley Braithwaite, *Anthology of Massachusetts Poets* (Boston: Small, Maynard, 1922), 4–8.

15. *Boston Daily Record*, 8 May 1950, 3; Wellesley College Archives, correspondence with the author.

16. *Christian Science Monitor*, 25 October 1923, 9.

17. For examples of coauthored poems later published in *Rhymes Grave and Gay*, see *Christian Science Monitor*, 8 August 1919, 15; 29 August 1919, 15; 13 September 1919, 19; 3 October 1919, 17; and 30 October 1919, 15. For examples of fiction published in the newspaper, see *Christian Science Monitor*, 15 January 1925, 6; 5 March 1925, 6; 23 April 1925, 10; 25 June 1925, 8; 19 August 1925, 6; 3 December 1925, 11; 29 April 1926, 10; 5 May 1927, 12; 16 June 1927, 8; 15 September 1927, 10; 29 December 1927, 8; and 26 April 1928, 9.

18. Fifteenth Census of the United States, 1930, Population Schedule, Brookline Town, MA (NARA microfilm publication T626), Roll 933, Sheet No. 8A (Washington: National Archives and Records Administration, 1930).

CHAPTER FIVE

1. *Boston Globe*, 23 January 1927, A14; 16 September 1928, B21; 5 June 1930, 13; 3 March 1931, 14; 29 December 1931, 18; 19 February 1932, 26; 9 April 1932, 4; 4 October 1932, 12; 3 February 1933, 31; 17 March 1933, 23; 4 April 1933, 16; 9 October 1933, 7; 1 November 1933, 19; *Universal Weekly*, 28 January 1933, 15. Quotes from *Boston Globe*, 5 February 1933, A39; 25 June 1935, 11. Hillman's reviews also appeared in more national literary journals, at least one coming in the July-August 1924 edition of *Voices: A Journal of Verse*, which also included poetic work from Robert Penn Warren and others. *Voices* was created by the noted Maine poet and editor Harold Vinal, and that specific issue was edited by the poet Kathryn White Ryan while Vinal was away in Europe (*New York Times*, 24 August 1924, BR17; "Robert Penn Warren to Allen Tate, 22 May 1926," in *Selected Letters of Robert Penn Warren*, vol. 1: *The Apprentice Years, 1924–1934*, ed. William Bedford Clark [Baton Rouge: Louisiana State University Press, 2000], 84–87).

2. Theodore Peterson, *Magazines in the Twentieth Century* (Urbana: University of Illinois Press, 1964), 1; James Playsted Wood, *Magazines in the United States: Their Social and Economic Influence* (New York: Ronald, 1949), 10, 22, 25, 27. Prior to these studies and others used in this general overview of the development of magazine fiction, modern magazine historiography began in 1930 with the first volume of Frank Luther Mott's five-volume *History of American Magazines* and continued with impact-

ful studies that were far more limited in their scope, such as Alfred Kazin's *On Native Grounds*. The final volume of Mott's series was published posthumously in 1968 (see Frank Luther Mott, *A History of American Magazines*, vol. 1: *1741-1850* [Cambridge, MA: Harvard University Press, 1930]; Frank Luther Mott, *A History of American Magazines*, vol. 5: *Sketches of 21 Magazines, 1905-1930* [Cambridge, MA: Belknap Press of Harvard University Press, 1968]; and Alfred Kazin, *On Native Grounds: An Interpretation of Modern American Prose Literature* [New York: Harcourt, Brace, 1942]).

3. *Godey's* lasted until 1898, eventually outpaced by the *Ladies' Home Journal*, founded in 1883 (Wood, *Magazines in the United States*, 45-46, 54, 59).

4. Wood, *Magazines in the United States*, 99, 100; Peterson, *Magazines in the Twentieth Century*, 1.

5. Matthew Schneirov, *The Dream of a New Social Order: Popular Magazines in America, 1893-1914* (New York: Columbia University Press, 1994), 257-58; Daniel A. Clark, *Creating the College Man: American Mass Magazines and Middle-Class Manhood, 1890-1915* (Madison: University of Wisconsin Press, 2010), 7. See also Theodore P. Greene, *America's Heroes: The Changing Models of Success in American Magazines* (New York: Oxford University Press, 1970), 3-15.

6. Peterson, *Magazines in the Twentieth Century*, 3. See also George Santayana, *The Genteel Tradition: Nine Essays by George Santayana* (1967; Lincoln: University of Nebraska Press, 1998).

7. David E. Sumner, *The Magazine Century: American Magazines since 1900* (New York: Peter Lang, 2010), 17-18; Peterson, *Magazines in the Twentieth Century*, 4-5; Tom Pendergast, *Creating the Modern Man: American Magazines and Consumer Culture, 1900-1950* (Columbia: University of Missouri Press, 2000), 3.

8. Richard Ohman, *Selling Culture: Magazines, Markets, and Class at the Turn of the Century* (New York: Verso, 1996), 6-8, 79-80, 232-35, 288-92; Peterson, *Magazines in the Twentieth Century*, 6-7; Sumner, *The Magazine Century* 19, 21; Wood, *Magazines in the United States*, 104; George Britt, *Forty Years—Forty Millions: The Career of Frank A. Munsey* (New York: Farrar and Rinehart, 1935), 39.

9. Ohman, *Selling Culture*, 28-29, 220, 231-35; Sumner, *The Magazine Century*, 24, 37-38, 40; Mike Ashley, *Age of the Storytellers: British Popular Fiction Magazines, 1880-1950* (London: British Library, 2006), 253.

10. Peterson, *Magazines in the Twentieth Century*, 12; Mary Ellen Zuckerman, *A History of Popular Women's Magazines in the United States, 1792-1995* (Westport, CT: Greenwood, 1998), 101.

11. First quotes from Peterson, *Magazines in the Twentieth Century*, 15. Final quote from Ellen Gruber Garvey, *The Adman in the Parlor: Magazines and the Gendering of Consumer Culture, 1880s to 1910s* (New York: Oxford University Press, 1996), 4.

12. Ohman, *Selling Culture*, 220, 225-30; Sumner, *The Magazine Century*, 25, 27-28; Zuckerman, *A History of Popular Women's Magazines in the United States*, 105-6.

13. Zuckerman, *A History of Popular Women's Magazines in the United States*, 107.

14. Zuckerman, *A History of Popular Women's Magazines in the United States*, 112. See also David Reed, *The Popular Magazine in Britain and the United States, 1880-1960* (Toronto: University of Toronto Press, 1997), 159.

15. Bigelow quoted in John E. Drewry, "Good Housekeeping—Men Read It Too," *Writer* (October 1937) and in Zuckerman, *A History of Popular Women's Magazines in the United States*, 179-80; McCall Corp., *A Qualitative Study of Magazines* (New York: McCall Corp., 1946), 41, 43.

16. Sumner, *The Magazine Century*, 28-29.

17. Robert Scholes and Clifford Wulfman, *Modernism in the Magazines: An Introduction* (New Haven, CT: Yale University Press, 2010), 61; David Minter, "A Cultural History of the Modern American Novel," in *The Cambridge History of American Literature*, vol. 6: *Prose Writing, 1910-1950*, ed. Sacvan Bercovitch (New York: Cambridge University Press, 2002), 135; Peterson, *Magazines in the Twentieth Century*, 44-45. See also Magazine Advertising Bureau, *Nationwide Magazine Audience Survey*, vol. 2: *Individuals* (New York: Magazine Advertising Bureau, 1948); and Magazine Advertising Bureau, *"The Profitable Difference": A Study of the Magazine Market* (New York: Magazine Advertising Bureau, 1960).

18. Among the magazines that did not survive the Depression was another of Hillman's publishers, *Smart Set*, which lasted from 1890 to 1930 (Sumner, *The Magazine Century*, 75, 78).

19. Peterson, *Magazines in the Twentieth Century*, 46.

20. Reed, *The Popular Magazine in Britain and the United States, 1880-1960*, 157; Peterson, *Magazines in the Twentieth Century*, 80.

21. Mike Ashley, "Spectral Memories," in *Phantom Perfumes and Other Shades: Memories of "Ghost Stories" Magazine* (Ashcroft, BC: Ash-Tree, 2000), xiii-xxvi, 187.

22. Peterson, *Magazines in the Twentieth Century*, 118-19, 120.

23. Minter, "A Cultural History of the Modern American Novel," 135-36. See also Robert Lynd and Helen Lynd, *Middletown: A Study in Modern American Culture* (New York: Harcourt, Brace, 1929).

24. Peterson, *Magazines in the Twentieth Century*, 122.

25. Peterson, *Magazines in the Twentieth Century*, 123.

26. J. K. Lasser, "How Good Publishing Management Works Today," *Magazine Industry* 1 (Winter 1950): 19-20; "Writers' Own Companion," *Newsweek*, 21 January 1946, 84; Peterson, *Magazines in the Twentieth Century*, 124-25.

27. Jonathan Norton Leonard, "Learning How to Write," in *Writing for Love or Money: Thirty-Five Essays Reprinted from "The Saturday Review of Literature,"* ed. Norman Cousins (New York: Longman, Greens, 1949), 14-18; Peterson, *Magazines in the Twentieth Century*, 125-26.

28. Peterson, *Magazines in the Twentieth Century*, 126.

29. Morton Sontheimer, introduction to *The Society of Magazine Writers: A Guide to Successful Magazine Writing*, ed. Clive Howard (New York: Scribner, 1954), 8-9; Peterson, *Magazines in the Twentieth Century*, 126.

30. Peterson, *Magazines in the Twentieth Century*, 127.

31. See Perry J. Ashley, ed., *Dictionary of Literary Biography*, vol. 29: *American Newspaper Journalists, 1926-1950* (Detroit: Gale Research, 1984); Sam G. Riley, ed., *Dictionary of Literary Biography*, vol. 137: *American Magazine Journalists, 1900-1960* (Detroit: Gale Research, 1994); Bobby Ellen Kimbel, ed., *Dictionary of Literary Biography*, vol. 86: *American Short-Story Writers, 1910-1945, First Series* (Detroit: Gale Research, 1989); Bobby Ellen Kimbel, ed., *Dictionary of Literary Biography*, vol. 102: *American Short-Story Writers, 1910-1945, Second Series* (Detroit: Gale Research, 1991); Sam G. Riley, ed., *Dictionary of Literary Biography*, vol. 91: *American Magazine Journalists, 1900-1960* (Detroit: Gale Research, 1990); and Perry J. Ashley, ed., *Dictionary of Literary Biography*, vol. 25: *American Newspaper Journalists, 1901-1925* (Detroit: Gale Research, 1984).

32. Zuckerman, *A History of Popular Women's Magazines in the United States*, 102; Peterson, *Magazines in the Twentieth Century*, 124.

33. Wood, *Magazines in the United States*, 273, 276.

34. Werner Sollors, "Ethnic Modernism," in *The Cambridge History of American Literature*, vol. 6: *Prose Writing, 1910-1950*, ed. Sacvan Bercovitch (New York: Cambridge University Press, 2002), 1, 4-5; Joan Shelley Rubin, *The Making of Middlebrow Culture* (Chapel Hill: University of North Carolina Press, 1992), xiii-xv.

35. Sollors, "Ethnic Modernism," 11.

36. Sollors, "Ethnic Modernism," 11; John Dewey, "Americanism and Localism," in *John Dewey: The Middle Works, 1899-1924*, vol. 12: *1920*, ed. Jo Ann Boydston (Carbondale: Southern Illinois University Press, 1982), 14.

37. Sollors, "Ethnic Modernism," 11; Mike Gold, "O Californians! O Ladies and Gentlemen!" *Gently, Brother* (March 1924), reprinted in *Mike Gold: A Literary Anthology*, ed. Michael Folsom (New York: International Publishers, 1972), 123.

38. Deborah Wynne, *The Sensation Novel and the Victorian Family Magazine* (New York: Palgrave, 2001), 1, 9, 168; Wilkie Collins, "The Unknown Public," *Household Words*, 21 August 1858; reprinted in Wilkie Collins, *My Miscellanies* (New York: Harper and Brothers, 1873), 126-42; R. G. Cox, "The Reviews and Magazines" in *The Pelican Guide to Victorian Literature*, vol. 6: *The Victorian Age* (Baltimore, MD: Penguin, 1958), 188-204; quote from 195.

CHAPTER SIX

1. John Twist and Gordon Malherbe HIllman, *The Great Man Votes*, script as shot, 8 January 1939 (Alexandria, VA: Alexander Street Press, 2007); F. Stinnette, The Great Man Votes—RKO, Synopsis, 6 December 1938; Stinnette, Lischka, and O'Neil, The Great Man Votes Analysis Chart, 6 December 1938, The Great Man Votes [RKO, 1938], Margaret Herrick Library.

2. *New York Times*, 24 September 1938, 17; 20 January 1939, 21; *Boston Globe*, 3 April 1938, B51; *Los Angeles Times*, 16 March 1938, 10.

3. Joseph I. Breen to J. R. McDonough, 20 September 1938; Joseph I. Breen to J. R. McDonough, 6 October 1938; Joseph I. Breen to J. R. McDonough, 18 October 1938; Joseph I. Breen to J. R. McDonough, 7 December 1938, in The Great Man Votes [RKO, 1938], Motion Picture Association of America, Production Code Administration Records, Department of Special Collections, Academy of Motion Picture Arts and Sciences, Margaret Herrick Library, Fairbanks Center for Motion Picture Study, Beverly Hills, California (hereinafter cited as The Great Man Votes [RKO, 1938], Margaret Herrick Library).

4. John Mosher, *New Yorker*, 21 January 1939; Daughters of the American Revolution Review on "The Great Man Votes"; "The Great Man Votes," *Time*, n.d., The Great Man Votes [RKO, 1938], Margaret Herrick Library.

5. "Barrymore Tops in Second Kanin Hit," *Hollywood Reporter*, 7 January 1939; "The Great Man Votes," *Film Daily*, 11 January 1939; Roscoe Williams, "The Great Man Votes," *Motion Picture Daily*, 12 January 1939; "The Great Man Votes," *Motion Picture Herald*, 14 January 1939; "Great Man Votes," *Variety*, 11 January 1939, The Great Man Votes [RKO, 1938], Margaret Herrick Library; "'Great Man' Sequel," *Hollywood Reporter*, 28 February 1939, 1.

6. *Hollywood Reporter*, 26 September 1938, 3. The archival record on Adams is limited. The one collection of his papers includes only his later screenplays (see Gerald Drayson Adams Scripts, ca.1949–ca. 1960s, PASC 221, UCLA Library, Performing Arts Special Collections, Los Angeles).

7. The unique place of adaptations in cinema history has led to the small but growing discipline of adaptation studies, beginning with George Bluestone's 1957 *Novels into Film*. While much of the scholarship in the field is concerned less with the history of the story-buying process and more with film and literary criticism that analyzes the production and reception of similar stories presented in different forms of media, its theoretical work can be instructive (see George Bluestone, *Novels into Film* [1957; Baltimore, MD: Johns Hopkins University Press, 2003]; Deborah Cartmell and Imelda Whelehan, *Adaptations: From Text to Screen, from Screen to Text* [New York: Routledge, 1999]; James John Griffith, *Adaptations as Imitations: Films from Novels* [Newark: University of Delaware Press, 1997]; and Rebecca Housel, ed., *From Camera Lens to Critical Lens: A Collection of Best Essays on Film Adaptation* [Newcastle: Cambridge Scholars Press, 2006]).

8. *Hollywood Reporter*, 13 February 1939, 1; 24 February 1939, 1; *New York Times*, 4 April 1939, 29; 30 September 1939, 11; *Los Angeles Times*, 1 April 1939, A16; Library of Congress, *Catalog of Copyright Entries*, Part 1, Group 3, 1940, New Series, Volume 13, No. 3 (Washington, DC: USGPO, 1940), 2064; *Boston Globe*, 9 October 1939, 9, 15 October 1939, B18.

9. Shurlock and Stinnette, Analysis Chart, Here I Am a Stranger, 11 September 1939; Harry Brand, Synopsis of "Here I Am a Stranger," 18 November 1940, in Here I Am a Stranger [20th-FOX, 1939], Motion Picture Association of America, Production Code Administration Records, Department of Special Collections, Academy of Motion

Picture Arts and Sciences, Margaret Herrick Library, Fairbanks Center for Motion Picture Study, Beverly Hills, California (hereinafter cited as Here I Am a Stranger [20th-FOX, 1939], Margaret Herrick Library).

10. Joseph I. Breen to Jason S. Joy, 15 May 1939; Harry Brand, Vital Statistics of "Here I Am a Stranger," Here I Am a Stranger [20th-FOX, 1939], Margaret Herrick Library; *Hollywood Reporter*, 2 June 1939, 1; 30 June 1939, 3.

11. *New York Times*, 30 September 1939, 11.

12. "'I Am a Stranger' Fair; 'Rio' Wanders Aimlessly," *Hollywood Reporter*, 21 September 1939; "Here I Am a Stranger," *Variety*, 21 September 1939; "Here I Am a Stranger," *Film Daily*, 3 October 1939; "Here I Am a Stranger," *Motion Picture Daily*, 25 September 1939; "Here I Am a Stranger," *Motion Picture Herald*, 30 September 1939, Here I Am a Stranger [20th-FOX, 1939], Margaret Herrick Library.

13. Sidney F. Hunter, "Thomas Y. Crowell & Co., New York, 1876–1979," The Lucile Project, University of Iowa Libraries, http://sdrc.lib.uiowa.edu/lucile/publishers/crowell/cr_intro.htm, accessed 26 November 2016; *New York Times*, 14 September 1941, BR22; *New Orleans Times-Picayune*, 19 October 1941, 38.

14. The book's title comes from Homer's *Iliad*, "The bitter dregs of Fortune's cup to drain" (Gordon Malherbe Hillman, *Fortune's Cup* [New York: Thomas Y. Crowell, 1941]; Homer, *Iliad*, book XX, line 85).

15. Ernest Poole, *His Family* (New York: Macmillan, 1917); and Edward Streeter, *Father of the Bride* (New York Simon and Schuster, 1949).

16. Edward Stanwood, *Boston Illustrated: Containing Full Descriptions of the City and Its Immediate Suburbs, Its Public Buildings and Institutions, Business Edifices, Parks and Avenues, Statues, Harbor and Islands* (Boston: Houghton, Mifflin, 1886) 104; Jim Vrabel, *When in Boston: A Time Line & Almanac* (Boston: University Press of New England, 2004), 247. For more on the *Record* in the period while Hillman was employed by the company, see William Randolph Hearst Papers, BANC MSS 77/121c, carton 23, folder 25–32, Bancroft Library, University of California at Berkeley.

17. *Boston Daily Record*, 8 May 1950, 3.

18. See Bainbridge Bunting, *Houses of Boston's Back Bay: An Architectural History, 1840–1917* (Cambridge, MA: Belknap Press of Harvard University Press, 1967); and Stephanie Schorow, *Boston on Fire: A History of Fires and Firefighting in Boston* (Beverly, MA: Commonwealth Editions, 2003).

CHAPTER SEVEN

1. *Boston Post*, 8 May 1950, 6.

2. "The Fairmont Copley Plaza, Boston, Massachusetts," Historic Hotels of America, http://www.historichotels.org/hotel/The_Fairmont_Copley_Plaza/1251, accessed 19 August 2008; Michael Kranish, Brian C. Mooney, and Nina J. Easton, *John F. Kerry: The Complete Biography by the "Boston Globe" Reporters Who Know Him Best* (New York: Public Affairs, 2004), 5–7.

3. James B. Hendryx, "Black John Pays a Debt," *Boston Sunday Globe Fiction Magazine*, 7 May 1950, 1-2.

4. *Boston Post*, 8 May 1950, 6.

5. *Boston Post*, 8 May 1950, 6.

6. Andrew Ryan, "Old Morgue Finds New Life As a Clinic for Homeless," *Boston Globe*, 31 May 2008, B1.

7. Leary would be replaced by Richard Ford, the head of Harvard's Department of Legal Medicine. Leary, for his part, could not remain idle, the octogenarian continuing research on cholesterol after his time as medical examiner had run its course (*Boston Herald*, 17 May 1950, 1; *Boston Daily Record*, 17 May 1950, 3; and *Boston Post*, 17 May 1950, 2; 25 May 1950, 15; 2 June 1950, 11; 4 June 1950, D3; 8 June 1950, 14).

8. *Boston Post*, 8 May 1950, 6; "Carolyn Hillman," Certified Copy of Record of Death in Office of the City Registrar, Registry Division, City of Boston, 15 May 1950. See also Anthony Mitchell Sammarco, *Forest Hills Cemetery* (Charleston, SC: Arcadia, 2009).

9. See Mike Ashley, ed., *Phantom Perfumes and Other Shades: Memories of "Ghost Stories" Magazine* (Ashcroft, BC: Ash-Tree, 2000).

10. "Death and Sunrise," *Ghost Stories* 7 (December 1929); "The Headless Shadow," *Ghost Stories* 7 (November 1929); "Stolen by Spirits" (true story), *Ghost Stories* 6 (February 1929); "The Thing That Limped," *Ghost Stories* 11 (July 1931); Mike Ashley, "Ghost Stories," in *Science Fiction, Fantasy and Weird Fiction Magazines*, ed. Marshall B. Tymn and Ashley, 315-31 (Westport, CT: Greenwood, 1985); Lee Server, *Encyclopedia of Pulp Fiction Writers* (New York: Facts on File, 2002), xii-xv.

11. Server, *Encyclopedia of Pulp Fiction Writers*, xiii; Rex Beach, "Captain Innocencio," *McClure's* 36 (February 1911): 365-75; Rex Beach, "The Colognizing of Kansas," *McClure's* 28 (March 1907): 525-34; Rex Beach, "The Pot-Hunters," *McClure's* 28 (January 1907): 327-38; Rex Beach, "Will You Sanction This?," *McClure's* 50 (May 1918): 56.

12. The case would take six years to run its course, but its eventual successful prosecution only bolstered Wilson's prestige. In 1958, that prestige would lead to Wilson's promotion to deputy superintendent, where he would lead the Bureau of Criminal Investigation. He would, however, die the following year, in 1959 (Correspondence with Margaret R. Sullivan, Records Manager and Archivist, Boston Police Department, 21 January 2012, in possession of the author; "Promote Boston Cop to Deputy Superintendent," *Jet*, 2 October 1958, 13; "Negro Helped Solve Nation's Biggest Cash Robbery," *Jet*, 16 April 1959, 44; Francis H. Mitchell, "The Man Who Cracked the Brink's Case," *Ebony* 14 [May 1959]: 148-54).

13. *Boston Globe*, Morning Edition, 8 May 1950, 1, 15; 9 May 1950, 16; *Boston Globe*, Evening Edition, 8 May 1950, 1, 11; 16 May 1950, 19; *New York Times*, 8 May 1950, 24; *Boston Herald*, 8 May 1950, 1, 15; 9 May 1950, 12; *Boston Daily Record*, 8 May 1950, 3; 9 May 1950, 11; *Boston Post*, 8 May 1950, 1, 6; 9 May 1950, 17. The story of the murder was picked up by the Associated Press and reprinted across the country. See, for example, *Richmond Times-Dispatch*, 8 May 1950, 1; *Los Angeles Times*, 8 May 1950, 11; and *Washington Post*, 9 May 1950, 9.

14. *Boston Globe*, Evening Edition, 16 May 1950, 19; *Boston Post*, 17 May 1950, 7.

15. *United States v. Chelsea Trust Co.*, 15 F.Supp. 139 (1936); *Nugent v. Murphy*, 84 F.2d 283 (1936); and *Clyde-Mallory Lines v. Cardillo*, 22 F.Supp. 40 (1938).

16. "Massachusetts State Board of Officers," Massachusetts Knights of Columbus, http://massachusettsstatekofc.org/StateOfficers.htm, accessed 30 January 2008; Christopher F. Small, *The Italian Home for Children* (San Francisco: Arcadia, 2005), 62; "Book Original Autography John F. Kennedy, JFK Signature," Worthpoint, http://www.worthpoint.com/worthopedia/book-original-autograph-john-kennedy-114837931, accessed 28 January 2012; "Tomasello, Frank W.," Political Graveyard, http://politicalgraveyard.com/bio/todhunter-tomlin.html, accessed 30 July 2008; *Lucky Bag Yearbook* (Annapolis, MD: United States Naval Academy, 1949), 342. He was still, however, under the stress of his new position, able to maintain his sense of humor. In one case where a defendant was accused of stealing five law books, Tomasello told him, "I have to throw the book at you," before sentencing him to thirty days in jail. The year prior to Hillman's appearance in his court, Tomasello's son graduated from the United States Naval Academy. He would eventually become a Middlesex Superior Court Justice. It was there that the judge had to announce to a stunned court that his friend and the president of the United States, John F. Kennedy, had been killed in Dallas. Those years would make Tomasello far more conservative, as he did his best to crack down on drug abuse and flag burning during the tumultuous 1960s ("Tomasello, Frank W.," Political Graveyard, http://politicalgraveyard.com/bio/todhunter-tomlin.html, accessed 30 July 2008; *Lucky Bag Yearbook* [Annapolis: United States Naval Academy, 1949], 342; Robert J. Samuelson, "Drugs at Harvard," *Harvard Crimson*, 11 March 1965, 1; "Miscellany," *Time*, 3 November 1952, 118; "Freedom March," *Time*, 30 November 1970, 16).

17. McDonough's political ambitions would never completely dissipate, and in 1956 he would serve as a Massachusetts delegate to the Democratic National Convention (Vincent A. Lapomarda, "Maurice Joseph Tobin: The Decline of Bossism in Boston," *New England Quarterly* 43 [September 1970]: 374–75; "McDonough, Joseph," Political Graveyard, http://politicalgraveyard.com/bio/mcdonell-mcdougle.html, accessed 30 July 2008).

18. Petition of the Defendant for the Appointment of Counsel," *Commonwealth v. Gordon M. Hillman*, Massachusetts Supreme Judicial Court, Archives and Records, Boston; City of Suffolk to Joseph M. McDonough, To Professional Services Rendered, 5 June 1950, Massachusetts Supreme Judicial Court, Archives and Records, Boston; Report of Investigation into the Mental Condition of Gordon Hillman, Commonwealth of Massachusetts, Department of Mental Health, Massachusetts Supreme Judicial Court, Archives and Records, Boston; Report to Department of Mental Health, Gordon Hillman, Suffolk County Jail, 22 May 1950, Massachusetts Supreme Judicial Court, Archives and Records, Boston.

19. Bill of Costs, Superior Court for the Transaction of Criminal Business, *Commonwealth v. Gordon M. Hillman*, Massachusetts Supreme Judicial Court, Archives and Records, Boston; True Bill, *Commonwealth v. Gordon M. Hillman*, Murder Second

Degree, Massachusetts Supreme Judicial Court, Archives and Records, Boston; State Prison Warrant vs. Gordon M. Hillman, 16 October 1950, Massachusetts Supreme Judicial Court, Archives and Records, Boston; *Boston Post,* 17 October 1950, 3; *Boston Herald,* 17 October 1950, 11; *Boston Globe,* 17 October 1950, 5.

20. *Boston Post,* 1 June 1950, 14; 4 June 1950, D4; 8 June 1950, 17; 15 June 1950, 15.

21. *Pittsburgh Press,* 26 February 1943, 14; *St. Petersburg Times,* 9 January 1943, 9; *New York Post,* 30 December 1942, 4.

22. John Breslin, "The Improbable Career of Mr. Blue," *Boston College Magazine* (Winter 2002), http://bcm.bc.edu/issues/winter_2002/ft_blue.html.

23. James Vinson, ed., *Twentieth Century Western Writers* (London: Macmillan, 1982), 388-91.

24. "Recapitulation of Homicides," *Forty-Fifth Annual Report of the Police Commissioner for the City of Boston,* Public Document No. 49 (Boston: Printed by order of the Police Commissioner, 1950), 20.

CHAPTER EIGHT

1. Kathleen M. Heide, *Understanding Parricide: When Sons and Daughters Kill Parents* (New York: Oxford University Press, 2013), 76-101. Information first published in Kathleen M. Heide and Autumn Frei, "Matricide: A Critique of the Literature," *Trauma, Violence, & Abuse* 11, no. 1 (2010): 3-17; Kathleen M. Heide, "Matricide and Stepmatricide Victims and Offenders: An Empirical Analysis of US Arrest Data," *Behavioral Sciences and the Law* 31 (2013): 203-14; Roberto Catanesi, Gabriele Rocca, Chiara Candelli, and Felice Carabellese, "Matricide by Mentally Disordered Sons: Gaining a Criminological Understanding beyond Mental Illness—A Descriptive Study," *International Journal of Offender Therapy and Comparative Criminology* 59, no. 14 (2015): 1551.

2. Sigmund Freud, "Dostoevsky and Parricide (1928)," *International Journal of Psycho-Analysis* 26 (January 1945): 1-8; Catanesi et al., "Matricide by Mentally Disordered Sons," 1551; Robert A. Schug, "Schizophrenia and Matricide: An Integrative Review," *Journal of Contemporary Criminal Justice* 27, no. 2 (2011): 207. For literature review of matricide case studies, see Heide, *Understanding Parricide,* 82-85, 92. Freud's comment came in contextualizing the literature of Dostoevsky, and studies of matricide have been far more likely to research the symbolic killing of the mother in fiction and in psychoanalysis. See, for examples, Alison Stone, "Against Matricide: Rethinking Subjectivity and the Maternal Body," *Hypatia* 27 (Winter 2012): 118-38; Amber Jacobs, *On Matricide: Myth, Psychoanalysis, and the Law of the Mother* (New York: Columbia University Press, 2007); and Christina Wieland, *The Undead Mother: Psychoanalytic Explorations of Masculinity, Femininity, and Matricide* (London: Rebus, 2000).

3. Gordon Malherbe Hillman, "The Wild Bunch," *Liberty* 22 (13 October 1945): 20-21, 88-96; Gordon Malherbe Hillman, "A Man Comes Home," *American Magazine* 137 (June 1944): 117. For more Hillman family stories, see, for example, Gordon

Malherbe Hillman, "Bath of Glory," *American Magazine* 116 (October 1933): 48–51, 132–35; Gordon Malherbe Hillman, "Beauty and the Butler," *Liberty* 24 (4 January 1947): 14–15, 64–68; Gordon Malherbe Hillman, "Benefit Performance," *American Magazine* 133 (April 1942): 32–34, 93–96; Gordon Malherbe Hillman, "Better Than Dreams," *Woman's Home Companion* 71 (March 1944): 26–27, 38, 40, 44; Gordon Malherbe Hillman, "Children in the House," *Ladies' Home Journal* 61 (November 1944): 32–33, 117–23; Gordon Malherbe Hillman, "Father's Day," *Holland's: The Magazine of the South* 55 (June 1936): 13–14, 49–52; Gordon Malherbe Hillman, "Happy-Go-Lucky Guy," *American Magazine* (December 1948): 32–33, 82–89; Gordon Malherbe Hillman, "The Kid Comes Home," *Cosmopolitan*, April 1939, 54–55, 132–37; Gordon Malherbe Hillman, "Something for Sis," *Liberty* 26 (July 1949): 24, 68–72.

4. Triple Feature: France's Greatest Detective, The Wild Bunch, The Witness, Cascadia Entertainment, DVD, CCE-1331; "Four Star Playhouse: The Wild Bunch," IMDB, http://www.imdb.com/title/tt0581948/, accessed 29 January 2012; Christopher Anderson, *Hollywood TV: The Studio System in the Fifties* (Austin: University of Texas, 1994), 260–61; Christine Becker, *It's the Pictures That Got Small: Hollywood Film Stars on 1950s Television* (Middletown, CT: Wesleyan University Press, 2008), 58–59.

5. *Boston Globe*, 14 April 1961, 6; *Bridgeport Telegram*, 5 October 1960, 1.

6. *Boston Globe*, 10 June 1965, 20; Ned Potter, "Edward M. Kennedy Escaped Death in 1964," ABC News, http://abcnews.go.com/Technology/story?id=8271369, accessed 28 January 2012. For more on the *Advertiser*, see William Randolph Hearst Papers, BANC MSS 77/121c, carton 23, folder 12–13, 29–32, Bancroft Library, University of California at Berkeley.

7. *Boston Globe*, 30 July 1972, B6.

8. *Boston Globe*, 31 July 1961, 19.

9. Diane Kessler, interview by the author, 12 January 2012.

10. Kessler interview.

11. Kessler interview.

12. Kessler interview; "Barbara Hillman," *Social Security Death Index*, 015-166-4995.

13. In lieu of flowers, contributions were encouraged to the Massachusetts General Hospital's Building Fund for Radial Therapy. Barbara died on 13 August 2002 in Boston. "Gordon M. Hillman," Certified Copy of Record of Death in Office of the City Registrar, Registry Division, City of Boston, 4 October 1968; *Boston Globe*, 5 October 1968, 20, 6 October 1968, 94, 95; "Gordon Hillman," *Social Security Death Index*, 024-12-1783; "Barbara Hillman," *Social Security Death Index*, 015-166-4995; "History of Boston Harborside Home of JS Waterman & Son-Waring-Langone," Boston Harborside Home of JS Waterman & Son-Waring-Langone, http://www.bostonharborsidehome.com/dm20/en_US/locations/46/4643/history.page, accessed 29 January 2012; Andrew Elder and Jeremy C. Fox, *Boston's Orange Line* (Charleston, SC: Arcadia, 2013), 76; John A. Buehrens, *Universalists and Unitarians in America: A People's History* (Boston: Skinner House, 2011), 173, 181, 184. See also Duncan Howlett, *No Greater Love: The James Reeb Story* (Boston: Skinner House, 1993).

BIBLIOGRAPHY

ARCHIVES

Gerald Drayson Adams Scripts, ca.1949–ca. 1960s. PASC 221, UCLA Library, Performing Arts Special Collections, Los Angeles.

William Stanley Braithwaite Collection. Houghton Library, Harvard University, Cambridge, MA.

Correspondence with the author. Boston Police Department Archives, Boston, MA.

Correspondence with the author. Wellesley College Archives, Wellesley, MA.

Course and Publication Records. Nobles Archives, Noble & Greenough School, Dedham, MA.

Court Records. *Commonwealth v. Gordon M. Hillman.* Massachusetts Supreme Judicial Court, Archives and Records, Boston.

William Randolph Hearst Papers. BANC MSS 77/121c, carton 23, folder 25–32. Bancroft Library, University of California at Berkeley.

Harold MacGrath Collection. Special Collections Research Center, Syracuse University, Syracuse, New York.

George Barr McCutcheon Papers. Harry Ransom Humanities Research Center, University of Texas at Austin.

Motion Picture Association of America. Production Code Administration Records, Department of Special Collections, Academy of Motion Picture Arts and Sciences, Margaret Herrick Library, Fairbanks Center for Motion Picture Study, Beverly Hills, CA.

Edward Streeter Papers, 1909–1976. MSS 39, Fales Library and Special Collections, New York University.

GOVERNMENT DOCUMENTS

Fifteenth Census of the United States, 1930.
Forty-Fifth Annual Report of the Police Commissioner for the City of Boston. Public Document No. 49. Boston: Printed by order of the Police Commissioner, 1950.
"Barbara Hillman." *Social Security Death Index*, 015-166-4995.
Carolyn Hillman. Certified Copy of Record of Death in Office of the City Registrar, Registry Division, City of Boston, 15 May 1950.
Clyde-Mallory Lines v. Cardillo, 22 F.Supp. 40 (1938).
"Gordon M. Hillman." Certified Copy of Record of Death in Office of the City Registrar, Registry Division, City of Boston, 4 October 1968.
"Gordon Hillman." Massachusetts, Social Security Death Index, Master File, 024-12-1783.
"Gordon Hillman." *Social Security Death Index*, 024-12-1783.
Marriages Registered in the City of Boston for 1899, p. 34. Massachusetts Vital Records, 1840-1911. New England Historic Genealogical Society, Boston, MA.
Nugent v. Murphy, 84 F.2d 283 (1936).
Carolyn Piper. Certification of Vital Record, State of New Hampshire, Department of State, Division of Vital Records Administration, Concord.
Tenth Census of the United States, 1890.
Thirteenth Census of the United States, 1910.
United States v. Chelsea Trust Co., 15 F.Supp. 139 (1936)
World War I Selective Service System. Gordon Hillman, Registration Card, Serial No. 3467, Order no. A748. National Archives and Records Administration, M1509, roll 1685167, Draft Board 4, Middlesex County, Massachusetts.

HILLMAN POEMS

Hillman, Carolyn, and Gordon Hillman. *Rhymes Grave and Gay*. Boston: Cornhill, 1919.
Hillman, Gordon Malherbe. "The Tankers." In *Contemporary Verse Anthology: Favorite Poems Selected from the Magazine, 1919-1920*, 143. New York: Dutton, 1920.

HILLMAN STORIES

"As Long As You Want Me." *American Magazine* 134 (August 1942): 38-41, 92-93.
"Bath of Glory." *American Magazine* 116 (October 1933): 48-51, 132-35.

"Beauty and the Butler." *Liberty* 24 (4 January 1947): 14–15, 64–68.
"Benefit Performance." *American Magazine* 133 (April 1942): 32–34, 93–96.
"Better Than Dreams." *Woman's Home Companion* 71 (March 1944): 26–27, 38, 40, 44.
"Broadway Doll." *Collier's*, 4 September 1948, 18–19, 56–58.
"But Never to Take Your Place." *McCall's*, May 1937, 18, 118–21.
"A Chair for the Captain." *Good Housekeeping*, December 1938, 34–35, 196–201.
"Children in the House." *Ladies' Home Journal* 61 (November 1944): 32–33, 117–23.
"Copy Girl." *American Magazine*, January 1952, 40, 123–26.
"Day to Remember." *McCall's*, June 1940, 20, 38–46.
"Death and Sunrise." *Ghost Stories* 7 (December 1929).
"Father's Day." *Holland's: The Magazine of the South* 55 (June 1936): 13–14, 49–52.
"For Your Own Good, Dear." *Woman's Home Companion* 71 (December 1944): 32, 68–70.
Fortune's Cup. New York: Crowell, 1941.
"From Now On." *American Magazine* 120 (July 1935): 18–21, 86, 88, 90.
"Gentleman's Estate." *American Magazine* 123 (January 1937): 126–30.
"The Great Man Votes." *American Magazine* 112 (November 1931): 24–27, 112, 114, 116–17.
"Guns at Shiloh." *Liberty* 15 (4 June 1938): 16–20.
"Happy-Go-Lucky Guy." *American Magazine*, December 1948, 32–33, 82–89.
"A Happy Man." *Liberty* 23 (7 September 1946): 31, 72–76.
"Hats Off to O'Hara." *Liberty* 21 (18 November 1944): 30–31, 79–82.
"The Headless Shadow." *Ghost Stories* 7 (November 1929).
"Infatuation." *Liberty* 24 (19 July 1947): 43, 82–85.
"Inside Story." *Woman's Home Companion*, April 1950, 22–23, 114–15, 118–20.
"It's All Over Now." *McCall's*, March 1940, 26–28, 83–89.
"Kid Brother." *American Magazine* 118 (July 1934): 58–61, 118–20, 123–24.
"The Kid Comes Home." *Cosmopolitan*, April 1939, 54–55, 132–37.
"Lead All—Baby." *Liberty* 24 (7 June 1947): 21, 71–74.
"A Man Comes Home." *American Magazine* 137 (June 1944): 44–45, 114–17.
"Miss Baby Intervenes." *American Magazine* 137 (March 1944): 34–36, 135–38.
"My Fair Lady." *American Magazine*, October 1943, 24–25, 91–94.
"A New Love for Freddy." *American Magazine* 137 (January 1944): 90–91, 134–36.
"Nine Lives to Love." *McCall's* 64 (January 1937): 18–19, 52–55.
"No Place for a Nice Girl." *American Magazine* 132 (December 1941): 10–13, 118–21.

"Panic in Wild Harbor." In *Supernatural Sleuths: Stories of Occult Investigators*, edited by Peter Haining, 162–71. London: William Kimber, 1986.
"Roman Holiday." *American Magazine* 133 (March 1942): 44–45, 93–98.
"Schoolboy's Return." *Liberty* 17 (5 October 1940): 36–42.
"A Ship Comes In." *Fiction Parade*, July 1935, 271–79.
"Something for Sis." *Liberty* 26 (July 1949): 24, 68–72.
"The Sound of Trumpets." *Liberty* 18 (9 August 1941): 22–25, 59–60.
"Square Peg." *American Magazine* 122 (July 1936): 50–53, 142–44.
"Stolen by Spirits." *Ghost Stories* 6 (February 1929).
"Storm Song." *Liberty* (23 January 1937): 26–30.
"The Thing That Limped." *Ghost Stories* 11 (July 1931).
"This Is Fair Warning." *American Magazine* 134 (December 1942): 38–41, 117–19.
"Tides of Memory." *American Magazine* 122 (October 1936): 30–32, 135–39.
"Tough Guy." *McCall's*, December 1935, 9–10, 25–26.
"Turn the Hour." *Good Housekeeping*, October 1937, 76–79, 191–99.
"The Unhappy Union Boss." *Liberty* 23 (1 June 1946): 26–27, 57–60.
"Visitors from Vermont." *Liberty* 19 (28 November 1942): 27–33.
"The Wild Bunch." *Liberty* 22 (13 October 1945): 20–21, 88–96.
"Wind in the Valley." *Liberty* 21 (3 June 1944): 16–17, 64–67.
"Woman Power." *Woman's Home Companion* 69 (January 1942): 16–17, 75–78.

NEWSPAPERS

Boston Daily Record (1950)
Boston Globe (1919–50, 2008)
Boston Herald (1950)
Boston Post (1950)
Bridgeport Telegram (1960)
Chicago Tribune (1896–1909)
Christian Science Monitor (1919–25)
Film Daily (1939)
Harvard Crimson (1965)
Hollywood Reporter (1938–39)
Los Angeles Times (1938–39, 1950)
Motion Picture Daily (1939)
Motion Picture Herald (1939)
New Orleans Times-Picayune (1941)
New York Post (1942)

New York Times (1924, 1938–41, 1950)
The Nobleman (1911)
Pittsburgh Press (1943)
Richmond Times-Dispatch (1950)
St. Petersburg Times (1943)
Universal Weekly (1933)
Variety (1939)
Washington Post (1950)
Wellesley College News (1921)

PRIMARY SOURCES

Brookline Directory (1915–18). Boston: Greenough, 1915–18.
Anderson, Sherwood. *Winesburg, Ohio.* New York: Huebsch, 1919.
Beach, Rex. "Captain Innocencio." *McClure's* 36 (February 1911): 365–75.
———. "The Colognizing of Kansas." *McClure's* 28 (March 1907): 525–34.
———. "The Pot-Hunters." *McClure's* 28 (January 1907): 327–38.
———. "Will You Sanction This?" *McClure's* 50 (May 1918): 56.
"Boston Transcript Folds after 111 Years of Genteel Journalism." *Life,* 12 May 1941, 34–35.
Braithwaite, William Stanley, ed. *Anthology of Magazine Verse for 1918.* Boston: Small, Maynard, 1918.
———, ed. *Anthology of Magazine Verse for 1919.* Boston: Small, Maynard, 1919.
———, ed. *Anthology of Massachusetts Poets.* Boston: Small, Maynard, 1922.
Bumstead's Evanston City and North Shore Directory, 1909–1910. Vol. 1. Chicago: Bumstead, 1909.
Burns, Robert Elliott. *I Am a Fugitive from a Georgia Chain Gang!* New York: Vanguard, 1932.
Carnegie, Dale. *How to Win Friends and Influence People.* New York: Simon and Schuster, 1936.
Collins, Wilkie. *My Miscellanies.* New York: Harper and Brothers, 1873.
The Concord Directory (1891, 1893, 1895–96). Boston: Littlefield Directory Publishing Co., 1891, 93, 95.
Dewey, John. *John Dewey: The Middle Works, 1899–1924.* Vol. 12: *1920,* edited by Jo Ann Boydston. Carbondale: Southern Illinois University Press, 1982.
Dreiser, Theodore. *An American Tragedy.* New York: Boni and Liveright, 1925.
Du Bois, W. E. B. "Book Reviews." *Crisis* 31 (February 1926): 193.
Eliot, T. S. *Prufrock and Other Observations.* New York: Knopf, 1920.
The Evanston Directory, 1901. Evanston, IL: Evanston Press, 1901.

The Evanston Directory, 1905. Evanston, IL: Evanston Press, 1905.

Farrell, James T. *Judgment Day.* New York: Vanguard, 1935.

———. *Young Lonigan.* New York: Vanguard, 1923.

———. *The Young Manhood of Studs Lonigan.* New York: Vanguard, 1934.

Federal Writers' Project of the Works Progress Administration. *New Hampshire: A Guide to the Granite State.* Boston: Houghton Mifflin, 1938.

Fitzgerald, F. Scott. *Tender Is the Night.* New York: Scribner's, 1934.

"Freedom March." *Time,* 30 November 1970, 16.

Freud, Sigmund. "Dostoevsky and Parricide (1928)." *International Journal of Psycho-Analysis* 26 (January 1945): 1–8.

Gibbons, Stella. *Cold Comfort Farm.* New York: Longman, 1932.

Gissing, George. *New Grub Street.* Troy, NY: Brewster, 1904.

Gold, Mike. *Mike Gold: A Literary Anthology.* Edited by Michael Folsom. New York: International Publishers, 1972.

Hecht, Ben, and Charles MacArthur. *The Front Page.* New York: Times Square Theatre, 1928.

Hendryx, James B. "Black John Pays a Debt." *Boston Sunday Globe Fiction Magazine,* 7 May 1950, 1–4.

Hughes, Thomas. *Tom Brown's Schooldays.* London: Macmillan, 1857.

Hurston, Zora Neale. *Their Eyes Were Watching God.* New York: Lippincott, 1937.

Kessler, Diane. Interview by the author. 12 January 2012.

Knowles, John. *A Separate Peace.* London: Secker and Warburg, 1959.

The Lakeside Annual Directory of the City of Chicago (1902–3, 1906–10). Chicago: Chicago Directory Co., 1902, 1903, 1906, 1907, 1908, 1909, 1910.

Lasser, J. K. "How Good Publishing Management Works Today." *Magazine Industry* 1 (Winter 1950): 19–20.

Library of Congress. *Catalog of Copyright Entries.* Part 1, Group 3, 1940, new series, vol. 13, no. 3. Washington, DC: USGPO, 1940.

Lucky Bag Yearbook. Annapolis, MD: United States Naval Academy, 1949.

Lynd, Robert, and Helen Lynd. *Middletown: A Study in Modern American Culture.* New York: Harcourt, Brace, 1929.

Magazine Advertising Bureau. *Nationwide Magazine Audience Survey.* Vol. 2: *Individuals.* New York: Magazine Advertising Bureau, 1948.

———. *"The Profitable Difference": A Study of the Magazine Market.* New York: Magazine Advertising Bureau, 1960.

Maurice, Arthur B. "A New Golden Age in American Reading." *The World's Work* 39 (March 1920): 488–507.

McCall Corp. *A Qualitative Study of Magazines.* New York: McCall, 1946.

"Miscellany." *Time,* 3 November 1952, 118.

Mitchell, Francis H. "The Man Who Cracked the Brink's Case." *Ebony* 14 (May 1959): 148–54.

"Negro Helped Solve Nation's Biggest Cash Robbery." *Jet*, 16 April 1959, 44.

"The New Golden Age of American Reading." *Wisconsin Library Bulletin* 16 (April 1920): 43.

Norris, Frank. *McTeague: A Story of San Francisco*. New York: Doubleday and McClure, 1899.

Poole, Ernest. *The Harbor*. New York: Macmillan, 1915.

———. *His Family*. New York: Macmillan, 1917.

"Promote Boston Cop to Deputy Superintendent." *Jet*, 2 October 1958, 13.

Repplier, Agnes. "In Case We Read: Thoughts about Books for the Vacation." *Weekly Review* 4 (25 June 1921): 602.

Selected Letters of Robert Penn Warren. Vol. 1: *The Apprentice Years, 1924–1934*, edited by William Bedford Clark. Baton Rouge: Louisiana State University Press, 2000.

Stanwood, Edward. *Boston Illustrated: Containing Full Descriptions of the City and Its Immediate Suburbs, Its Public Buildings and Institutions, Business Edifices, Parks and Avenues, Statues, Harbor and Islands*. Boston: Houghton, Mifflin, 1886.

Steinbeck, John. *The Grapes of Wrath*. New York: Viking, 1939.

Streeter, Edward. *Father of the Bride*. New York: Simon and Schuster, 1949.

Triple Feature: France's Greatest Detective, The Wild Bunch, The Witness. DVD, CCE-1331. Cascadia Entertainment.

Twain, Mark. *Editorial Wild Oats*. New York: Harper and Brothers, 1905.

Waugh, Alec. *The Loom of Youth*. 1917. London: Methuen, 1984.

Waugh, Evelyn. *Scoop*. London: Chapman and Hall, 1938.

Widdemer, Margaret. "Message and Middlebrow." *Saturday Review*, 18 February 1933, 433–34.

"Writers' Own Companion." *Newsweek*, 21 January 1946, 84.

SECONDARY SOURCES

Anderson, Christopher. *Hollywood TV: The Studio System in the Fifties*. Austin: University of Texas, 1994.

Ashley, Mike. *Age of the Storytellers: British Popular Fiction Magazines, 1880–1950*. London: British Library, 2006.

———. "Ghost Stories." In *Science Fiction, Fantasy and Weird Fiction Magazines*, edited by Marshall B. Tymn and Mike Ashley, 315–31. Westport, CT: Greenwood, 1985.

BIBLIOGRAPHY

———, ed. *Phantom Perfumes and Other Shades: Memories of "Ghost Stories" Magazine.* Ashcroft, BC: Ash-Tree, 2000.

———. "Spectral Memories." In *Phantom Perfumes and Other Shades: Memories of "Ghost Stories" Magazine,* xiii–xxvi. Ashcroft, BC: Ash-Tree, 2000.

Ashley, Perry J., ed. *Dictionary of Literary Biography.* Vol. 25: *American Newspaper Journalists, 1901–1925.* Detroit: Gale Research Co., 1984.

———, ed. *Dictionary of Literary Biography.* Vol. 29: *American Newspaper Journalists, 1926–1950.* Detroit: Gale Research Co., 1984.

Avrich, Paul. *The Haymarket Tragedy.* Princeton, NJ: Princeton University Press, 1986.

Bacon, Edwin M. *The Book of Boston: Fifty Years' Recollections of the New England Metropolis.* Boston: Book of Boston Company, 1916.

Barrett, James. *Work and Community in the Jungle: Chicago's Packinghouse Workers, 1894–1922.* Urbana: University of Illinois Press, 1987.

Baym, Nina. "Again and Again, the Scribbling Women." In *Hawthorne and Women: Engendering and Expanding the Hawthorne Tradition,* edited by John L. Idol Jr. and Melinda M. Ponder, 20–35. Boston: University of Massachusetts Press, 1999.

Becker, Christine. *It's the Pictures That Got Small: Hollywood Film Stars on 1950s Television.* Middletown, CT: Wesleyan University Press, 2008.

Bederman, Gail. *Manliness and Civilization: A Cultural History of Gender and Race in the United States, 1880–1917.* Chicago: University of Chicago Press, 1995.

Bluestone, George. *Novels into Film.* 1957. Baltimore, MD: Johns Hopkins University Press, 2003.

Boyer, Paul S. "Boston Book Censorship in the Twenties." *American Quarterly* 15 (Spring 1963): 3–24.

Braithwaite, William Stanley. Introduction to *Anthology of Magazine Verse for 1958 and Anthology of Poems from the Seventeen Previously Published Braithwaite Anthologies,* edited by Braithwaite and Margaret Haley Carpenter, xxxix–xli. New York: Schulte, 1950.

Breslin, John. "The Improbable Career of Mr. Blue." *Boston College Magazine,* Winter 2002. http://bcm.bc.edu/issues/winter_2002/ft_blue.html.

Britt, George. *Forty Years—Forty Millions: The Career of Frank A. Munsey.* New York: Farrar and Rinehart, 1935.

Brooks, Van Wyck. *The Flowering of New England.* Boston: Dutton, 1936.

Buehrens, John A. *Universalists and Unitarians in America: A People's History.* Boston: Skinner House, 2011.

Bunting, Bainbridge. *Houses of Boston's Back Bay: An Architectural History, 1840–1917.* Cambridge, MA: Belknap Press of Harvard University Press, 1967.

Carpenter, Margaret Haley. Foreword to *Anthology of Magazine Verse for 1958 and Anthology of Poems from the Seventeen Previously Published Braithwaite Anthologies,* edited by William Stanley Braithwaite and Carpenter, xv–xxviii. New York: Schulte, 1950.

Carpenter, William Lant. *A Treatise on the Manufacture of Soap and Candles, Lubricants and Glycerin.* 2nd ed. Edited by Henry Leask. London: Spon and Chamberlain, 1895.

Cartmell, Deborah, and Imelda Whelehan. *Adaptations: From Text to Screen, from Screen to Text.* New York: Routledge, 1999.

Catanesi, Roberto, Gabriele Rocca, Chiara Candelli, and Felice Carabellese. "Matricide by Mentally Disordered Sons: Gaining a Criminological Understanding beyond Mental Illness—A Descriptive Study." *International Journal of Offender Therapy and Comparative Criminology* 59, no. 14 (2015): 1551.

Chamberlin, Joseph Edgar. *The Boston Transcript: A History of Its First Hundred Years.* Freeport, NY: Books for Libraries Press, 1930.

Clark, Daniel A. *Creating the College Man: American Mass Magazines and Middle-Class Manhood, 1890–1915.* Madison: University of Wisconsin Press, 2010.

Cox, R. G. "The Reviews and Magazines." In *The Pelican Guide to Victorian Literature,* vol. 6: *The Victorian Age,* 188–204. Baltimore, MD: Penguin, 1958.

Currey, J. Seymour. "Chicago's North Shore." In *Transactions of the Illinois State Historical Society for the Year 1908,* 101–14. Springfield: Illinois State Journal Co., 1909.

Elder, Andrew, and Jeremy C. Fox. *Boston's Orange Line.* Charleston, SC: Arcadia, 2013.

Felix, David. *Protest: Sacco-Vanzetti and the Intellectuals.* Bloomington: Indiana University Press, 1965.

Fink, Leon. *Workingmen's Democracy: The Knights of Labor and American Politics.* Urbana: University of Illinois Press, 1983.

Flood, Richard T. *The Story of Noble and Greenough School, 1866–1966.* Dedham, MA: Noble and Greenough School, 1966.

Garvey, Ellen Gruber. *The Adman in the Parlor: Magazines and the Gendering of Consumer Culture, 1880s to 1910s.* New York: Oxford University Press, 1996.

Gibbs, F. W. "The History of the Manufacture of Soap." *Annals of Science* 4 (April 1939): 169–90.

Goodman, Susan. *Republic of Words: The "Atlantic Monthly" and Its Writers, 1857–1925*. Hanover, NH: University Press of New England, 2011.

Green, James. *Death in the Haymarket: A Story of Chicago, the First Labor Movement and the Bombing that Divided Gilded Age America*. New York: Anchor, 2006.

Greene, Theodore P. *America's Heroes: The Changing Models of Success in American Magazines*. New York: Oxford University Press, 1970.

Griffith, James John. *Adaptations as Imitations: Films from Novels*. Newark: University of Delaware Press, 1997.

The Handbook of Private Schools. 83rd ed. Boston: Porter Sargent, 2002.

Heide, Kathleen M. "Matricide and Stepmatricide Victims and Offenders: An Empirical Analysis of US Arrest Data." *Behavioral Sciences and the Law* 31 (2013): 203–14.

———. *Understanding Parricide: When Sons and Daughters Kill Parents*. New York: Oxford University Press, 2013.

Heide, Kathleen M., and Autumn Frei. "Matricide: A Critique of the Literature." *Trauma, Violence, & Abuse* 11, no. 1 (2010): 3–17.

Henry, Gilles. *Francois de Malherbe: Gentilhomme et poète, 1555–1628*. Paris: Cheminements, 2005.

"The History of Soap." https://blog.udemy.com/history-of-soap/. Accessed 8 September 2016.

Homer. *Iliad*.

Housel, Rebecca, ed. *From Camera Lens to Critical Lens: A Collection of Best Essays on Film Adaptation*. Newcastle: Cambridge Scholars Press, 2006.

Howlett, Duncan. *No Greater Love: The James Reeb Story*. Boston: Skinner House, 1993.

Hunter, Sidney F. "Thomas Y. Crowell & Co., New York, 1876–1979." The Lucile Project, University of Iowa Libraries. http://sdrc.lib.uiowa.edu/lucile/publishers/crowell/cr_intro.htm. Accessed 26 November 2016.

Jacobs, Amber. *On Matricide: Myth, Psychoanalysis, and the Law of the Mother*. New York: Columbia University Press, 2007.

James, Nancy C. *The Pure Love of Madame Guyon: The Great Conflict in King Louis XIV's Court*. Lanham, MD: University Press of America, 2007.

Janssen, Marian. *Not at All What One Is Used To: The Life and Times of Isabella Gardner*. Columbia: University of Missouri Press, 2010.

Johns-Heine, Patricke, and Hans Gerth. "Values in Mass Periodical Fiction, 1921–1940." *Public Opinion Quarterly* 13 (Spring 1949): 105–13.

Kazin, Alfred. *On Native Grounds: An Interpretation of Modern American Prose Literature*. New York: Harcourt, Brace, 1942.

Keefer, Truman Frederick. *Ernest Poole*. New York: Twayne, 1966.
——. *Ernest Poole*. New Haven, CT: College and University Press, 1966.
Kessler, Sidney H. "The Organization of Negroes in the Knights of Labor." *Journal of Negro History*, July 1937, 248–76.
Kimbel, Bobby Ellen, ed. *Dictionary of Literary Biography*. Vol. 86: *American Short-Story Writers, 1910–1945, First Series*. Detroit: Gale Research, 1989.
——, ed. *Dictionary of Literary Biography*. Vol. 102: *American Short-Story Writers, 1910–1945, Second Series*. Detroit: Gale Research, 1991.
Klapper, Joseph T. "The Mass Media and the Engineering of Consent." *American Scholar* 17 (Autumn 1948): 419–29.
Kranish, Michael, Brian C. Mooney, and Nina J. Easton. *John F. Kerry: The Complete Biography by the "Boston Globe" Reporters Who Know Him Best*. New York: Public Affairs, 2004.
Lapomarda, Vincent A. "Maurice Joseph Tobin: The Decline of Bossism in Boston." *New England Quarterly* 43 (September 1970): 374–75.
Larson, Erik. *Devil in the White City: Murder, Magic, and Madness at the Fair That Changed America*. New York: Crown, 2003.
Leonard, Jonathan Norton. "Learning How to Write." In *Writing for Love or Money: Thirty-Five Essays Reprinted from "The Saturday Review of Literature*," edited by Norman Cousins, 14–18. New York: Longman, Greens, 1949.
Levine, Susan. "Labor's True Woman: Domesticity and Equal Rights in the Knights of Labor." *Journal of American History* 70 (September 1983): 323–39.
Lieberwitz, Risa. "The Use of Criminal Conspiracy Prosecutions to Restrict Freedom of Speech: The Haymarket Trial." In *In the Shadow of the Statute of Liberty: Immigrants, Workers, and Citizens in the American Republic, 1880–1920*, edited by Marianne Debouzy, 275–91. Urbana: University of Illinois Press, 1992.
Loving, Jerome. *The Last Titan: A Life of Theodore Dreiser*. Berkeley: University of California Press, 2005.
McElrath, Joseph R., Jr., and Jesse S. Crisler. *Frank Norris: A Life*. Urbana: University of Illinois Press, 2006.
Miller, Donald L. *City of the Century: The Epic of Chicago and the Making of America*. New York: Simon and Schuster, 1996.
Miller, Neil. *Banned in Boston: The Watch and Ward Society's Crusade against Books, Burlesque, and the Social Evil*. Boston: Beacon, 2010.
Miller, Ross. *American Apocalypse: The Great Fire and the Myth of Chicago*. Chicago: University of Chicago Press, 1990.
Minter, David. "A Cultural History of the Modern American Novel." In *The Cambridge History of American Literature*, vol. 6: *Prose Writing, 1910–*

1950, edited by Sacvan Bercovitch, 3–281. New York: Cambridge University Press, 2002.

Morison, Elizabeth Forbes, and Elting E. Morison. *New Hampshire: A Bicentennial History*. New York: Norton, 1976.

Mott, Frank Luther. *A History of American Magazines*. Vol. 1: *1741–1850*. Cambridge, MA: Harvard University Press, 1930.

———. *A History of American Magazines*. Vol. 5: *Sketches of 21 Magazines, 1905–1930*. Cambridge, MA: Belknap Press of Harvard University Press, 1968.

Ohmann, Richard. *Selling Culture: Magazines, Markets, and Class at the Turn of the Century*. New York: Verso, 1996.

Paradis, Wilfrid H. *Upon This Granite: Catholicism in New Hampshire, 1647–1997*. Portsmouth, NH: Peter E. Randall, 1998.

Paraschos, Manny E. "Boston." In *Encyclopedia of Journalism*, vol. 1: *A–C*, edited by Christopher H. Sterling, 176–77. Los Angeles: Sage, 2009.

Pendergast, Tom. *Creating the Modern Man: American Magazines and Consumer Culture, 1900–1950*. Columbia: University of Missouri Press, 2000.

Peterson, Theodore. *Magazines in the Twentieth Century*. Urbana: University of Illinois Press, 1964.

Porter, Katherine Anne. "Go Little Book . . ." In *The Collected Stories of Katherine Anne Porter*, v–vi. New York: Harcourt, Brace, 1965.

———. "Pale Horse, Pale Rider." In *The Collected Stories of Katherine Anne Porter*, 269–317. New York: Harcourt, Brace, 1965.

Private Independent Schools. 43rd ed. Wallingford, CT: Bunting and Lyon, 1990.

Reed, David. *The Popular Magazine in Britain and the United States, 1880–1960*. Toronto: University of Toronto Press, 1997.

Riley, Sam G., ed. *Dictionary of Literary Biography*. Vol. 91: *American Magazine Journalists, 1900–1960*. Detroit: Gale Research, 1990.

———, ed. *Dictionary of Literary Biography*. Vol. 137: *American Magazine Journalists, 1900–1960*. Detroit: Gale Research, 1994.

Rubin, David Lee. *Higher, Hidden Order: Design and Meaning in the Odes of Malherbe*. Chapel Hill: University of North Carolina Press, 1972.

Rubin, Joan Shelley. *The Making of Middlebrow Culture*. Chapel Hill: University of North Carolina Press, 1992.

Sammarco, Anthony Mitchell. *Forest Hills Cemetery*. Charleston, SC: Arcadia, 2009.

Santayana, George. *The Genteel Tradition: Nine Essays by George Santayana*. 1967. Lincoln: University of Nebraska Press, 1998.

Schneider, Mark R. *Boston Confronts Jim Crow, 1890–1920*. Boston: Northeastern University Press, 1997.

Schneirov, Matthew. *The Dream of a New Social Order: Popular Magazines in America, 1893–1914*. New York: Columbia University Press, 1994.

Scholes, Robert, and Clifford Wulfman. *Modernism in the Magazines: An Introduction*. New Haven, CT: Yale University Press, 2010.

Schorow, Stephanie. *Boston on Fire: A History of Fires and Firefighting in Boston*. Beverly, MA: Commonwealth, 2003.

Schug, Robert A. "Schizophrenia and Matricide: An Integrative Review." *Journal of Contemporary Criminal Justice* 27, no. 2 (2011): 207.

Sedgewick, Ellery. *A History of the "Atlantic Monthly," 1857–1909: Yankee Humanism at High Tide and Ebb*. Amherst: University of Massachusetts Press, 1994.

Server, Lee. *Encyclopedia of Pulp Fiction Writers*. New York: Facts on File, 2002.

Sinclair, Upton. *The Jungle*. New York: Doubleday, 1906.

Slap, Andrew Leonard. "Transforming Politics: The Liberal Republican Movement and the End of Civil War–Era Political Culture." PhD diss., Pennsylvania State University, 2002.

Small, Christopher F. *The Italian Home for Children*. San Francisco: Arcadia, 2005.

Smith, Carl. *Urban Disorder and the Shape of Belief: The Great Chicago Fire, the Haymarket Bomb, and the Model Town of Pullman*. Chicago: University of Chicago Press, 1995.

Sollors, Werner. "Ethnic Modernism." In *The Cambridge History of American Literature*, vol. 6: *Prose Writing, 1910–1950*, edited by Sacvan Bercovitch, 1–11. New York: Cambridge University Press, 2002.

Sontheimer, Morton. Introduction to *The Society of Magazine Writers: A Guide to Successful Magazine Writing*, edited by Clive Howard, 1–11. New York: Scribner, 1954.

Stone, Alison. "Against Matricide: Rethinking Subjectivity and the Maternal Body." *Hypatia* 27 (Winter 2012): 118–38.

Sumner, David E. *The Magazine Century: American Magazines since 1900*. New York: Peter Lang, 2010.

Taylor, Welford Dunaway, ed. *The Newsprint Mask: The Tradition of the Fictional Journalist in America*. Ames: Iowa State University Press, 1991.

Temkin, Moshik. *The Sacco-Vanzetti Affair: America on Trial*. New Haven, CT: Yale University Press, 2009.

Terkel, Studs. *Division Street, America*. New York: Pantheon, 1967.

Vinson, James, ed. *Twentieth Century Western Writers*. London: Macmillan, 1982.

Vrabel, Jim. *When in Boston: A Time Line & Almanac*. Boston: University Press of New England, 2004.

Ward, Patricia A. *Experimental Theology in America: Madame Guyon, Fénelon, and Their Readers*. Waco, TX: Baylor University Press, 2009.

Warner, Sam Bass. *Streetcar Suburbs: The Process of Growth in Boston, 1870–1900*. 2nd ed. Cambridge, MA: Harvard University Press, 1978.

Wieland, Christina. *The Undead Mother: Psychoanalytic Explorations of Masculinity, Femininity, and Matricide*. London: Rebus, 2000.

Wilson, Harold Fisher. *The Hill Country of Northern New England: Its Social and Economic History, 1790–1930*. New York: Columbia University Press, 1936.

Wilson, R. Lucock. *Soap through the Ages*. London: Unilever Educational Booklets, 1959.

Wood, James Playsted. *Magazines in the United States: Their Social and Economic Influence*. New York: Ronald Press, 1949.

Wynne, Deborah. *The Sensation Novel and the Victorian Family Magazine*. New York: Palgrave, 2001.

Zuckerman, Mary Ellen. *A History of Popular Women's Magazines in the United States, 1792–1995*. Westport, CT: Greenwood, 1998.

INDEX

Academy Awards, 38, 150
Adams, Gerald Drayson, 122
Adams, Henry, 29
Amasa Howe Award, 161
"America the Beautiful," 82
American Magazine, 6, 35, 78, 79, 103, 121, 123, 146
American Magazine (1787), 96
American Soap Manufacturing Association, 15
American Tragedy, An, 57
Anderson, Sherwood, 57
Arlington Street Church, 163–164
"Around the Year," 76
Arthur B. Spingarn Award for Outstanding Achievement in Literature, n184
"As Long As You Want Me," 78–79
Ashford, Daisy, 2
Associated Press, 55, n192
Atlanta University, n184
Atlantic Monthly, 6, 29, 62, 97–98, 103, 108
"Auld Lang Syne," 35

Barnes Memorial Airport, 162
Barrymore, John, 120, 121
Bates, Katharine Lee, 82

Baxter, Warner, 123
Beach, Rex, 2–3, 4, 147
Beale, Edith, 81
Becker, Mary Lamberton, 62
Becky Sharp, 96
Beethoven, Ludwig von, 31
Berube, Tom, 161, 162
Bigelow, William Frederick, 100
Binford, Jessie, 13
Bissell, Israel, 162
B. J. Johnson Company, 14
Bluestone, George, n190
Bok, Edward, 99, 103
Boston Advertiser, 54, 96, 127, 161
Boston American, 54, 55, 127
Boston College, 29
Boston Evening Transcript, 54–58, 61–64, 82, 127, n184
Boston Globe, 55, 77, 143, 144, 150
Boston Municipal Court, 147, 149
Boston Police Department, 56–57, 144, 146–149, 151
Boston Post, 100, 142, 149
Boston Press Club, 161
Boston Record, 54, 55, 127, 160–161
Boston Symphony Orchestra, 31
Boyer, Charles, 160
Brady, Frederick, 160

211

INDEX

Braithwaite, William Stanley, 61–64, 76, 82, 83, n184
Bridgewater State Hospital, 150
Brink's Building, 147
Brink's Robbery, 147, n192
"Broadway Doll," 16–17, 81
Brown, Sterling, 62
Bryan, Michael Neely, 150
Buffalo Express, 3, 57
Bump on Brannigan's Head, The, 150
Burnham, Daniel, 13
Burns, Robert Elliott, 38
Burton, Harry Payne, 100

Capra, Frank, 150
Carnegie, Dale, 38
Carpenter, Margaret Haley, 63
Carpenter, William Lant, 14
Cavalcade, 96
CBS, 159–160, 165
Century, 4, 97
Chamberlin, Joseph Edgar, 55, 57
Channing, William Ellery, 164
Charles Street Jail, 147–148, 149
Chicago Tribune, 14, 102
Chicago White Sox, 82
Christian Science Monitor, 82
Christie, Agatha, 103
Civil Rights Act of 1964, 161
Civil War, 10, 12, 29, 97
Clark, Daniel A., 97
Claus, Henry Turner, 57
Clyde-Mallory Lines v. Cardillo, 148
Cold Comfort Farm, 39
Colgate, William, 14, 15
Collier's, 104
Collins, Wilkie, 107
Colonial Inn, 81
Columbus, Christopher, 13
Connolly, Myles, 150, 151, 165
Conrad, Joseph, 2
Contemporary Verse, 64

Coolidge, Calvin, 56–57, 120
Copley Plaza Hotel, vii, 1, 142–147, 159, 165
Cornhill Company, 62, 76
Cosmopolitan, 98–99, 102, 103, 104
Cotter, Joseph S., 62
Cottolene, 15
Cox, R. G., 108
Crane, Hart, 63
Crane, Stephen, 100
Crowell Publishing Company, 99, 125
Cullen, Countee, 62
cummings, e.e., 146
Currie, Barton, 99
Curtis, Cyrus H. K., 97, 99, 100
Curtis Company, 99
Cutter, R. Ammi, 32

Daily Except Sundays, 3
Daughters of the American Revolution, 121
"Day to Remember," 34, 40
"Death and Sunrise," 146
Del Ruth, Roy, 123
Democratic National Convention, 148, n193
Democratic Party, 148, 161, n193
Dewey, John, 107
Dexter Field, 32
Dictionary of Literary Biography, 106
Divorcee, The, 150
Dix, Richard, 124
Dostoevsky, Fyodor, n194
Dreiser, Theodore, 57
Drums along the Mohawk, 123
Du Bois, W. E. B., 62
Dudley, Albertus T., 31

Eastern Airlines, 161
Echdoy, Theodore G., 144
Eddy, Mary Baker, 82
Edgett, Edwin Francis, 56

212

INDEX

Eiffel Tower, 14
Eliot, T. S., 55, 106, n183
Ellison, Jerome, 104
Emerson College, 29
Eton College, 30
Ex-Wife, 150

Fairbank, N. K., 11, 14–15, n180
Fairbank, Peck & Co., 14
Fallon, Edward W., 146
Farrell, James T., 38
Father of the Bride, 127, 160
Faulkner, William, 100
Faust, Frederick S., 105, 106
Federal Bureau of Investigation, 161
Fenway Theatre, 124
Ferris, George W., 14
Film Daily, 122
Fisher Building, 15
Fiske, George H., 31, 32
Fitzgerald, F. Scott, 39, 100
Fletcher, John Gould, 62
Flood, Richard, 31–32
"For Your Own Good, Dear," 17, 81
Ford, Richard, n192
Forest Hills Cemetery, 145–146
Fortune's Cup, 8, 125–126, n191
Four Star Playhouse, 159, 160, 165
Franklin, Benjamin, 96, n184
"From Now On," 38
Front Page, The, 58
Frost, Robert, 62, 64

Galsworthy, John, 2
Gamble, James, 14
Gandil, Chick, 82
Garrison, William Lloyd, 146
Gaudette, Albert, 144
General Magazine, 96
"Gentleman's Estate," 35
George, Gladys, 124
Gettell, Richard G., 102

Ghost Stories, 103, 146, 151
Gibbons, Stella, 39
Gilded Age, 10–12, 14, 16, 30, 55, 83, 97, 146
Ginn and Company, 62
Gissing, George, 57
Glasgow, Ellen, 2
Gleason, Russell, 124
Godey's Lady's Book, 97, n187
Gold, Mike, 107
Gold Dust Washing Powder, 15
Good Housekeeping, 31, 35, 99, 102, 142
Goodman, Benny, 150
Gould, Beatrice Blackmar, 99
Gould, Bruce, 99
Grapes of Wrath, The, 38
Great Depression, 2, 8, 38, 63, 106, 164, n184, n188
Great Fire of 1871, 13
"Great Man in Politics, The" 122
"Great Man Votes, The" (story), 120–121
Great Man Votes, The (film), 120–123
Greene, Richard, 123, 124
Greenough, James Jay, 30
Grey, Zane, 2, 100
Grey Gardens, 81
Guyon, Madam, 16

"Happy Man, A" 60–61
Harbor, The, 33
"Harbor Lights," 77–78
Hardenbergh, Henry Janeway, 142
Harlem Renaissance, 62
Harper's, 97–98, 103, 108
Harrow School, 30
Harvard University, 29, 30, 33, 35, 64; Harvard Department of Legal Medicine, n192; Harvard Medical School, 163
Haymarket Riot, 12–13
"Headless Shadow, The," 146
Hearst, William Randolph, 55, 98–99, 127

213

INDEX

Hecht, Ben, 57–58
Heller, Frank, 125
Hellman, Sam, 122, 123
Henderson, Ernest G., 32
"Here I Am a Stranger" (story), 122
Here I Am a Stranger (film), 123–125
Higgins, John P., 149
Hillman, Barbara Tibbets, 162–164
Hillman, Carolyn (Piper), 161, 164;
    early life of, 10–11, 17; marriage of, 11;
    delusions of grandeur of, 16, 96, 146;
    educating Gordon, 33; life with Gordon, 81–83, 127; death of, 144–145
Hillman, Frank, 11, 29, 33
Hillman, Gordon Malherbe
—Life (general): early life of, 11, 16, 29, 32–33; financial trouble of, 127, 142–143, 150; life with Carolyn, 80–83, 127; murder committed by, 1, 9, 144–145; legal ordeal of, 149–151; delusions of grandeur of, 7, 16; newspaper work, 54, 57–58, 96, 160–162; and Hollywood, 120–125; later life of, 159–163; death of, 163–164
—Fiction of, 1, 58–61, 78–80, 96, 106, 108, 159–160. *See also specific titles of works*
—Poetry of, 63–64, 76–77. *See also specific titles of works*
His Family, 3, 126, 160
His Second Wife, 3
History of American Magazines, n186–187
Holden, Peter, 121
Hollywood Reporter, 121, 125
Holmes, Oliver Wendell, 29
Home for Italian Children, 148
Homer, n191
Hotel Buckminster, 82
Hotel Oxford, 11
Hotel Vendome, 127, 143
Houghton Mifflin, 29

How to Win Friends and Influence People, 38
Howe, Julia Ward, 29
Hughes, Langston, 62
Hughes, Thomas, 39
Hurd, Charles E., 56
Hurston, Zora Neale, 38–39
Hendryx, James B., 143, 144, 150–151

I Am a Fugitive from a Georgia Chain Gang, 38
Ibañez, Vicente Blasco, 2
Iliad, n191
Industrial Revolution, 10
Italian American Charitable Society, 148

Johnson, Georgia Douglas, 62
Johnson, James Weldon, 62
Joyce, James, 106
J. S. Waterman & Sons Funeral Home, 163
Jungle, The, 12

Kazin, Alfred, n187
Kelly, Francis E., 149
Kelly, Nancy, 123
Kennedy, Edward, 161–162
Kennedy, John F., 148–149, n193
Kerry, Frederick, 142
Kerry, John, 142
Kessler, Diane, 162
King, Martin Luther, 164
Kipling, Rudyard, 2
Klondike Gold Rush, 2
Knights of Columbus, 148
Knights of Labor, 12
Knowles, John, 8, 39

Ladies' Home Journal, 99–100, 102, 103, n187
Lasser, J. K., 104
"Lead All—Baby," 59, 64
Leary, Timothy, 144–145, n192

INDEX

Leland Powers School, 162
Leonard, Jonathan Norton, 104
Lewis, Sinclair, 100
Liberty, 6, 37, 59, 60, 102–103, 123, 146, 160
Lindsay, Vachel, 64
Little, Royal, 32
Logan Airport, 161
London, Jack, 100
Long, Ray, 99, 103
Longfellow, Henry Wadsworth, 125
Longshoremen's and Harbor Workers' Compensation Act, 148
Lonigan, Studs, 38
Loom of Youth, The, 39, 126
Lorimer, George Horace, 100, 103, 104
Lowell, Amy, 63
Lowell, Francis Cabot, 146
Lowell, James Russell, 29
Lupino, Ida, 160
Lynd, Helen Merrell, 103

MacArthur, Charles, 58
MacBride, Donald, 120
Macfadden, Bernarr, 102–103
MacGrath, Harold, 2, 3, 4, 57, 126, 165
Magazine Advertising Bureau, 100
Malherbe, Francois, 16
Mallory Institute of Pathology, 145
Manufacturers and Liberal Arts Building, 13
Masefield, John, 2
Massachusetts Bureau of Criminal Investigation, n192
Massachusetts Division of Employment Security, 162
Massachusetts General Hospital, 163; Building Fund for Radial Therapy, 195
Massachusetts Institute of Technology, 29
Massachusetts Investors Trust, 32
Massachusetts Supreme Court, 32
Masters, Edgar Lee, 62

Masuret, Leo, 149
Maurice, Arthur B., 2
McCabe, Bruce, 162, 163
McCall's, 6, 34, 36, 59, 100–102, 108, 122–123, 146
McCarthy, James J., 150
McClure, S. S., 98
McClure's, 3, 97–98
McCormick, Robert, 102
McCutcheon, George Barr, 2, 3, 4, 57, 165
McDonough, Joseph M., 147, 149
McKay, Claude, 62
McMahon, James, 15
McTeague, 57
Medical Legal Society, 145
Mendelsohn, Jack, 164
Middlesex Superior Court, 150, n193
Millay, Edna St. Vincent, 62, 64
Milton, John, 125
Minter, David, 103
"Miss Baby Intervenes," 17, 81
Monroe, Harriet, 82–83
Monroe, James, 34
Moore, Victor, 120
Moss, Edward, 162
Motion Picture Daily, 122
Motion Picture Herald, 122
Mott, Frank Luther, n186–187
Munsey, Frank, 98, 99, 100
Munsey's, 80, 97, 98, 99
"My Fair Lady," 79

N.K. Fairbank Soap Company, 11, 14–15, n180
Nation, 6
National Association for the Advancement of Colored People, n184
National Home for Disabled Volunteer Soldiers, 148
New Grub Street, 57
New Hampshire Board of Health, 10
"New Love for Freddy," 81

INDEX

New Orleans Times-Picayune, 126
New York Daily News, 102
New York Times, 121, 124, 125
New York Times Book Review, 63
New Yorker, 6, 121
"Nine Lives to Love," 36
Nivin, David, 160
Noble, George Washington Copp, 29–32
Noble and Greenough Battalion, 32
Noble and Greenough School, 1, 29–37, 54–55, 82, n182; in Hillman's biography and stories, 63, 77, 79
Nobleman, The, 54
Norris, Frank, 57
Norris, Kathleen, 100
North American Review, The, 62, 97, 108
Novels into Film, n190
Nugent, Frank S., 124
Nugent v. Murphy, 148

Office of Special Investigation, 161
Ohmann, Richard, 6, 80
Olmsted, Frederick Law, 13
On Native Grounds, n187
O'Neill, Eugene, 146

Pale Horse, Pale Rider, 4
Palmolive, 14
"Panic in Wild Harbor," 151
Paramount Theatre, 124
Paraschos, Manny, 54
Parkman, Francis, 29
Parrott, Ursula, 150, 151
Patterson, Joseph M., 102
Pendergast, Tom, 98
Peterson, Theodore, 5–6, 99, 104
Phillips Exeter Academy, 39
Picasso, Pablo, 106
Piper, Carolyn, 10
Piper, Joseph, 10
Plaza Hotel, 142
Poetry: A Magazine of Verse, 82

Poetry Society of America, 63
Poole, Ernest Cook, 2–4, 32–33, 38, 39, 57, 64, 126, 160, 165
Porter, Katherine Anne, 4–5, 7, 9, 165
Powell, Dick, 160
Princeton University, 33
Procter and Gamble, 14, 15
Procter, William, 14
Production Code Administration, 120, 121, 124
Pulitzer Prize, 3, 33, 38, 127, 165
Purdue University, 3

Rains Came, The, 123
Ratoff, Gregory, 123
Reeb, James, 164
Reid, Walter, 62
Renaissance, 106
Repertory Theater of Boston, 82
Revolutionary War, 162
Rhymes Grave and Gay, 76–77, 83
Ridge, Lola, 63, 64
Rinehart, Mary Roberts, 2
RKO Pictures, 120–122
Robinson, Dwight P., 32
Rocky Mountain News, 4
Rollins, Leighton, 82, n185
"Roman Holiday," 81
Roosevelt, Franklin, 148
Rubin, Joan Shelly, 6, 146
Rugby School, 30, 39
Russian Revolution, 57
Ryan, Kathryn White, n186

Sacco, Nicola, 30, 147
Santayana, George, 98
Sargent, John Singer, 142
Saturday Evening Post, 6, 97, 99–104, 107, 123
Schneirov, Matthew, 97
"Schoolboy's Return," 35
Scoop, 57, 126

Scribner's, 62, 97
Seiter, William A., 160
Separate Peace, A, 8, 39
Server, Lee, 147
Sexton, Anne, 146
Shearer, Norma, 150
Sheraton Corporation, 32
"Ship Comes In, A," 83
Simmons University, 29
Sinclair, Upton, 12, 103
Sisk, Bob, 120
Smart Set, n188
Smedley, Peck & Co., 14
Society of Magazine Writers, 105
Sollors, Werner, 106–107
Sontheimer, Morton, 105
"Sound of Trumpets, The," 37–38
Southern Mortuary, 145
Sperling, Milton, 122–123
Spoilers, The, 2–3
Stanley and Livingston, 123
Steinbeck, John, 38, 39
Stevens, Wallace, 62
"Stolen by Spirits," 146
"Storm Song," 80
Streeter, Edward, 2–4, 57, 126–127, 160, 165
Suffolk Superior Court, 149
Sullivan, Joseph "Sport," 82
Sullivan, Thomas F., 146
Sumner, David, 98
Syracuse Herald, 3, 57
Syracuse University, 162

"Tankers, The," 64
Tarkington, Booth, 2, 100, 165
Tender Is the Night, 39
Tennyson, Alfred Lord, 125
Terkel, Studs, 13
Textron, 32
Their Eyes Were Watching God, 38–39
"Thing That Limped, The," 146

"This Is Fair Warning," 17, 81
Thomas Y. Crowell Company, 99, 125
Tibbetts, G. Wallace, 162
Tibbetts, Maude, 162
Time, 102, 121
"Tides of Memory," 78
Tobin, Maurice Joseph, 149
Tom Brown's School Days, 39
Tomasello, Frank W., 147–149, n193
"Tough Guy," 59, 108
Treatise on the Manufacture of Soap and Candles, A, 14
Tribune Building, 11, 15
True Story, 103
Tufts College, 145
"Turn the Hour," 31, 35
Tutenkamen, 145
Twentieth Century-Fox, 122–124
Twist, John, 120, 122

"Unhappy Union Boss, The," 60
United Press International Newspaper Editors of Massachusetts, 162
United States Air Force, 161
United States Employees' Compensation Commission, 148
United States Naval Academy, n193
United States v. Chelsea Trust Co., 148
University School for Boys, 3, 33

Van Doren, Carl, 4
Vanzetti, Bartolomeo, 30, 147
Variety, 122
Vinal, Harold, n186
"Visitors from Vermont," 17
Voices: A Journal of Verse, n186
Volkmann, Arthur, 31
Volkmann School, 31, 34

Waban Hall, 82
Waban Hotel, 82
Walker, Cornelia Wells, 55, 56

Walker, John Brisben, 98–99
Wallace, Margaret, 125
Walpole, Hugh, 2
Warren, Robert Penn, 62, n186
Washington, George, 97
Waugh, Alec, 39, 126
Waugh, Evelyn, 57, 126
"Weather Vane," 83
Webster, Noah, 96
Weidler, Virginia, 121
Weird Tales, 146
Wellesley College, 82, 143
Wells, H.G., 2
White, Stanford, 82
Whitman, Walt, 2
Widdemer, Margaret, 6
"Wild Bunch, The" (story), 9, 160, 165
"Wild Bunch, The" (television episode), 160

Willis, Nathaniel, 56
Wilson, Francis G., 146, 147, 149, n192
Winesburg, Ohio, 57
Woman's Home Companion, 99–100, 102
Wood, James Playsted, 96–97, 106
Wood, Natalie, 160
"Woman Power," 81
Works Progress Administration, 145
World War I, 3, 31, 37–38, 82, 99, 107, 148, n184
World War II, 2, 39, 60, 106, 121
World's Columbian Exhibition, 13–14

Young, Brigham, 123
Young, Rida Johnson, 123
Young, Roland, 124

Zanuck, Darryl, 122–124
Zuckerman, Mary Ellen, 100

CPSIA information can be obtained
at www.ICGtesting.com
Printed in the USA
LVHW020546090721
692214LV00004B/272